HORTICULTURE AND ECOLOGY
STUDIES AND MANAGEMENT

ENV BOOKS SERIES

HORTICULTURE AND ECOLOGY

STUDIES AND MANAGEMENT

Editors

Dr. Alka Chauhan

Society for Environment, Health Awareness of Nutrition & Toxicology (SEHAT)
B-225/5D, Top Floor, Subhash Gali, Road No. 7, Block B
Ashok Nagar, Shahdara, Delhi - 110 093

&

Dr. Pawan Kumar 'Bharti'

Society for Environment, Health Awareness of Nutrition & Toxicology (SEHAT)
B-225/5D, Top Floor, Subhash Gali, Road No. 7, Block B
Ashok Nagar, Shahdara, Delhi - 110 093
(India)

DPH

DISCOVERY PUBLISHING HOUSE PVT. LTD.
INDIA

Published by:
Namit Wasan
DISCOVERY PUBLISHING HOUSE PVT. LTD.
4383/4B, Ansari Road, Darya Ganj
New Delhi-110 002 (India)
Phone : +91-11-23279245; 23253475; 43596065
E-mail : discoverybooksindia@gmail.com
discoverypublishinghouse@gmail.com
namitwasan9@gmail.com
web : www.discoverypublishinggroup.com

***First Edition:* 2019**

ISBN: 978-93-88854-09-2

Horticulture and Ecology: ***Studies and Management***

Printed at:
Infinity Imaging Systems
Delhi

FOREWORD

M.S. Swaminathan
Founder Chairman
Ex-Member of Parliament (Rajya Sabha)

I am very glad to know that a several books are being edited under the aegis of ENVBOOKS series Delhi, India on various sub-themes of Agriculture and environment like:

- Heavy Metals and Pesticides in Environment
- Heavy conservation and renewable sources Climate Change and Agriculture Production
- Geospatial Technology and Ecosystem Assessment
- Food Technology and Agriculture Advancement
- Vermicompost and Vermitechnology
- Pest Control and Management
- Plant Response to Environmental Stress
- Bioremediation and Biotechnology
- Noise and Air Pollution
- Risk and Disaster Management
- Agro-ecology and Environmental Biotechnology
- Water and Wastewater Management
- Soil Pollution and Lithosphere
- Earth Ecosystem and Pollution
- Microbial Ecology
- Waste Recycling and Product Development

I am very happy to learn that a number of editors and authors from different institutions and university of different nations are involved in editing these books. The books are the compendium of screened-in manuscripts received from different countries like UK, Canada, Egypt, Nigeria, Ghana, Ethiopia, China, South Africa, Japan, Guyana, PNG, Nepal, South America and various parts of India. I am feeling delighted in writing forward to these books and congratulate to Dr. Pawan Kumar 'Bharti', Editor-in-Chief and founder of ENVBOOKs series and of course his team for their tenacity and hard work in compiling these valuable compendiums.

I hope these books will be beneficial for academician, researchers, industrialist policy makes and students as study material and will work as reference for further research work.

M.S. Swaminathan

M.S. Swaminathan

PREFACE

Horticulture is the area of agriculture involving the science of growing and caring for plants. Horticulture is socially important because it improves how we use plants, for food and other human purposes, as well as repairing the environment and personal aesthetics. Plants are also very important in environmental protection. They are used to re-vegetate and restore land disturbed by human or natural activities, they control erosion and they help to clean the air and water. Plants also have an important role in the beautification of urban and rural landscapes and recreation areas.

Ecology is not synonymous with environmentalism, natural history, or environmental science. It overlaps with the closely related sciences of evolutionary biology, genetics, and ethology. An important focus for ecologists is to improve the understanding of how biodiversity affects ecological function.

Ecology has practical applications in conservation biology, wetland management, natural resource management (agroecology, agriculture, forestry, agroforestry, fisheries), city planning, community health, economics, basic and applied science, and human social interaction.

The present book updates the subject content of irrigation methods and water quality for horticultural crops, Effect of foliar spray of organic and inorganic nutrients on the growth and yield of crops, Water management in fruit crops, Post harvest technology, Ecological status of pteridophytes, Ecology and ethnobotany of few plants, Ecological status of wild life sanctuary.

Thanks are due to publisher and contributors from various institutions and universities.

The book will be helpful for the researchers, academia working in the field of irrigation methods and water quality for horticultural crops, Effect of foliar spray of organic and inorganic nutrients on the growth and yield of crops, Water management in fruit crops, Post harvest technology, Ecological status of pteridophytes, Ecology and ethnobotany of few plants, Ecological status of wild life sanctuary.

Editors
(envbooks@gmail.com)

CONTENTS

Horticulture and Ecology - *Studies & Management*
***Edited by:* Dr. Alka Chauhan and Dr. Pawan Kumar 'Bharti'**
ISBN: 978-93-88854-09-2
***Edition:* 2019**
***Published by:* Discovery Publishing House Pvt. Ltd., New Delhi (India)**
Pages 1-5

1 Introduction

Horticulture has been defined as the culture of plants for food, comfort and beauty. A more precise definition can be given as "The cultivation, processing, and sale of fruits, nuts, vegetables, ornamental plants and flowers as well as many additional services". It also includes plant conservation, landscape restoration, soil management, landscape and garden design, construction, and maintenance, and arboriculture. In contrast to agriculture, horticulture does not include large-scale crop production or animal husbandry.

Horticulturists apply their knowledge, skills, and technologies used to grow intensively produced plants for human food and non-food uses and for personal or social needs. Their work involves plant propagation and cultivation with the aim of improving plant growth, yields, quality, nutritional value, and resistance to insects, diseases, and environmental stresses. They work as gardeners, growers, therapists, designers, and technical advisors in the food and non-food sectors of horticulture. Horticulture even refers to the growing of plants in a field or garden.

Horticulture has a very long history. The study and science of horticulture dates all the way back to the times of Cyrus the Great of ancient Persia, and has been going on ever since, with present-day horticulturists such as Freeman S. Howlett and Luther Burbank. The practice of horticulture can be retraced for many thousands of years. The cultivation of taro and yam in Papua New Guinea dates back to at least 6950–6440 cal BP. The origins of horticulture lie in the transition of human communities from nomadic hunter-gatherers to sedentary or semi-sedentary horticultural communities, cultivating a variety of crops on a small scale around their dwellings or in specialized plots visited occasionally during migrations from one area to the next (such as the "milpa" or maize field of Mesoamerican cultures). In the Pre-Columbian Amazon Rainforest, natives are believed to have used biochar to enhance soil productivity by smoldering plant waste. European settlers called it Terra Preta de Indio. In forest areas such horticulture is often carried out in swiddens ("slash and burn" areas). A characteristic of horticultural communities is that useful trees are often to be found planted around communities or specially retained from the natural ecosystem. Horticulture primarily differs from agriculture in two ways. First, it generally encompasses a smaller scale of cultivation, using small plots of mixed crops rather than large fields of single crops. Secondly, horticultural cultivations generally include a wide variety of crops, even including fruit trees with ground crops. Agricultural cultivations however as a rule focus on one primary crop. In pre-contact North America the semi-sedentary horticultural communities of the Eastern Woodlands (growing maize, squash and sunflower) contrasted markedly with the mobile hunter-gatherer communities of the Plains people. In Central America, Maya horticulture involved augmentation of the forest with useful trees such as papaya, avocado, cacao, ceiba and sapodilla. In the cornfields, multiple crops were grown such as beans (using cornstalks as supports), squash, pumpkins and chilli peppers, in some cultures tended mainly or exclusively by women.

Horticulture is the area of agriculture involving the science of growing and caring for plants. Horticulture is socially important because it improves how we use plants, for food and other human purposes, as well as repairing the environment and personal aesthetics. Plants are also very important in environmental protection. They are used to re-vegetate and restore land disturbed by human or natural activities, they control erosion and they help to clean the air and water. Plants also have an important role in the beautification of urban and rural landscapes and recreation areas.

Examples of horticulture include the following:

- landscaping
- gardening
- growing crops for food, fiber and fuel
- horticultural therapy—using horticultural methods to treat patients
- Arboriculture—the care of trees

Horticulture, the branch of plant agriculture dealing with garden crops, generally fruits, vegetables, and ornamental plants. The word is derived from the Latin hortus, "garden," and colere, "to cultivate." As a general term, it covers all forms of garden management, but in ordinary use it refers to intensive commercial production. In terms of scale, horticulture falls between domestic gardening and field agriculture, though all forms of cultivation naturally have close links.

Horticulture is divided into the cultivation of plants for food (pomology and olericulture) and plants for ornament (floriculture and landscape horticulture). Pomology deals with fruit and nut crops. Olericulture deals with herbaceous plants for the kitchen, including, for example, carrots (edible root), asparagus (edible stem), lettuce (edible leaf), cauliflower (edible flower), tomatoes (edible fruit), and peas (edible seed). Floriculture deals with the production of flowers and ornamental plants; generally, cut flowers, pot plants, and greenery. Landscape horticulture is a broad category that includes plants for the landscape, including lawn turf, but particularly nursery crops such as shrubs, trees and climbers.

The specialization of the horticulturist and the success of the crop are influenced by many factors. Among these are climate, terrain, and other regional variations.

Ecology, also called bioecology, bionomics, or environmental biology, study of the relationships between organisms and their environment. Some of the most pressing problems in human affairs—expanding populations, food scarcities, environmental pollution including global warming, extinctions of plant and animal species, and all the attendant sociological and political problems—are to a great degree ecological.

The word ecology was coined by the German zoologist Ernst Haeckel, who applied the term oekologie to the "relation of the animal both to its organic as well as its inorganic environment." The word comes from the Greek oikos, meaning "household," "home," or "place to live." Thus, ecology deals with the organism and its environment. The concept of environment includes both other organisms and physical surroundings. It involves relationships between individuals within a population and between individuals of different populations. These interactions between individuals, between populations, and between organisms and their environment form ecological systems, or ecosystems. Ecology has been defined variously as "the study of the interrelationships of organisms with their environment and each other," as "the economy of nature," and as "the biology of ecosystems.

Ecology is the branch of biology which studies the interactions among organisms and their environment. Objects of study include interactions of organisms with each other and with abiotic components of their environment. Topics of interest include the biodiversity, distribution, biomass, and populations of organisms, as well as cooperation and competition within and between species. Ecosystems are dynamically interacting systems of organisms, the communities they make up, and the non-living components of their environment. Ecosystem processes, such as primary production, pedogenesis, nutrient cycling, and niche construction, regulate the flux of energy and matter through an environment. These processes are sustained by organisms with specific life history traits. Biodiversity means the varieties of species, genes, and ecosystems, enhances certain ecosystem services.

Ecology is not synonymous with environmentalism, natural history, or environmental science. It overlaps with the closely related sciences of evolutionary biology, genetics and ethology. An important focus for ecologists is to improve the understanding of how biodiversity affects ecological function. Ecologists seek to explain:

- Life processes, interactions, and adaptations.
- The movement of materials and energy through living communities.
- The successional development of ecosystems.
- The abundance and distribution of organisms and biodiversity in the context of the environment.

Ecology has practical applications in conservation biology, wetland management, natural resource management (agroecology, agriculture, forestry, agroforestry, fisheries), city planning (urban ecology), community health, economics, basic and applied science, and human social interaction (human ecology). For example, the Circles of Sustainability approach treats ecology as more than the environment 'out there'. It is not treated as separate from humans. Organisms (including humans) and resources compose ecosystems which, in turn, maintain biophysical feedback mechanisms that moderate processes acting on living (biotic) and non-living (abiotic) components of the planet. Ecosystems sustain life-supporting functions and produce natural capital like biomass production (food, fuel, fiber, and medicine), the regulation of climate, global biogeochemical cycles, water filtration, soil formation, erosion control, flood protection, and many other natural features of scientific, historical, economic, or intrinsic value.

The word "ecology" ("Ökologie") was coined in 1866 by the German scientist Ernst Haeckel. Ecological thought is derivative of established currents in philosophy, particularly from ethics and politics. Ancient Greek philosophers such as Hippocrates and Aristotle laid the foundations of ecology in their studies on natural history. Modern ecology became a much more rigorous science in the late 19th century. Evolutionary concepts relating to adaptation and natural selection became the cornerstones of modern ecological theory.

Ecology, or ecological science, is the scientific study of the distribution and abundance of living organisms and how the distribution and abundance are affected by interactions between the organisms and their environment.

The environment of an organism includes both physical properties, which can be described as the sum of local abiotic factors such as insolation (sunlight), climate, and geology, as well as the other organisms that share its habitat.

Ecology is usually considered a branch of biology, the general science that studies living organisms.

Organisms can be studied at many different levels, from proteins and nucleic acids (in biochemistry and molecular biology), to cells (in cellular biology), to individuals (in botany, zoology and other similar disciplines), and finally at the level of populations, communities and ecosystems, to the biosphere as a whole; these latter strata are the primary subjects of ecological inquiries.

Ecology is a Multi-disciplinary Science

Because of its focus on the higher levels of the organization of life on earth and on the interrelations between organisms and their environment, ecology draws heavily on many other branches of science, especially geology and geography, meteorology, pedology, chemistry and physics.

Thus, ecology is considered by some to be a holistic science, one that over-arches older disciplines such as biology which in this view become sub-disciplines contributing to ecological knowledge.

REFERENCES

https://en.wikipedia.org/wiki/Horticulture

https://www.merriam-webster.com/dictionary/horticulture

https://articles.extension.org/pages/64847/what-is-horticulture

https://www.britannica.com/science/horticulture

https://www.britannica.com/science/ecology

https://en.wikipedia.org/wiki/Ecology

https://www.sciencedaily.com/terms/ecology.htm

Horticulture and Ecology - *Studies & Management* Pages 6-33
Edited by: Dr. Alka Chauhan and Dr. Pawan Kumar 'Bharti'
ISBN: 978-93-88854-09-2
Edition: 2019
Published by: Discovery Publishing House Pvt. Ltd., New Delhi (India)

2 Irrigation Methods for Vegetable Crops

[1]A. Solaimalai, [2]M. Jayakumar, [3]Dr. A. Rajkumar and [4]S. Irulandi

Introduction

About 83% of the fresh water resources in India are currently being used for agriculture. However, tomato crop requires 400-800 mm water per total growing period in an open field. So, there is a tremendous pressure on agriculture sector to reduce its share of water and at the same time to improve total production by enhancing productivity with increased water use efficiency (Pandey *et al.*, 2013). Although, we know water scarcity is the most common problem in many areas creating problem in growing crops. Water productivity at the all India level is very low and needs to be enhanced through tapping, harvesting and recycling water, efficient on-farm water management practices, micro irrigation, use of waste water and resource conservation technologies. The overall irrigation efficiency of the major and medium irrigation projects in India is estimated at around 38%, says the survey, adding that efficiency of the surface irrigation system can be improved from 35-40% to around 60% and that of groundwater from 65 to 75% (Source: the third-pole.net). Drip irrigation can be very effectively utilized in such land situation of the region. Drip irrigation provides an efficient method of water/fertilizer delivery and allows precise timing and uniform distribution of water and applied nutrients (Pandey *et al.*, 2013). Drip irrigation is an effective way to supply water to roots of plant and save water, while maintaining high yield and excellent product quality.

Water molecules are integral part of living systems being the solvent for metabolites and structural component of proteins and nucleic acids. Transpiration lowers water potential at evaporative sites within leaves. This

1 Associate Professor (Agronomy), Department of Fruit Crops, Horticultural College & Research, TNAU, Periyakulam–625 604, Tamil Nadu, India.
2 Corresponding author: Scientist, Regional Coffee Research Station, Thandikudi, Dindugul-District, Tamil Nadu, India.
3 Assistant Professor (Horticulture), Krishna College of Agriculture & Technology, Sree Rangapuram, Usilampatti (TK), Madurai (Dt), Tamil Nadu, India.
4 Assistant Professor (Agricultural Entomology), Department of Fruit Crops, Horticultural College & Research, TNAU, Periyakulam–625 604, Tamil Nadu, India.

effect is immediately translated to root system through creating tension in plants vascular system. This demand of water must be satisfied continuously to maintain leaf water potential. The internal water balance of plants depends on relative rates of water absorption and water loss. Despite stomatal resistance, the steep gradient in vapour pressure from leaf to air favours transpiration rate well in excess of CO_2 fixation. Transpiration rate normally ranges from 500 to 2500 mg H_2O/dm^2-h, whereas CO_2 fixation rates range generally 5 to 25 mg CO_2/dm^2-h. This physiological phenomenon amply justifies high water requirement to maintain high dry matter productivity. For this reason, actively growing plants as the case of all the vegetable crops need to maintain liquid phase continuity from soil water through its vascular system and all the way to evaporative sites in leaves.

Vegetables contain large amount of water and the product qualities like tenderness, succulence, crispness and flavor are very much related to water supply at proper stages. In fact, texture of vegetables is determined by combination of tissue structure, cell wall properties and turgor pressure.

The phenology of the growing plant can be characterized by vegetative, flowering, fruiting and other distinctive characteristics in vegetative stage like, curding in cauliflower, heading in cabbage and lettuce, bulbing in onion and garlic and tuberization in potato and sweet potato. During vegetative stage, consumptive use continues to increase till the end of this stage of growth and flowering occurs near and during the peak of consumptive use. The fruiting stage is accompanied by a decrease in consumptive use until the transpiration ceases during the later part of development of seeds inside the fruit.

Stomata are the compulsory passage way for CO_2 and H_2O gas exchange between plant and atmosphere. Therefore, to fix carbon, the plant losses water to the atmosphere, the ratio being variable depending on species and growing conditions. This ratio is called water use efficiency i.e. quantity water transpired/ unit of carbon fixed in dry matter.

Water use efficiency increases as amount of water required /unit of dry matter production decreases. Transpiration ratio is used express water use efficiency. Transpiration ratio refers to the quantity of water transpired by plant to accumulate 1 g of dry matter. This ratio ranges from 200 to 1000 (200:1 to 1000:1) depending on crop species, cultivation conditions and vegetation period. Vegetable crops can be categorized in to four groups according to such index of water exchange. Leaf vegetables require more water to produce 1 g dry matter than pumpkin. Vegetable crops showing high transpiration ratio cannot endure water stress, and any shortage of water during the period of growth severely affects yield. On the other hand, vegetable crops characterized by very low transpiration ratio can somewhat endure water stress condition and can give satisfactory yield even in moisture deficit condition.

Critical Stages of Crop Growth

Optimal soil moisture for plant growth varies with the stage of crop growth. Certain periods during the crop growth and development are most sensitive to soil moisture stress compared with other. These periods are known as moisture sensitive periods. The term critical period is commonly used to define the stage of growth when plants are most sensitive to shortage of water. Inadequate water supply during moisture sensitive periods will irrevocably reduce the yield and provision of adequate water and other management practices at other growth stages will not help in recovering the yield lost.

In case of vegetables, when they are young, though transpire less water, need a stress free moisture condition because of the very weak root system which is sparsely distributed and located in upper 15 to 20 cm layer of soil that gets quickly dried. Vegetable crops utilize and transpire more water in the later stages of growth during which moisture stress markedly reduces yield (Table 2.1).

Table 2.1: Water Requirement of Vegetable Crops

Crop	Water requirement (mm)
Tomato	600-800
Potato	500-700
Pea	350-500
Onion	350-550
Bean	300-500
Cabbage	380-500

Water is a vital component of vegetable crop production. An adequate water supply is essential to maximize both quality and crop yield for a given date. It is also an important management tool enhancing crop establishment, chemical weed control and harvesting of root vegetables. However, water has to be applied at the correct time, in sufficient quantities but without waste and with sympathy for the environment as a whole.

Seasonal Water Requirements and Storage

In a survey carried out in connection with these farmers, 75% of vegetable growers said that they had been short of irrigation water at some time in the last 10 years and 40% had insufficient in at least one season during the last 5 years. As a result these experiences many had been active in installing water storage facilities. Indeed the need for businesses to store reasonable quantities of water is likely to become even more important as water costs rise and competition for supplies increases. The feasibility of water storage will relate to water availability and source.

Reservoirs

Storage reservoirs are most commonly formed using an off-stream, earth embankment construction, filled by gravity or pumping. This avoids the need to make provisions for flood flows, with any surplus water being returned via an overflow pipe. Occasionally, reservoirs are made by damming an existing water course. This option can be expensive, requiring overflow and bypass arrangements.

Storage Tanks

Water for immediate use on glass house plant-raising units should be stored in a covered tank to prevent contamination. The storage tank can be an elevated sectional metal tank, a ground level reinforced concrete tank or a ground level corrugated metal tank. The latter is the most cost effective.

System Installation and Equipment

The scale and cropping type dictates the system to be used, as well as the level of investment in underground mains and water storage. While hose reel systems still predominate, centre pivot and linear systems are also of significance on some large-scale farms. Trickle irrigation schemes, at least at present, are usually tailored for small areas or specialist applications. There are several stages to work through in designing and installing an irrigation scheme such as (*a*) water source and quality, (*b*) volume of water required, (*c*) planning the irrigation layout and (*d*) application equipment.

Water Source and Quality

Most water sources are suitable for the whole range of crops and systems, but physical water quality is crucially important for trickle irrigation, to avoid blockages. Given sufficient investment, virtually all water can be adequately filtered. Use of trickle irrigation may be advantageous in saline water areas, as it delivers the water at ground level, avoiding foliage scorch.

Volume of Water Required

The frequency of water application at peak summer demand should be decided at the design stage. The volume required at each application depends on the water holding capacity of the soil, evapotranspiration rate and the cropping. The water volume needed, combined with the area being irrigated, the pressure required by the system and the land levels dictate the size and type of irrigation mains and the pump specification. It is crucial to get these design points right from the outset because it is difficult and expensive to alter later. Allowing for expansion, e.g. by using larger mains near the pump is advantageous, if finances will allow.

Planning the Irrigation Layout

Irrigation mains are sized on the flow required, allowing for acceptable pressure drops. For larger schemes, a ring main is a great advantage, enabling the water to flow from each direction to a hydrant. This limits the pipe size needed and reduces pump size but is more suited to farms that are broadly rectangular in shape rather than long and narrow. Sufficient hydrants should be incorporated in the design to permit flexible use. Very few farms have more than they need. Mains piping should be specified for the task involved for hose reel irrigation standard. To plan the most efficient systems, filed need to be individually considered for the soil type, slope and especially row length. For hose reel requirement, the mains and hydrants are usually laid to suit the length of pipe on the hose reel as far as practically possible. Large fields may need hydrants in the middle of fields but usually they are at the side or corners of fields, alongside a farm track etc. hopefully serving land on both sides. Where a field is on the perimeter of the form and only to be irrigated say once in year in a rotation, it is normally practicable to use portable above ground pipe (Table 2.2). Trickle mains and especially the header pipes are often fabricated in black polyethylene and are either buried or laid on the soil surface.

Table 2.2: Potential Water Use Efficiency of Irrigation Systems

Irrigation systems	Water use efficiency (%)	Pump pressure (psi)
Hand move (sm sprinkler)	75	60-100
Hand move (gun sprinkler)	70	80-130
Solid set	80	60-100
Centre pivot (med. Pressure)	90	70-110
Centre pivot (high Pressure)	92	40-80
Linear move	92	40-80
Hose pull traveler	70	30-200
Drip irrigation	90+	5-75

Application Equipment

The consideration should be the needs and value of the cropping set against the annual cost of the equipment. Few farms are now completely new to irrigation. However, most have the potential to improve some aspect of performance with existing equipment and can consider further improvements when additional purchases are being considered.

Potentially, the most water efficient method of application is drip irrigation, but apart from use on very high value vegetable crops or where water supplies are very limited, the investment is currently difficult to justify ton field vegetable crops. When comparing different application systems, the factors that should be considered are:

(*a*) Relative energy requirements.

(*b*) The uniformity of distribution and therefore potential water saving.

(*c*) Types of hose reel: rain gun versus booms.

(*d*) Irrigation management e.g. lane spacing maximizing night time irrigation.

(*e*) Capital cost versus the crop value.

(*f*) Tied ridge machines to retain water within the rooting zone.

Selection of Suitable Crops and Varieties

In vegetable crops like dolichos bean, cowpea, cluster bean, lima bean, chilli, drumstick, brinjal and okra are suitable for rainfed cultivation. Among these, legume vegetables can be recommended for contingency crop-planning in an eventuality of late monsoon rains. Varieties having good root system and capacity to recoup after the alleviation of stress need to be selected. Depending upon situation, it is recommended to use short duration varieties.

Improved Method of Seedling Production

Improved method of seedling production such as Protray grown seedling using coco peat, nylon net protection and bio-fertilizers/bio-pesticide inoculation at nursery stage has good potential for obtaining sturdy, uniform and healthy seedlings. These seedlings when transplanted in the main-field will establish better with less root damage and fare better in overcoming biotic and abiotic stresses particularly during water stress conditions.

Adoption of Soil and Moisture Conservation Techniques

Contour cultivation, contour trip cropping, mixed Cropping, tillage, mulching, zero tillage, are some of the agronomical measures for the in-situ soil moisture conservation. Mechanical measures like contour bunding, graded bunding, bench terracing, vertical mulching etc. also need to be followed for effective soil and moisture conservation in dry lands. Another technology for efficient utilization of runoff is water harvesting recycling. Rainwater harvesting includes collecting runoff water into dug out ponds or tanks in small depressions, gullies and into storage dams of earth or masonry structures. Rain water harvesting is possible in areas having rainfall as little as 500 to 800 mm. Depending on the rainfall and soil characteristics, 10-50 % of the runoff can be collected in farm pond. Surface run off thus collected in a farm pond can be used to provide protective irrigation in the period of prolonged dry spell or through microirrigation techniques.

Enhancing Soil Organic Matter Content

Constant efforts must be made to improve the soil organic carbon. Incorporation of crop residues and farm yard manure to soil improves the organic matter status, improves soil structure and soil moisture storage capacity. Organic matter content of the soil can also be improved by fallowing alley cropping, green manuring, crop rotation and agro forestry. Vegetable being short duration crop and having faster growth phases, the available organic matter needs to be properly composted. Vermicomposting can be followed for quicker usage of available organic matter in the soil and improving the soil moisture holding capacity.

Application of Foliar Nutrition

The foliar application of nutrients during water stress conditions helps in the better growth by quick absorption of nutrients. The spraying of K and Ca induces drought tolerance in vegetable crops. Spraying of micronutrients and secondary nutrients improves crop yields and quality.

Use of Drip Irrigation

Drip irrigation has proved its superiority over other conventional method of irrigation, in Horticulture due to precise and direct application of water in root zone. A considerable saving in water, increased growth, development and yields of fruits and vegetables and control of weeds, saving in labour under drip irrigation are the added advantages. Drip irrigation can be adopted in fruit crops and also to all vegetable crops including closed spaced crops like onions and beans. The saving in water is to the tune of 30-50 % depending on the crop and season. Generally inline drip laterals having emitting point spaced at 30cm distance and emitting at the rate of 2LPH is selected for vegetable crops. In crops like chilli, brinjal, cauliflower and okra paired row planting is practiced and one drip lateral is used for two crop rows. High frequency water management by drip irrigation provides daily requirement of water to a portion of the root zone of each plant and maintains a high soil matric potential in the rhizosphere to reduce plant water stress (Nakayama and Bucks, 1986).

Maisiri *et al.* (2005) compared water productivity of low cost drip irrigation system and surface irrigation system for vegetable cultivation. Drip irrigation method used 7.87 m^3 of water which led to > 50% of water saving compared to surface irrigation method (23.88 m^3). The lower percentage wetted area in drip irrigation systems (up to 30%) compared to surface irrigation (100%) might be the major reason for difference in water use. This led to water productivity of 10.8 kg m^{-3} in drip irrigation and 2.4 kg m^{-3} in conventional surface irrigation for vegetable cultivation.

Use of Micro Sprinkler Irrigation

Depending upon situation and availability of water, this technology can be used for fruits and vegetable crops. The cost of initial establishment is lower compared to drip system. Further in summer the sprinkling of water helps in reducing the microclimate temperature and increasing the humidity, thereby improving the growth and yield of the crop. The water saved is to the tune of 20 to 30 per cent.

Moisture Saving Methods under Limited Water Resource Conditions

The following methods may be adopted under limited water conditions to save water.

Water Saving Irrigation Method

Under limited water situations, water-saving irrigation methods like alternate furrow irrigation or widely spaced furrow irrigation and drip irrigation systems can be adopted. Studies conducted on methods of irrigation in capsicum, tomato, okra and cauliflower indicated that adopting alternate-furrow irrigation and widely-spaced furrow irrigation saved 35 to 40 per cent of irrigation water without adversely affecting yield.

Mulching Practices in Vegetable Production

The technique of covering the soil with natural crop residues or plastic films for soil and water conservation is called mulching. Mulching can be practiced in fruits and vegetable crops using crop residues and other organic material available in the farm. Recently plastic mulches have come into use due to the inherent advantages of efficient moisture conservation, weed suppression and maintenance of soil structure. Wide variety of vegetables can be successfully grown using mulches. In addition to soil and water conservation, improved yield and quality, suppression of weed growth , mulches can improve the use efficiency of applied fertilizer nutrients and also use of reflective mulches are likely to minimize the incidence of virus diseases. For vegetable production generally polyethylene mulch film of 30 micron thick and 1 to 1.2 m width is used. Generally raised bed with drip irrigation system is followed while laying the mulch film.

Wind Breaks, Hedges and Intercropping

To overcome the adverse effect of high temperature and dry winds, tall growing trees need to be planted all along the boundary of the farm. Inter cropping of vegetable crops of the area can be practiced in orchards during summer months. Maize/ Sorghum can be grown all along the border of the plot to mitigate the effect of desiccating winds.

Use of Protected Cultivation of Vegetables

In peri-urban regions where climate does not favour year round production of crops in the open field, vegetable production can be taken up in protected environment (Figure 2.1). Protective structure is a facility to protect crop from biotic and abiotic constraints. Structures for protected cultivation include green houses, plastic/net houses and "tunnels". Commonly used protected structures are polyhouses and net or shade houses. Rain-shelter is a simple structure covered with polyethylene sheet which helps in producing the crops which are affected by excessive rainfall. The productivity of tomato, onions and melons are adversely affected in the event of high rainfall due to difficulty in managing the foliar diseases, lack of proper soil aeration and drainage and also depending on the nature of crop physical damage of the foliage and flower drop. Net house cultivation and shade net cultivation provide better microclimate especially during summer in minimizing the high temperature effect and improving the relative humidity. The productivity of tomato, French bean and capsicum can be improved during high temperature period by using net/shade net on the top.

Efficient use of available irrigation water is essential for increasing agricultural production for the alarming Indian population. Water availability for irrigation is going to be a major constraint for agriculture in the near future. Hence, judicious use of the available water resources through more efficient methods of water application like drip irrigation under conditions of protected cultivation becomes necessary to enhance the yield and water use efficiency (Dunage *et al.*, 2009). Protected cultivation of vegetables provides the best way to increase the productivity and quality of vegetables, especially cucurbits. Naturally ventilated greenhouses are highly suitable for year round cultivation of parthenocarpic cucumber varieties.

Fig. 2.1: Drip irrigation in polyhouse

Irrigation Methods

Tomato

Hebbar *et al.* (2004) recorded that the fertigation with 100 per cent water soluble fertilizer (WSF) increased the fruit yield significantly (79.2 q/ ha) over furrow-irrigated control (52.1 q /ha). The increase in fruit yield was due to the improvement in fruit weight of tomato under drip fertigation, possibly due to enhanced water utilization through drip, better nutrients uptake and excellent soil-water-air environment in the root zone (Singandhupe *et al.*, 2003). Gupta *et al.* (2010) recorded drip irrigation at 80 per cent ET water along with 80 per cent recommended dose of NPK as fertigation was found significantly superior over all other treatment combinations with maximum fruit yield (366.48 q /ha) in hybrid tomato. Ngouajio *et al.* (2007) showed that drip irrigation reduced water consumption by 20%compared to the furrow irrigation.

Waldir *et al.* (2007) proved that in tomato maximum fruit yield was reached when irrigations were performed at SWT thresholds of 35, 12, and 15 kPa during vegetative, fruit development, and maturation growth stages. Harmanto *et al.* (2005) concluded that the drip irrigation at 75% of ETc provided the maximum crop yields and irrigation water productivity in tomato variety Troy 489 under tropical greenhouse conditions. Mahajan *et al.* (2007) revealed that drip irrigation at 0.5 pan evaporation with fertigation at 100 per cent recommended nitrogen resulted in increased tomato fruit yield by 59.5 per cent compared to conventional method. Hebbar *et al.* (2002) revealed that the total dry matter production and leaf area index of tomato were significantly higher in drip irrigation (165.8 g and 3.12 respectively) over furrow irrigation with the higher fruit yield of 19.9 per cent in drip irrigation (71.9 Mg /ha) over furrow irrigation (59.50 Mg/ha).

Ananta (2006) reported that higher fruit yield of tomato was noticed when nitrogen was supplied in 8 or 10 split doses with 100 per cent ET through drip irrigation. Subba Reddy *et al.* (2015) reported that in tomato highest water use efficiency (1.44) was observed in drip + polythene mulch + trellising followed by drip + polythene mulch (1.26). Manish (2007) conducted an experiment to evaluate the agro techniques *viz.*, growing media, irrigation regime, fertigation and mulching on productivity of tomato. Growing media of soil: compost: sand (2: 1:1), irrigation regime of 20 kPa, 50kg /ha as basal dose with straight fertilizers and fertigation at the rate of 250 kg /ha with water soluble fertilizer with black polythene mulched recorded significantly higher number of flower cluster per plant (12.16), fruit per plant (48.33) and fruit yield (2.85 kg / plant).

At Abohar (Punjab), drip irrigation at80% pan evaporation applied gave significantly higher fruit yield (45.57 t/ha) compared with the surface irrigation (29.43 t/ha) (Table 3). Use of black polyethylene mulch + drip irrigation further raised the fruit yield to 57.87 t/ha. Plant height, leaf area index, dry matter production, fruit weight and yield increased significantly with the use of drip irrigation alone and in conjunction with polyethylene mulch compared to surface irrigation alone or with mulch. Water-use efficiency under drip irrigation alone, drip irrigation + polyethylene mulch and surface irrigation was 0.97, 1.23 and 0.42 t/ha-cm, respectively. Among different irrigation levels,drip irrigation at 80% PE resulted in higher net returns (Rs.34431 /ha) and B: C ratio (1.76) into mato. However, maximum net returns (51386 Rs/ha) and B: C ratio (2.03) was found with drip irrigation at 80% PE+ polyethylene mulch compared to other treatments. Drip irrigation besides giving a saving of 38% water resulted into 55% higher fruit yield compared to surface irrigation (Rajbir Singh *et al.*, 2009).

Table 2.3: Effect of Different Irrigation Levels and Mulching on Fruit Yield, Water Use Efficiency and Economics of Tomato

Treatments	Fruit weight (g)	Yield (t/ha)	Water applied (cm)	WUE (kg/ ha-mm)	Net returns (Rs./ha)	B: Cratio
Drip irrigation with 100 % PE	76.4	42.02	52.4	0.80	27909	1.61
Drip irrigation with 80 % PE	79.6	45.57	43.1	1.06	34431	1.76
Drip irrigation with 60 % PE	69.8	34.52	33.7	1.02	15407	1.34
surface irrigation	62.3	29.43	70.0	0.42	19146	1.59
Drip irrigation with 100 % PE + BPM	81.7	52.58	52.4	1.00	41819	1.83
Drip irrigation with 80 % PE + BPM	86.6	57.87	43.1	1.34	51386	2.03
Drip irrigation with 60 % PE + BPM	75.9	43.75	33.7	1.30	26989	1.54
surface irrigation + BPM	68.1	36.06	70.0	0.51	26183	1.71
CD 5 %	5.0	2.85	-	-	-	-

(Rajbir Singh *et al.*, 2009). PE: Pan evaporation, BPM: black polyethylene mulch

A considerably saving in water, increased growth, development and yield of tomato under drip irrigation has been reported (Bhella 1988; Bafna *et al.*, 1993; Imtiyaz *et al.*, 2000). Elknerand Kaniszewski (1995) also observed significantly higher fruit weight of tomato under drip irrigation as compared to control practices. Locascio *et al.* (1989) reported the water requirement of tomato under drip irrigation is about 50% of pan evaporation on fine sandy soil but between 50 to 100% pan evaporation values on the fine sandy loam soil. Maximum water use efficiency was observed with 80% of PE both under mulched and unmulched conditions (Raina *et al.*,1999).

Machado *et al.* (2003) compared yield and root distribution among surface and subsurface drip irrigation (at two different depths) of tomato cultivars. Yields were 88 and 114 t/ha (with surface), 108 and 128 t/ha (subsurface at 20 cm depth), 105 and 125 t/ha (subsurface at40 cm depth) for the first and second year, respectively. Dalvi *et al.* (1999) revealed that drip irrigation in tomato scheduled at every second day frequency, led to better root elongation compared to daily irrigation with irrigation at 0.79 ET. It saved water to the tune of 21% and increased yield up to 27%as compared to traditional method of cultivation. Significantly higher uptake of nutrients was observed under drip fertigation over conventional surface irrigation in tomato (Sharma *et al.*, 2009).

Chillies

Muralikrishnaswamy *et al.*, (2006) recorded the significant effect of drip irrigation at 75 per cent PE (pan evaporation) + 100 per cent N and K through fertigation recorded 67.5% pod yield and drip irrigation at 50 per cent PE + 100 per cent N and K through fertigation recorded 65.8 percent increased pod yield when compared to surface irrigation 0.90 IW/CPE ratio + entire NPK as soil application. Pandey *et al.*, (2013) showed that drip irrigation enhanced the fruit yield, net income and minimized the time, weeds and diseases of the crop. Fertigation resulted in maximum yield (10.20 kg m^{-2}), minimal disease and saved water and total irrigation time as compared to top dressing. The drip irrigation had significantly increased yield (10.50 kg m^{-2}) and net income (60.30 %) as compared to flood irrigation. Darwish *et al.*, (2003) reported that irrigation at 100 per cent PE + fertigation with 100 per cent N and K and 50 per cent PE + fertigation with 100 per cent N and K being at par recorded 67.06 and 65.78 per cent, respectively higher pod yield of chilli as compared to surface irrigation at 0.90 IW/CPE ratio + entire NPK as soil application. Swarajyalakshmi *et al.* (2005) reported that the highest green chilli yield (21.56 t ha^{-1}) was recorded through drip method scheduled at 0.8 ET under black polythene mulch. This increase was accounted to 34 per cent over conventional method of irrigation practiced.

Brinjal

Aujla *et al.*, (2007) reported that 50% water saving could be achieved through drip irrigation in brinjal while obtaining 4% yield increase as compared to furrow irrigation. At Bhavanisagar (Tamil Nadu), Vijayakumar *et al.* (2010) noted higher yields (42.33 t/ha in I crop and 37.90 t /ha in II crop) and maximum shoot length of 45.2, 82.0 and 111.3 cm at 30, 60 and 90 days after planting (DAP) and number of branches per plant of 8.3, 12.1 and 16.0 at 30, 60 and 90 DAP, respectively by drip irrigation at 75% of PE with 75% of recommended N and K. Chauhan *et al.* (2013) concluded drip irrigation at 1.0 Et, an optimum irrigation schedule for brinjal. It gave 30.95% higher fruit yield of brinjal and saved 24.62 per cent irrigation water over conventional surface irrigation. Ughade and Mahadkar (2014) reported that the brinjal crop under Field water use efficiency (FWUE) was maximum under treatment 80% ET with 100% RDF drip fertigation while comparing with 100 and 60% ET with RDF drip fertigation. Singandupe *et al.* (2007) reported in brinjal that irrigation at 80 per cent ET (6.3 t/ha) has given at par yield with 100 per cent ET (6.45 t/ha).Yadav *et al.* (2004) found in brinjal that maximum plant height of 61.7 cm, number of branches per plant of 11.1 and biological yield of 405.7g with 80 mm CPE irrigation treatment and 100 kg of N, 50 kg P_2O_5 and 25 kg K_2O/ha.

Table 2.4: Effect of Drip Irrigation on Yield Parameters and Yield of Brinjal for Low Fertility Area

Treatments	Fruit length (cm)	Fruit diameter (cm)	Fruit weight (gm)	Yield (t/ ha)	Water Required (cm)	WUE (kg/ ha-mm)
50% drip irrigation level	13	6.7	57	6252	5.5	1.136
65% drip irrigation level	11	5.0	46	6950	6.5	1.069
75% drip irrigation level	11	4.5	44	7323	7.5	0.964
80% drip irrigation level	12	5.5	52	10745	8.0	1.343
90% drip irrigation level	9.5	6.0	52	9841	8.5	1.157
100% drip irrigation level	10.5	6.2	54	11159	9.5	1.220

(Ram Kumar *et al.*, 2016)

At Moradabad (Uttar Pradesh), maximum yield of crop 900 gm/plant and minimum of yield 600 g/plant and total yield (52270 kg/ha) (Table 2.4). The increase in water use efficiency for drip irrigation system. Higher field water use efficiency (1.343 kg /ha-cm) was found at 65% irrigation level, indicating comparatively more efficient use of irrigation water with a possibility of water saving of 35% water by adopting 80% drip irrigation plot (1.58 litre/plant/day) (Ram Kumar *et al.*, 2016).

Onion

Subsurface fertigation had similar effects on yield as did surface fertigation. Irrigation and fertilization had little effect on total N concentration in spring sown onion (cvs. Riviera F1 and Utopia F1 (Rumpel *et al.*, 2004). Dingre *et al.*, (2012) showed that drip fertigation resulted into 12 to 74 per cent increase in the productivity of onion seed as compared to conventional method. The total irrigation water applied through surface and drip system was 840 mm and 520.45 mm indicating 39 per cent water saving whereas, field water use efficiency of drip fertigation was more by 2.5 times as that of control. Dingre *et al.* (2012) showed that drip fertigation resulted into 12 to 74% increase in the productivity of onion seed as compared to conventional method. The total irrigation water applied through surface and drip system was 840 mm and 520.45 mm indicating 39% water saving whereas, field water use efficiency of drip fertigation was more by 2.5 times as that of control.

At Dharwad (Karnataka), shorter interval of irrigation (one day interval) recorded significantly higher bulb yield (46.93 t/ha)due to significantly higher performance of growth and yield parameters (Table 2.5). The 100% PE recorded significantly higher bulb yield (50.92 t/ha) compared to 80 and 60% PE and flood irrigation and this reflected in growth and yield parameters also. Significantly higher bulb yield was recorded in one day interval of irrigation at 100 % PE (54.91 t/ha)which was on par with two days interval of irrigation at 100% PE (52.83 t/ha). Both one day and two days interval of irrigation and 60 per cent PE recorded significantly higher WUE. The intervals and levels of irrigation and their combinations were significantly superior for WUE, compared to flood irrigation (Bagali *et al.*, 2012)

Table 2.5: Effect of Scheduling of Drip Irrigation on Bulb Yield, Yield Parameters, Yield and Water Use Efficiency in Summer Onion

Treatment	Equatorial diameter (cm)	Polar diameter(cm)	Bulb weight (g)	Yield(t ha)	WUE(t /ha cm)
Interval of irrigation					
1 day interval	5.15	5.41	53.29	46.93	1.02
1 day interval	5.09	5.32	52.80	46.47	1.01
1 day interval	4.87	5.22	48.64	42.80	0.94
CD 5%	0.21	NS	2.48	2.17	0.05
Level of irrigation					
60% PE	4.52	4.81	43.34	38.16	1.09
80% PE	5.23	5.46	53.53	47.12	1.01
100% PE	5.36	5.67	57.86	50.92	0.87
CD 5%	0.21	0.23	2.83	2.48	0.05

(Bagali *et al.*, 2012)

The shorter interval of irrigation ensure the moisture in the crop root zone nearly at 15-20 % depletion from field capacity which increased number of leaves per plant and plant height (Batra and Pandita, 1984; Palled *et al.*, (1988), leaf area and LAI (Neeraja *et al.*, 2000; Channagoudar and Janawade 2004) and neck thickness (Haque *et al.*, 2004; Gethe *et al.*, (2006). Improved crop growth with irrigation or re-watering near field capacity was reported (Satyendra Kumar *et al.*, 2007).

Cucumber

Ibrikci and Buyuk (2002) obtained higher yield and leaf N, P and K content in drip fertigated cucumber than furrow irrigated plants. Beyaert *et al.*, (2007) showed that drip irrigation coupled with fertigation showed significant advantages in terms of yield and economic returns of cucumber compared with overhead irrigation and conventional fertilization practices.

Table 2.6: Effect of Drip Irrigation Levels on Yield of Salad Cucumber

Treatment	Fruits /plant	Fruit yield (t/ha)	Water used (cm)	WUE (kg / ha-cm)
50 % drip irrigation level	35b	62.26b	11.11	5603.35
65 % drip irrigation level	49a	88.8a	14.44	6148.31
80 % drip irrigation level	44a	88.06a	17.78	4953.65
95 % drip irrigation level	45a	82.77a	21.11	3920.90
100 % drip irrigation level	44a	81.79a	22.22	3680.57

(Abdul Hakkim and Jisha Chand, 2014)

At Tavanur (Kerala), *d*rip irrigation applied at the rate of 2 litre/ plant/ day to the control plants was reduced by 5, 20, 35 and 50% by applying corresponding irrigation rates of 1.9, 1.6, 1.3 and 1 litre/plant/day under different treatments (Table 2.6). Lowering irrigation level to 65% sustained the production and increased water use efficiency without decreasing the yield of cucumber. However, irrigation level of less than 65% reduced the yield without increasing water use efficiency. Maximum fruit number (49), fruit weight (7.194 kg/ plant) and fruit yield (88.8 t /ha) were obtained from drip irrigation level of 65% (1.3 litre/plant/day) and the lower fruit number (35), fruit weight (5.043 kg/plant) and fruit yield (62.26 t/ha) from drip irrigation level of 50% (1 litre/plant/ day), with the lowest water application rate total quantity of water applied through 65% drip irrigation level was 144.4 mm and which showed 35 % water saving over control with higher water use efficiency (6148.31 kg /ha-cm) and B:C ratio (3.41)under naturally ventilated polyhouse (Abdul Hakkim and Jisha Chand, 2014).

Wang *et al.* (1999) studied the relationship between irrigation amount, yield and quality of cucumber under greenhouse. Xiaobo *et al.* (2002) studied the water requirement of cucumber for different cropping in solar greenhouse. Reducing water supply at seedling stage, controlling water supply at flowering stage and increasing water supply at fruiting stage of cucumber can increase yield and water use efficiency (Shao *et al.*, 2010).

Okra

Rekha and Mahavishnan (2008) reported the water and fertilizer saving by 40-70 and 30-50 per cent, respectively through drip fertigation in okra. Tiwari *et al.*(1998) reported higher fresh yield of okra crop under dripirrigation compared to furrow irrigation. Based on the average yield of three years, all the drip irrigated at 40% deficit water supply resulted in 45% higher yield of okra as compared to furrow irrigation.

Subsurface drip application in Okra crop resulted in greater yield and water use efficiency by 41.82 and 40% as compared to that of furrow irrigation.

Experiments were conducted to evaluate the soil moisture dynamics under subsurface drip for the Okra crop in four soil layers 0-20, 20-40, 40-60, and 60-90 cm. Temporal variations of soil moisture in the root zone are affected by irrigation treatments. Depletion in soil moisture was relatively rapid in 0-20 cm layer whereas it was gradual 20-40 cm, 40-60 cm and 60-90 cm soil layers. The soil moisture variation within root zone of the crop was greatly influenced due to water extraction by roots and their growth. Soil moisture variation was more prominent in 0cm soil profile this may also be due to evaporation. In addition to this some part of applied irrigation water may get percolated to the lower layers. Cumulative deep drainage throughout the Okra crop growing season was less than 1 m for 20% maximum allowable deficit (MAD) (Tiwari, 2017). Significantly higher uptake of nutrients was observed under drip fertigation over conventional surface irrigation in okra (Bhanu and Mahavishan, 2008).

Sweet Pepper

Kaushal *et al.,* (2011) reported that the drip irrigation adoption increased water use efficiency (60-200%), saved water (20-60%), reduced fertilization requirement (20-33%) through fertigation, produced better quality crop and increased yield (7-25%) as compared with conventional irrigation. At Ludhiana (Punjab), dry matter accumulation, number of fruit per plant, fruit size, total yield and water use efficiency were observed higher under drip irrigation with IW/CPE ratio of 0.75 (Table 2.7). Higher plant height and leaf area index were observed in drip irrigation with IW/CPE ratio of 0.90. The minimum number of days to flowering, fruit initiation and fruit maturity were observed drip irrigation with IW/CPE ratio of 0.60. Best drip irrigated treatment I2 gave an increase of 30.67% over furrow irrigation with paired row planting and an increase of 33.74% over furrow irrigation with single row planting. The percentage of water saving for drip irrigation 0.60, 0.75 and 0.90 were 51.01%, 39.72% and 28.73% respectively over the furrow irrigation treatment. Drip irrigation with IW/CPE ratio of 0.75 gave maximum yield and higher WUE (Lodhi *et al.,* 2014).

Table 2.7: Effect of Irrigation Regimes on Yield Attributes and Yield of Sweet Pepper

Treatments	Fruits/ plant	Fruit length (cm)	Fruitgirth (cm)	Sweet pepper yield (q/ ha)	Irrigation water applied (cm)	WUE (q/ha-cm)
Drip irrigation with IW/CPE ratio 0.60	9.56	5.78	18.17	222.46	38.21	5.82
Drip irrigation with IW/CPE ratio 0.75	10.07	6.38	20.41	288.11	47.01	6.12
Drip irrigation with IW/CPE ratio 0.90	9.70	5.83	18.98	276.95	55.82	4.96

Furrow irrigation with paired row planting	9.48	5.65	17.99	220.48	78.00	2.82
Furrow irrigation with single row planting	9.38	5.53	17.88	215.42	78.00	2.76
CD 5 %	0.12	0.14	0.39	5.00	-	0.09

(Lodhi *et al.*, 2014)

Khan *et al.* (2005) reported that the plants under any kind of stressed conditions tends to shortened their life span and try to complete their life cycle in hasten which causes the lowest days to flowering, fruiting.Moisture in optimum level enhances the cell metabolism resulting in an increase in released energy which induces growth and yield of capsicum (Pandey *et al.* 2005; Lodhi *et al.* (2013).Antony and Sing and hupe (2004) concluded that the drip irrigation at 100 per cent CPE recorded the maximum capsicum yield of 99.97 g plant^{-1} compared to drip irrigation at 80 and 60 per cent CPE.Paul *et al.* (2013) studied that the capsicum yield (28.7 t/ha) was recorded maximum under 100% net irrigation volume with drip irrigation (VD) and plastic mulching and net seasonal income by 57% and 54% respectively as compared to conventional surface irrigation without mulch. Judicious application of irrigation at a regulated interval through drip irrigation which aims to supply only required amount of water of fruit yield of capsicum (Mahajan *et al.*, 2007). Significantly higher uptake of nutrients was observed under drip fertigation over conventional surface irrigation in capsicum (Tumbare and Bhoite, 2002; Tumbare, 2004). At Jorhart (Assam), higher uptake of P_2O_5 by plants (7.37 kg/ha) and by fruits (3.64 kg/ha) K_2O by plant (47.05 kg/ ha) and by fruits (26.07 kg/ha) recorded in 100% EPR + application of 75% RD of N and K through drip (Kohire Patil and Das, 2015).

Lettuce

Hanson *et al.* (1997) indicated that the consumed water in the drip method is 40% less than that of the furrow method.

Pea

Singh *et al.*(2006) showed that the increase in N through fertigation caused increased in green pea yield at all the levels of drip irrigation (0.5 Epan, 0.75 Epan and 1.0 Epan), but the magnitude of increase was highest at lowest level of water supply.

Potato

Patel and Rajput (2007) reported that the potato yield was Maximum when irrigation was applying at the 100% of the crop evapotranspiration (23.6 cm of irrigation water) and by placing the drip tape at 10.0 cm depth followed by 15.0 cm and 20.0 cm depth. Yuan *et al.* (2003) reported that the amount of increasing irrigation water had significant effects on decreasing the canopy temperature and increasing the Total fresh tuber yields and marketable tuber yields (>85 g).

Significant interaction between irrigation and nitrogen application through drip irrigation on potato yield was reported by Badra *et al.* (2012). The reduction in yield by27.3 and 44.6% was attributed to applying 40and 60%less amount of water compared to full irrigation, respectively. An Experiment was conducted at PFDC IIT Kharagpur to study the effect of fertilizer application through sub surface drip irrigation on potato crop. Result of this showed that the daily crop water requirement of potato (cv. KufriJyoti) is 0.22 litre/plant at its initial growth stage and 0.32 litre/plant at peak stage. About 220 mm of water is needed for irrigating one hectare of potato crop through drip irrigation. The maximum yield(26.74 t /ha) of potato was obtained for the lateral pipe at 7.5cm below the soil surface in sandy loam soil with fertigation schedule of nitrogen applied at 10 days interval from 20 to 70days after sowing (Tiwari, 2017).

Ahire *et al.* (2000) found that trickle irrigation system had higher values for number of tubers /plant (5.58), size of tubers (16.08 cm), weight of tubers/plant (145.5 g) and tuber yield (20.43 t/ ha) compared to surface irrigation. Trickle irrigation saved 46% irrigation water compared to surface irrigation. The wider spacing of 60 cm increased tuber yield (20.29 t /ha) compared with the narrow spacing of 45 cm (17.86 t/ha). Normal planting resulted in higher growth and yield components compared to paired row. At Meerut (Uttar Pradesh), Singh *et al.* (2002) recorded total yield of potato was higher with sprinkler irrigation at 150 % CPE (272 q /ha), earthing + weeding (270 q ha^{-1}) and N application in 3 splits (284 q /ha). N drip irrigation at 100 % resulted in the highest total tuber yield (316 q /ha) and water use efficiency (1.01 q/ ha-mm), whereas N drip irrigation at 50 % resulted in the higher nitrogen use efficiency (2.58 q N /kg). Agrawal *et al.* (2009) found that drip irrigation saves water by 30 - 50 percent as compared to conventional mode of irrigation. It increased yield of potato crop upto 30-40% in Chhattisgarh.

Bakeer *et al.* (2009) indicated that wetted soil volume (more than or equal 100 % of field capacity) in root zone "WSV e–100 % FC", application efficiency, yield and water use efficiency of potato were increased by increasing number of irrigation pulses where 100% FC in root zone. Shiri-e-Janagard *et al.* (2009) reported that maximum and minimum values of most traits studied were observed at 100 and 60% crop evapotranspiration levels, respectively. Number of tubers with 28-50 mm and larger than 50 mm diameter in size were higher at 80 and 100% of full irrigation, respectively, and total tuber yield was higher with 100% irrigation of evapotranspiration by drip irrigation. Estimating of amount of water irrigation during irrigation period for 100, 80 and 60% of water irrigation were 558.7, 445.96 and 335.22 mm respectively.

Badra *et al.* (2012) recorded that plants grown under irrigation supply (100% crop ET) resulted in higher tuber yield and there were significant reductions in total yield and yield components when applying less amount of water (80, 60 and 40% crop ET). Tuber weight was more sensitive to water deficit than tuber number, where the decrease in potato yield in the deficit water treatments was mainly due to a decrease in tuber weight. Sahebi *et al.* (2012) showed that minimum performance (19.168 t/ha) was related to the drip irrigation method with 50 percent evaporation from the A-class pan and maximum one (34.455 t/ha) was related to the drip irrigation method with 100% evaporation from the A-class pan. The maximum number of stolons, number of tubers, tuber dry weights and plant growths were found maximum in drip irrigation method with 100 % of evaporation from A class pan. Minimum percent (number of tubers) of tubers smaller than 35 mm (26.47%) and maximum tuber production (37.17%) in the size of food and market-friendly (tuber bigger than 55 mm) were attained by drip irrigation method with 100% evaporation from the A-class pan.

At New Delhi, drip irrigation increased water use efficiency three times as compared with furrow irrigation (conventional method of irrigation) (Table 2.8). Black Polyethylene mulch (25μm) conserved soil moisture, raised soil temperature by 9°C, stimulated shoot, solon and root growth, increased the total tuber number and yield but reduced the grade of tubers. Drip irrigation may prove a viable tool for source-sink alteration; stimulating early stolon initiation combined with ability to quick ground cover and sustained leaf growth for new tuber initiation for seed production as well as extended tuber bulking of early formed tubers for obtaining maximum yield with 50% saving of irrigation water and efficient use of nitrogen fertilizer (Santosh Kumari, 2012).

Table 2.8: Influence of Irrigation Methods and Mulch on Water Use, Tuber Yield and WUE of Potato

Treatments	Water use (cm)	Tuber yield (t/ha)	WUE (kg/ha-cm)
Furrow	36.79	12.78	34.73
Furrow +mulch	35.7	12.83	35.92
Alternate furrow	37.87	10.35	27.33
Alternate furrow + mulch	35.67	11.10	31.12
Drip irrigation	21.90	24.95	113.93
Drip + mulch	16.83	26.02	154.60
CD 5%	10.87	1.95	9.41

Santosh Kumari (2012)

Carrot

Quezada *et al.* (2011) showed that higher crop yield was obtained with 100% Epan treatment. However, higher WUE was found in the 75% Epan treatment equivalent to 3864 m^3/ha, which is the recommended water application level in irrigation scheduling. Regarding carrot crop yield and quality parameters, statistical differences between the different water treatments were non-significant, but the increase of applied water (125% Epan) reduced plant density and root length.

Table 2.9: Yield, Water Used and WUE of Carrot under Different Irrigation Levels

Treatments	Root yield (t /ha)	water used (m^3/ha)	Water use efficiency (kg/ m^3)
60 per cent ET irrigation under drip	39.97	2595	15.4
80 per cent ET irrigation under drip	52.36	3450	15.1
100 per cent ET irrigation under drip	42.81	4304	9.9
120 per cent ET irrigation under drip	37.90	5159	7.3
Control with sunken bed	33.06	6260	5.2

(Longwe, 2015)

At Raichur (Karnataka), root yield was higher in 80 per cent ET irrigation under drip (52.36 t/ha) and lower in control with sunken bed (33.06 t /ha) (Table 2.9). Higher water use efficiency was observed in 60 per cent ET irrigation under drip (15.4 kg m^{-3}) and lowest in control with sunken bed (5.2 kg m^{-3}) (Longwe, 2015).

Broccoli

Erdem *et al.* (2010) studied response of drip irrigated broccolito different water regimes and N fertilizer applications. Higher yield (11t/ha) was recorded with irrigation at 125% of pan evaporation (Epan) and 200 kg N /ha application in springand 4.55 t/ha at 125% of Epan with 250 kg N /ha application in autumn.

Muskmelon

Chun-Zhi Zeng *et al.,* (2009) showed that fruit quality and quantity of muskmelon yield under 90% of field water capacity is the suitable soil irrigation which can save irrigation water and improve the quality of fruit. Seyfi and Rashidi (2007) reported that the highest fruit weight and fruit thickness was obtained for the drip irrigation + polyethene mulch treatment and lower for the conventional irrigation treatment. The crop yield was higher (27.07 t/ha) for the drip irrigation + polyethene mulch treatment was found to be more effective irrigation method in improving WUE and increasing muskmelon yield.

Cabbage

Imtiyaz *et al.* (2000) recorded that the higher marketable cabbage yield of 74.26 t/ha was observed in drip irrigation at 11 mm CPE compared to 22 mm CPE (72.39 t/ha) and 33 mm CPE (45.23 t/ha). Tiwari *et al.* (2003) stated that 54% higher yield at 40% reduced water application through drip irrigation compared to furrow irrigation.

Economics

Narayanan *et al*. (1994) reported that maximum gross return was obtained with drip irrigation compared to furrow irrigation. It was reported that the net profit per ml of water used in tomato crop under drip irrigation and conventional system were 278.43 and 66.47, respectively. Singh *et al*. (2006) stated that under unlimited water supply, drip irrigation in cauliflower-hybrid chilli sequence gave a net return of ₹ 37565 /ha against ₹ 18618/ha in check basin method of irrigation. However, under limited water supply or in water hunger areas, drip irrigation boosted the net return to the tune of ₹ 1,00,077 due to increase in yield resulted from additional area covered under irrigation.

Narayanan *et al*. (1994) reported that maximum gross return was obtained with drip irrigation compared to furrow irrigation in sweet pepper. It was reported that the net profit per ml of water used in tomato crop under drip irrigation and conventional system were 278.43 and 66.47, respectively and the water use efficiencies were 123.80 and 27.95 kg/ha-cm, respectively (Anonymous, 1995). Asokaraja (1998) recorded higher benefit cost ratio of 9.89 due to drip irrigation than surface irrigation (5.44) in tomato. The cost of micro irrigation system and optimization was performed to assess minimum input cost of tomato,considering the advent of mechanically moved portable drip sets, with every second day irrigation approximately 50 percent saving on initial investment of drip set can be achieved as the same set will irrigate double the area (Dalvi *et al*.,1999). Drip irrigation at 100 per cent WRc with 100 per cent RDF registered the highest additional net income of ₹ 1,23,679 and BCR of 3.30 in chilli which was closely followed by drip irrigation at 80 per cent WRc with 100 percent RDF registering an additional net income of ₹ 1,19,488and BCR of 3.23 over surface irrigation (Selvakumar, 2006).

Do's and Don'ts for Vegetable Crops

- Establishing vegetation-free strips under the trees and between tree rows before growth begins.
- In crop like Onion, drum seeder may be used for direct sowing.
- Postpone transplanting of seedlings in the main field and also fertilizer application till the favorable soil moisture is prevailed.
- Once the soil moisture condition becomes favorable transplanting of the seedlings may be taken up.
- Resorting to foliar application of (water soluble) major nutrients.
- Protection of young plants with partial shade.
- In the inter spaces of crops weeding and inter-culture practices may be followed.
- Thinning may be taken up to reduce the plant population.

- Alternate furrow Irrigation may be taken up based on the availability of water.
- Drip Irrigation may be followed. Pitcher irrigation wherever drip is unavailable for protective maintenance.
- Plastic mulching and drip irrigation may be followed for better soil and moisture conservation and weed control.
- Adopting the conjunctive use of surface and ground water as well as the use of non-conventional sources such as brackish water.
- Waste water should not be utilized without pretreatment & safe reuse may be ensured.
- Minimise use of those fertilizers which promote vegetative growth like nitrogen, use K and B as foliar spray to maintain plant turgor.
- Reducing water losses during conveyance and distribution.
- Use of super absorbent polymers such as Luquasorb for water absorption and slow release.

At Kharagpur (West Bengal), increase in yield, saving in water, higher water use efficiency and net increase in profit were observed in vegetable fruit crops (Tiwari *et al.*, 1998; Tiwari *et al.*, 1998a; Tiwari *et al.*, 2003). Wetting per cent (Wp) was decided based on average canopy growth of the plant (which was 40% of the area of each plant). As the canopy area increases the wetting fraction also increased (Cetin and Uygan, 2008).

Conclusion

Water is a major input for agricultural production. About 83% of the fresh water resources in India are currently being used for agriculture. In the current situation, it is a scarce resource and there exists a large gap in terms of water available and its requirement for irrigation of crops. Adoption of innovative irrigation techniques can increase the efficiency of water usage. In vegetables production water and nutrients are two most critical and costly inputs and are interrelated in their effects on plant growth and yield. Their efficient management is most important for improving productivity. Every effort must be made to enhance water and fertilizer use efficiency by reducing their wastage. Drip irrigation is the most effective way to supply water and nutrients to the plant, which not only saves water but also increases yield of fruits and vegetable crops. This water saving is because maximum amount of water is stored in the root zone and deep percolation losses are minimized.

Desirable effects of plastic mulching are Weed control, temperature moderation, salinity reduction, which increases the utilization of plastic mulching in vegetable cultivation. The notable advantage of the use of plastic mulch is its impermeability which prevents direct evaporation of moisture from the soil and thus reduces the water losses. Drip irrigation is at present economically feasible in high value crops. The use efficiency of these key inputs is currently very low in India leading to a lot of problems such as low crop productivity,degradation of soil health and increased environmental pollution apart from the wastage of substantial quantity of these costly and scarce inputs, increasing the efficiency of water and fertilizer use can itself go a long way in meeting the growing demand for food and other plant products consequent to rapidly escalating population. Although, we know water scarcity is the most common problem in many areas creating problem in growing crops. Water productivity at the all India level is very low and needs to be enhanced through tapping, harvesting and recycling water, efficient on-farm water management practices, micro irrigation, use of waste water and resource conservation technologies.

In drip fertigation system, waterfalls onto the soil surface drop by drop and fertilizers can also be applied along with water. From the review study of different literature, it should be concluded that if water and nutrients are applied according to crop demand in adequate amount and at right time then plant can grow much better in a congenial environment without more losses. At the rate of 75% ETc through drip irrigation and 75% RDF through fertigation could help in attaining more yields with higher uptake and nutrient use efficiency thus enhanced the quality of the produce and we get more economic returns. However, it is very difficult to obtain maximal water use efficiency and maximal yield simultaneously because reduction in the amount of irrigation water results in higher water use efficiency; but at lower irrigation rate higher yield can't be achieved. Thus, higher water use efficiency is achieved at lower irrigation rate.

REFERENCES

Abdul Hakkim, V.M. and A.R. Jisha Chand (2014). Effect of Drip Irrigation Levels on Yield of Salad Cucumber under Naturally Ventilated Polyhouse. IOSR Journal of Engineering, 4 (4): 18-21.

Agrawal, N., H. K. Panigrahi, C. R. Gupta, P. Singh, D. Sharma, S. K. Rahangdale and R. Agrawal (2009). Hitech Production of Potato through Drip Irrigation. Lead Papers & Abstract Summary, State Level Workshop on Promotion of Potato Cultivation in Chhattisgarh. 29-30 January. Pp.95.

Ahire, N.R., P.G. Bhoi and A.V. Solanke (2000). Effect of Row Spacing and Planting System on Growth and Yield of Potato under Surface and Drip Irrigation. *Journal of Indian Potato Association*, **27**(1&2): 59-60.

Ananta, B. (2006). Effect of Solid Soluble Fertilizer Applied through Fertigation on Growth and Yield of Tomato. *Veg. Sci.*, 33(1): 26 - 28.

Anonymous (1995). Drip Irrigation Studies on Tomato. Annual Report. Plasticulture Dev. Centre, A.P.A.U. Hyderabad (Telungana), India.

Antony, E. and R.B. Singandhupe (2004). Impact of Drip and Surface Irrigation on Growth, Yield and WUE of Capsicum (Capsicum Annuum L.). Agr Water Manag., 65: 121–132.

Asokaraja, N. (1998). Drip Irrigation and Mulching in Tomato. In: Proc. Workshop on Micro Irrigation and Sprinkler Irrigation Systems. New Delhi, India.

Aujla, M.S., H. S. Thind and G.S. Buttar (2007). Fruit Yield and Water use Efficiency of Eggplant as Influenced by Different Quantities of Nitrogen and Water Applied through Drip and Furrow Irrigation. *Scientia Horticul-turae,* 112: 142-148.

Badra, M.A., W.A. El-Tohamyb and A.M. Zaghloulc (2012). Yield and Water use Efficiency of Potato Grown under Different Irrigation and Nitrogen Levels in an Arid Region. *Agricultural Water Management,* 110: 9-15.

Bafna, A.M., S.Y. Daftardar, K.K. Khade, P.V. Patel and R.S. Dhotre (1993). Utilization of Nitrogen and Water by Tomato under Drip Irrigation System. J. Water Manage., 1(1): 1-5.

Bagali, A. N. H. B. Patil, M. B. Guled and R. V. Patil (2012). Effect of Scheduling of Drip Irrigation on Growth, Yield and Water use Efficiency of Onion (Allium cepaL.). Karnataka J. Agric. Sci., 25 (1): 116-119.

Bakeer, G.A.A., F.G. El-Ebabi, M.T. El-Saidi and A. R. E. Abdelghany (2009). Effect of Pulse Drip Irrigation on Yield and Water Use Efficiency of Potato Crop Under Organic Agriculture in Sandy Soils. *Journal of Agriculture Engineering* 26 (2): 736 - 765.

Batra, B. R. and M. L. Pandita(1984), Response of Onion to Irrigation and Nitrogen Levels. *Haryana J. Hort. Sci.,* 13 (1-2): 55-61.

Beyaert, R.P., R.C. Roy and B.B.R. Coelho (2007). Irrigation and Fertilizer Management Effects on Processing Cucumber Productivity and Water use Efficiency. Canadian J Plant Sci., 87: 355-363.

Bhanu, R.K. and K. Mahavishnan (2008). Drip Fertigation in Vegetable Crops with Emphasis on Lady's Finger [Abelmoschusesculentous (L.) Moench].Agric. Rev., 29(4): 298-305.

Bhella, H.S. (1988). Tomato Response of Trickle Irrigation and Black Polyethylene Mulch. J. Am. Soc. Hort. Sci., 113(4): 543-546.

Cetin, O. and D. Uygan (2008). The Effect of Drip Line Spacing, Irrigation Regimes and Planting Geometries of Tomato on Yield, Irrigation Water use Efficiency and Net Return. Agric. Water Manage 95: 949-958.

Channagoudar, R. F. and A. D.Janawade(2004). Effects of Different Levels of Irrigation and Sulphur on Growth, Yield and Quality of Onion *(Allium cepa*L.). *Karnataka J. Agric. Sci.,* 19 (3): 489- 492.

Chauhan, R.P.S., B.S. Yadav and R.B. Singh (2013). Irriga-tion Water and Fertigation Management in Brinjal Crop with Drip Irrigation. *Journal of Rural and Agricultural Research,* 13 (1): 53-56.

Chun-Zhi Zeng, Z. L. Bie and B. Z. Yuan (2009). Determination of Optimum Irrigation Water Amount for Drip-irrigated Muskmelon (Cucumismelo L.)in Plastic Greenhouse, *Agricultural Water Manage.,* 96: 595 – 602.

Dalvi, V.B., K.N.Tiwari, M.N. Pawade and P.S. Phire (1999). Response Surface Analysis of Tomato Production under Micro Irrigation. *J. Water Mgmt.,* 41 (1): 11-19.

Darwish, T., T. Atallah, S. Hajhasan and A. Chranek (2003). NutrCycl in Agroecosystem, 67 (1): 1-11.

Dingre, S.K, D.D. Pawar and K.G. Kadam (2012). Productivity Water use and Quality of Onion (*Allium Cepa*) Seed Production Under Different Irrigation Scheduling through Drip. Indian J Agron., 57: 186-190.

Dunage, V.S., P. Balakrishnan and M.G. Patil (2009). Water use Efficiency and Economics of Tomato using Drip Irrigation under Net House Conditions. Karnataka J. Agric. Sci., 22 (1):133-136.

Elkner, K. and S. Kaniszewski (1995). Effect of Drip Irrigation and Mulching on Quality to Tomato Fruits. Acta Hort., 379: 175-180.

Erdem, T., L. Arýn, Y. Erdem, S. Polat, M. Deveci, H. Okursoy and H.T. Gültas (2010). Yield and Quality Response of Drip Irrigated Broccoli (Brassica Oleracea L. Var. Italica) under Different Irrigation Regimes, Nitrogen Applications and Cultivation Periods. Agricultural Water Management, 97(5): 681-688.

Gethe, R. M., V. S. Pawar, S. H.Pathan, D. A. Sonawane and A. D.Kadlag(2006), Influence of Planting Layouts, Irrigation Regimes and Fertilizer Levels on Growth and Yield of Onion Under Micro-Sprinkler. *J. Maharashtra Agric. Univ.*, 31(3) : 272-274.

Gupta, V.J., M.A. Chattoo and F.N. Bhat (2010). Techno-economic Evaluation of Drip Irrigation and Fertigation Practices in Tomato under Kashmir Conditions. *Vegetable Science*, 36: 309 - 314.

Gupta, V.J., M.A. Chattoo and L. Singh (2015). Drip Irrigation and Fertigation Technology for Improved Yield, Quality, Water and Fertilizer Use Efficiency in Hybrid Tomato. *Journal of Agriculture Research*, 2 (2): 94 - 99.

Hanson, B.R., L.J. Schwankl, K.F. Schulbach and G.S. Pettygrove (1997). A Comparison of Furrow, Surface Drip, and Subsurface Drip Irrigation on Lettuce Yield and Applied Water. Agricultural Water Management, 33: 139–57.

Haque, M. I., M. M.Zaman, M. K.Hasan, M. Begum and F. Pervin(2004). Growth and Yield of Onion as Influenced by Nitrogen and Irrigation. *J. Agric. Rural Dev.*, (Gazipur), 2(1): 151-153.

Harmanto, V.M. Salokhe, M.S. Babel and S.J. Tantau (2005). Water Requirement of Drip Irrigated Tomatoes Grown in Greenhouse in Tropical Environment, *Agri. Water Manage,*, 71: 225–242.

Hebbar, S.S., B.K. Ramachandroppa, H.V. Nanjappa and M. Prabhakar (2004). Studies on NPK Drip Fertgation in Field Grown Tomato (*Lycopersicumesculantum*Mill.). *European Journal of Agronomy*, 21:117-127.

Hebbar, S.S., B.K., Ramachandrappa, H.V. Nanjappa, M. Prabhakar (2002). Studies on NPK Drip Fertigation in Field Grown Tomato. *Europe J. Agron.*, 221: 117–127.

Ibrikci, G.S and H. Buyuk (2002). Yield and Elemental Composition of Cucumber as Affected by Drip and Furrow Irrigation. Acta Hort., 34: 51-57.

Imtiyaz, M., N.P. Mgadla, B. Chepete and E.O. Mothobi (2000). Yield and Economic Returns of Vegetable Crops under Varying Irrigation. Irrigation Sci., 19: 87-93.

Kaushal, A., A.S. Lodhi and K.G. Singh (2011). Economics of Growing Sweet Pepper under Low Tunnels. Prog Agri., 14: 67-72.

Khan, M.H., T.H. Chattha and N. Saleem (2005). Influence of Different Irrigation Intervals on Growth and Yield of Bell Pepper (Capsicum Annuumgrossum Group). Res J Agric. Biol. Sci., 1:125 - 128.

KohirePatil V.O and J.C Das (2015). Effect of Drip Irrigation and Fertilizer Management on Capsicum (Capsicum Annum L). IOSR Journal of Agriculture and Veterinary Science, 8, (1): 10-13.

Locascio, S.J., S.M. Olsen and F.M. Rhoads (1989). Water Quantity and Time of N and K Application of Tickle Irrigated Tomatoes. J. Am. Soc. Hort. Sci., 114(2): 265 - 268.

Lodhi, A. S., A. Kaushal and K. G. Singh (2014). Impact of Irrigation Regimes on Growth, Yield and Water Use Efficiency of Sweet Pepper. Indian Journal of Science and Technology, 7(6), 790 - 794.

Lodhi, A.S., A. Kaushal and K.G. Singh (2013). Effect of Irrigation Regimes and Low Tunnel Heights on Microclimatic Parameters in the Growing of Sweet Peppers. International Journal of Engineering Science Invention, 2 (7): 20–29.

Longwe, B. B. (2015). Evaluation of Drip Irrigation Levels on the Productivity of Carrot (Daucuscarota L.) under Raichur Agro Climatic Conditions. M.E (Thesis), Department of Soil and Water Engineering, College of Agricultural Engineering, University of Agricultural Sciences, Raichur, Karnataka.

Machado, R.M., M. Do RosArio, G. Oliveira and C.A. Portas (2003). Tomato Root Distribution, Yield and Fruit Quality under Subsurface Drip Irrigation. In Roots: The Dynamic Interface between Plants and The Earth, Springer, Netherlands, pp. 333-341.

Mahajan, G., K.G. Singh, R. Gharda and M.Siag (2007).Response or Red Hot Pepper (Capsicum Annum L.) to Water and Nitrogen under Drip and Check Basin Method of Irrigation. Asian Journal of Plant Science, 6(5): 815-820.

Maisiri, N., A. Senzanje, J. Rockstrom and S.J. Twomlow (2005). On Farm Evaluation of the Effect of Low Cost Drip Irrigation on Water and Crop Productivity Compared to Conventional Surface Irrigation System. Physics and Chemistry of The Earth, Parts A/B/C, 30(11): 783-791.

Manish (2007). Effect of Growing media, Irrigation Regime, Fertigation and Mulching on Productivity of Tomato. *Indian J. Agric. Sci.*, 75(5): 302-304.

Muralikrishnaswamy, S., V. Veerabadran, S. Krishnasamy, V.Kumar and S. Sakthivel (2006). Drip Irrigation and Fertigation in Chillies (*Capsicum Annum*). In: Porc. of *7th Inter-national Micro-irrigation Congress, Kaula Lumpur, Malaysia*.P: 88-89.

Nakayama, F.S. and D.A. Bucks (1986). Trickle Irrigation for Crop Production, Design, Operation and Management. Elsevier Scientific Publishers, Netherlands.

Narayanan, T.A., S. Thimmegowda, A.G. Bandi and N.Devakumar, (1994). Economic Feasibility of Adopting Drip irrigation in Sweet Pepper. *Indian Journal of Agronomy*, 39 (1): 150-151.

Neeraja, G., K.Mallareddy, M. Suryanarayan Reddy and I. Prabhakar Reddy (2000). Studies on Uptake of Secondary Nutrients at Different Stages of Growth of Onion in different Levels of Irrigation and Nitrogen. J. *Res. ANGRAU.*, 28 (1&2): 13-18.

Ngouajio, M., G. Wang and R. Goldy (2007). Withholding of Drip Irrigation between Transplanting and Flowering Increases The Yield of Field-Grown Tomato under Plastic Mulch. Agricultural Water Management, 87: 285 – 291.

Palled, Y. B., M. D. Kachapur, A. M. Chandrashekhar and A. S. Prabhakar (1988). Response of Onion to Irrigation and Nitrogen. *Indian J. Agron.*, 33(1): 22-25.

Pandey, AK., AK. Singh, A. Kumar and S.K. Singh (2013). Effect of Drip Irrigation, Spacing and Nitrogen Fertigation on Productivity of Chilli (*Capsicum Annuum* L.). *Environment and Ecology*, 32 (1): 139-142.

Pandey, V., Z. Ahmed, H.C. Tewari and N. Kumar (2005). Effect of Greenhouse Models on Plant-growth and Yield of Capsicum in Northwest Himalayas. Indian Journal of Horticulture, 62: 312– 313.

Patel, N. and T.B.S. Rajput (2007). Effect of Drip Tape Placement Depth and Irrigation Level on Yield of Potato, *Agricultural Water Manage.*, 88: 209 – 223.

Paul, J.C., J.N. Mishra, P.L. Pradhan and B. Panigrahi (2013). Effect of Drip and Surface Irrigation on Yield, Water Use-efficiency and Economics of Capsicum (Capsicum Annum L) Grown under Mulch and Non Mulch Conditions in Eastern Coastal India. *European J. Sustainable Development*, 2 (1): 99-108.

Quezada, C., S. Fischer, J. Campos and D. Ardiles (2011). Water Requirements and Water Use Efficiency of Carrot under Drip Irrigation in a Haploxer Soil. *Journal of Soil Science and Plant Nutrition*, 11(1): 16-28.

Raina, J.N., B.C. Thaku and M.L. Verma (1999). Effect of Drip Irrigation and Polyethylene Mulch on Yield, Quality and Water-Use Efficiency of Tomato. Indian J. Agric. Sci., 69: 430-433.

Rajbir Singh, Satyendra Kumar, D. D. Nangare and M. S. Meena (2009). Drip Irrigation and Black Polyethylene Mulch Influence on Growth, Yield and Water-Use Efficiency of Tomato. African Journal of Agricultural Research, 4 (12): 1427-1430.

Ram Kumar, H. Trivedi, R. Yadav, B. Das and A. S. Bist (2016). Effect of Drip Irrigation on Yield and Water use Efficiency on Brinjal (Solanum Melongena) Cv. Pant Samrat. International Journalof Engineering Sciences& Research Technology, 5 (10): 7-18.

Rekha, K.B. and K. Mahavishnan (2008). Drip Fertigation in Vegetable Crops with Emphasis on Lady's Finger (*Abelmoschusesculentus*(L.) Moench) - A Review. Agricultural Review,29: 298-305.

Rumpel, J., S. Kaniszewski and J. Dyśko (2004). Effect of Drip Irrigation and Fertilization Timing and Rate on Yield of Onion.Journal of Vegetable Crop Production, 9 (2): 65-73.

Sahebi, F. G., H. Masoud and P. Eman (2012). Effect of Under Irrigation Management on Potato Performance Components. *International Journal of Agricultural Management & Development,* 2(2): 143-148.

Santosh Kumari (2012). Influence of Drip Irrigation and Mulch on Leaf area Maximization, Water use Efficiency and Yield of Potato (*Solanum Tuberosum* L.). Journal of Agricultural Science, 4 (1): 71- 80.

SatyendraKumar, M. Imtiyaz, Ashwani Kumar and Ranbir Singh (2007), Response of Onion to Different Levels of Irrigation Water. *Agric. Water Mgnt.,* 89(1-2) : 161-166.

Selvakumar, T. (2006). Performance Evaluation of Drip Fertigation on Growth, Yield and Water Use in Hybrid Chilli (*Capsicum Annuum*L.). (Ph.D.) Thesis, Tamil Nadu Agricultural University, Coimbatore, Tamil Nadu. (India).

Seyfi and Rashidi(2007). Effect of Drip Irrigation and Plastic Mulch on Crop Yield and Yield Components of Muskmelon. *International J. Agri. Biol.,* 247–249.

Shao, L.I., X.U.E. Xu-zhang, G.U.O Wen-shan, L.I. Xia and C. Fei (2010). Effects of Water Supply Tension on Yield and Water use Efficiency of Greenhouse Cucumber. Journal Scientia AgriculturaSinica, 2: 77- 81.

Sharma, I.S., M.Z. Sahar and A.A. Yassen (2009). Effect of Method and Rate of Fertilizer Application Under Drip Irrigation on Yield and Nutrient Uptake by Tomato. Ozean Journal of Applied Sciences, 2(2):139.

Shiri-e-Janagrad, M., A. Tobeh, S. Hokmalipour, S. Jamaati-e-Somarin, A. Abbasi and K.Shahbazi (2009). Potato (*Solanum Tuberosum*L.) Response to Drip Irrigation Regimes and Plant Arrangements During Growth Periods. *Asian Journal of Plant Sciences,* 8(6): 390-399.

Singandhupe, R.B., B.K. James, Edanna, Anthony, P. Nanda and M.S. Behera(2007). Response of Fertigation and Mulching on Growth and Fruit Yield of Brinjal. *Indian J. Agric. Sci.,* 77(1): 8-13.

Singandhupe, R.B., G.G.S.N Rao, N.G. Patil and P.S. Brahmanand (2003). Fertigation Studies and Irrigation Scheduling in Drip Irrigation System in Tomato Crop (*Lycopersiconesculentum* L.). European J. Agron., 19: 327-340.

Singh, K.G., G. Mahajan and M. Siag (2006). Evaluation of Drip Irrigation System in Cauliflower - Hybrid Chilli Sequence. *Haryana Journal of Horticultural Sciences,* 35: 326-328.

Singh, N., M.C. Sood and R.C. Sharma (2002). Effect of Irrigation Levels, Cultural Practices and Nitrogen Application on Potato Production under Drip and Sprinkler Methods of Irrigation. Potato, Global Research and Development Proceedings of The Global Conference on Potato, New Delhi, India, 6-11 December, Volume - 2, pp. 923-925.

Subba Reddy, G.V., B.V. Patil, B.Srihari Rao and B. Nagendraprasad (2015). Effect of Different Types of Irrigation and Growing Methods on Growth, Yield and Water-Use Efficiency of Tomato (Lycopersiconesculentum Miller). *The Bioscan,* 10 (1): 243 - 246.

Swarajyalakshmi, K.M., Reddy, Deva Muni, M. Shivashankar, K. Suresh Babu and P. Nageswara Rao (2005). Studies on Response of Chilli to Different Levels of Drip Irrigation and Mulching as Compared to Basin Method of Irrigation. In: International Conference on Plasticulture and Precision Farming, New Delhi, India.

Tiwari, K.N. (2017). Improving Water and Fertilizer use Efficiency using Microirrigation. J. Indian Water Resour. Soc., 17 (1): 33-42.

Tiwari, K.N., A. Singh and P.K. Mal (2003). Effect of Drip Irrigation on Yield of Cabbage (Brassica Oleracea L. Var. Capitata) under Mulch and Non-mulch Conditions. Agricultural Water Management, 58 (1): 19-28.

Tiwari, K.N., P.K. Mal, R.M. Singh and A. Chattopadhyay (1998). Response of Okra (Abelmoschusesculentus (L.) Moench.) to Drip Irrigation under Mulch and Nonmulch Condition. Agr Water Manage., 38: 91-102.

Tiwari, K.N., P.K. Mal, R.M. Singh and A. Chattopadhyay (1998a). Feasibility of Drip Irrigation under Different Soil Covers in Tomato. J. Agric. Engg., 35: 41-49.

Tumbare, A.D. (2004). Effect of Planting and Fertigation on Growth and Yield of Green Chilli (Capsicum Annuum).India Journal of Agriculture Science, 74(5): 242-245.

Tumbare, A.D. and S.U. Bhoite (2002). Effect of Solid Soluble Fertilizer Applied through Fertigation on Growth and Yield of Chilli (Capsicum Annuum). Indian Journal of Agricultural Sciences, 72 (2): 109-111.

Ughade, S.R. and U.V. Mahadkar (2014). Effect of Planting Density, Irrigation and Fertigation Levels on Water Saving and Water Use Efficiency of Brinjal (Solanum Melongena L). *Adv. Res. J. Crop Improv.,* 5 (2): 114-117.

Vijayakumar, G., D. Tamilmani and P.K. Selvaraj (2010). Irrigation and Fertigation Scheduling under Drip Irrigation in Brinjal (*Solanum MelongenaL.*) Crop. *Indian Journal of Bio-resource Management,* 1: 72 - 76.

Waldir, A., W.Marouelli and L.C. Silva (2007). Water Tension Thresholds for Processing Tomatoes under Drip Irrigation in Central Brazil. *Irrig. Sci.,* 25: 411–418.

Wang, X., .iDengshun and Z. Xiying (1999). Relationship Between Irrigation Amount and Yield of Cucumber in Solar Greenhouse. *J. China Vegetables,* 3 (1): 12-16.

Xiaobo, P., Z. Fuman and G. Lihong (2002). Study on Water Requirement of Cucumber of Different Cropping in Solar Greenhouse. J. Chinese Agricultural Science Bulletin, 4: 26-29.

Yadav, A.C., A. Singh, K.S. Baswana, N.K. Sharma and M.S. Dahiya (2004). Effect of Various Irrigation and Fertility Levels on the Production of Newly Developed Brinjal Cultivars. *Haryana J. Hort. Sci.,* 3(3&4): 284-286.

Yuan, B.Z., S. Nishiyama and Y.Kang (2003). Effects of Different Irrigation Regimes on the Growth and Yield of Drip Irrigated Potato. *Agricultural Water Manage.,* 63: 153–167.

Horticulture and Ecology - *Studies & Management* Pages 34-60
Edited by: Dr. Alka Chauhan and Dr. Pawan Kumar 'Bharti'
ISBN: 978-93-88854-09-2
Edition: 2019
Published by: Discovery Publishing House Pvt. Ltd., New Delhi (India)

3 Water Quality for Irrigation in Horticultural Crops

[1]A. Solaimalai, [2]M. Jayakumar, [3]S. Irulandi and M. [4]Theradimani

Introduction

Understanding knowledge of irrigation water quality is critical to the management of water for long-term productivity. Irrigation water quality is related to its effects on soils and crops and its management. High quality crops can be produced only by using high-quality irrigation water keeping other inputs optimal. Characteristics of irrigation water that define its quality vary with the source of the water (APHA, 2005). There are area differences in water characteristics, based mainly on geology and climate. There may also be great differences in the quality of water available on a local level depending on whether the source is from surface water bodies such as rivers and ponds or from groundwater aquifers with varying geology, and whether the water has been chemically treated (Ayers and Westcot, 1994; Nahid *et al.*, 2009). The chemical constituents of irrigation water can affect plant growth directly through toxicity or deficiency, or indirectly by altering nutrient availability to the plants (Ayers and Westcot, 1985; Rowe *et al.*, 1995; Islam and Shamsad, 2009).

Analytical procedures for the laboratory determinations of water quality have been given in several publications (USDA Handbook 60 by Richards, 1954; FAO Soils Bulletin 10 by Dewis and Freitas 1970; APHA, 2005). Table 3.1 shows the guidelines for interpretations of water quality for irrigation as given by Ayers and Westcot (1985). The chemicals guidelines given in Table 3.1 act as the management tools and practical guidelines that have been used successfully in general irrigated agriculture for evaluation of the common constituents in

1 Associate Professor (Agronomy), Department of Fruit Crops, Horticultural College & Research, TNAU, Periyakulam–625 604, Tamil Nadu, India.
2 Corresponding author: Scientist, Regional Coffee Research Station, Thandikudi, Dindugul-District, Tamil Nadu, India.
3 Assistant Professor (Agricultural Entomology), Department of Fruit Crops, Horticultural College & Research, TNAU, Periyakulam–625 604, Tamil Nadu, India.
4 Professor (Plant Pathology), Department of Floriculture, Horticultural College & Research, TNAU, Periyakulam–625 604, Tamil Nadu, India.

surface water, ground water, drainage water, sewage effluent and waste water. They are the first step in pointing out the quality limitations of the water supply. Also shown in Table 3.1 is the degree of restriction of chemical parameters on the use of irrigation water. A restriction on use indicates that there may be a limitation in choice of crop or special management need to maintain full production capability. However, a "restriction on use" does not indicate that the water is unsuitable for use.

Table 3.1: Guidelines for Interpretations of Water Quality for Irrigation

Potential Irrigation Problem				Units	Degree of restriction on use		
					None	Slight to moderate	Severe
Salinity							
ECw				dS/m	< 0.7	0.7 – 3.0	> 3.0
TDS				mg/l	< 450	450 – 2000	> 2000
SAR	= 0 – 3	ECw	=		> 0.7	0.7 – 0.2	< 0.2
	= 3 – 6		=		> 1.2	1.2 – 0.3	< 0.3
	= 6 – 12		=		> 1.9	1.9 – 0.5	< 0.5
	= 12 – 20		=		> 2.9	2.9 – 1.3	< 1.3
	= 20 – 40		=		> 5.0	5.0 – 2.9	< 2.9
Specific Ion Toxicity							
	Sodium (Na)						
	Surface irrigation			SAR	< 3	3 – 9	> 9
	Sprinkler irrigation			me/l	< 3	> 3	
	Chloride (Cl)						
	Surface irrigation			me/l	< 4	4 – 10	> 10
	Sprinkler irrigation			me/l	< 3	> 3	
	Boron (B)			mg/l	< 0.7	0.7 – 3.0	> 3.0
	Nitrogen (NO_3 – N)			mg/l	< 5	5 – 30	> 30
	Bicarbonate (HCO_3)						
	pH				Normal Range 6.5 – 8.4		

Ayers and Westcot (1985)

Effect of Water Quality on Crop Production

Irrigation water whether of good quality or not, can have effect on plant growth, for example poor irrigation water quality with excess salt can damage plants in various ways, but the most common problems are caused by salts effecting osmotic relationship between the root and the soil moisture (Malash *et al.*, 2005).Water with high amount of salts can hinder the conversion of ammonium salts to nitrate by nitrifying micro-organisms in soil when used for irrigation. Furthermore, most of tomato plants are more sensitive to salt during seed germination, seedling growth and when flowering or fruiting (Breckle, 1995). According to Breckle (1995) the seed and seedling stages are vulnerable not only because the plant structures are immature and delicate, but also because tiny roots system draw moisture and nutrients from the soil surface where salts tend to concentrate. A severe reduction in water infiltration rate due to water quality is usually related to either very low water salinity or to a high sodium adsorption ratio (SAR). In either case, the calcium content of the water may be at a relatively low concentration. If the calcium in the soil-water taken up by the crop is less than 2 me/l, there is a strong probability that the crop yield will be reduced due to a calcium deficiency (Rhoades, 1982).

Salinity is a measure of the total amount of salt in the water. When the salt levels are too high, a salinity hazard may exist. Salts in soil and/or water can reduce water availability to the crop to such an extent that yield can be affected. Electrical conductivity or Total Dissolved Solids (TDS) tests are two means of measuring salinity. Electrical conductivity is a useful and reliable index for the measurement of water salinity or TDS in water. Electrical conductivity in water is due to ionization of dissolved inorganic solids (minerals, salts, elements both cations and anions). The total amount of TDS should be used together with SAR. TDS levels below 700 mg/L and SAR below 4 are considered safe; TDS levels between 700 and 1,750 mg/L and SAR levels between 4 and 9 are considered slightly safe, while levels above these are considered hazardous to any crop. The properties of the soil, the ground water and the landscape interact with the salinity of the irrigation water to either increase or decrease the salinity hazard (Peterson, 1999).

Effect of Water Quality on Soil Properties

The normal pH range for irrigation water is from 6.5 to 8.4. Abnormally low pHs may cause accelerated irrigation system corrosion where they occur. High pH's above 8.5 are often caused by high bicarbonate (HCO_3^-) and carbonate (CO_2^-) concentrations, known as alkalinity. High carbonates cause calcium and magnesium ions to form insoluble minerals leaving sodium as the dominant ion in solution. According to Mass (1990), this alkaline water can intensify sodic soil conditions. While ECwis an assessment of all soluble salts in a sample, sodium hazard is defined separately because of sodium's specific detrimental effects on soil physical properties. The SAR index quantifies the proportion of sodium (Na^+) to calcium (Ca^{++}) and magnesium (Mg^{++}) ions in a sample. Calcium will flocculate (hold together), while sodium disperses (pushes apart) soil particles. This dispersed soil will readily crust and have water infiltration and permeability problems. General classifications of irrigation water based upon SAR values calculated using Equation 1, are presented in Table 3.2.

Equation 1. Equation used to calculate SAR

$$SAR = \frac{Na}{\sqrt{\frac{(Ca+Mg)}{2}}}$$

Where

meq/L = mg/litre divided by atomic weight of ion divided by ionic charge (Na^{+} = 23.0 mg/meq, Ca^{++} = 20.0 mg/meq, Mg^{++} =12.15 mg/meq)

Table 3.2: Classification of Sodium Hazard of Water Based on SAR Values

SAR values	Sodium hazard of water	Comments
1-9	Low	Use on sodium sensitive crops must be cautioned.
10-17	Medium	Amendments (such as gypsum) and leaching needed.
18-25	High	Generally unsuitable for continuous use.
≥26	Very High	Generally unsuitable for use.

Mass (1990)

Sodium in irrigation water can also cause toxicity problems for some crops, especially when sprinkler is used. However, crops vary in their susceptibility to sodium toxicity damage (Mass, 1990).

Effect of Water Sources for Irrigating Crops

Biernbaum (1994) both irrigation water quality and proper irrigation management are critical to successful crop production. In addition, the quality of the irrigation water may affect both crop yields and soil physical conditions, even if all other conditions and cultural practices are favourable or optimal. Different crops require different irrigation water qualities. Therefore, testing the irrigation water prior to selecting the site and the crops to be grown is critical (Shahinasi and Kashuta, 2008). The quality of some water sources may change significantly with time or during certain periods such as in dry or rainy seasons (Islam and Shamad, 2009). So it is recommended to have more than one sample taken, in different time periods. Growth of plants is frequently limited by imbalances in electrical conductivity (EC), alkalinity, sodium (Na), and boron (B). High EC levels inhibit the germination of seeds, the rooting of cuttings, and root growth of some established crops. Alkalinity directly influences the pH of the root medium; as alkalinity in irrigation water increases, so does root medium pH. High levels of Na can antagonize the uptake of potassium (K), calcium (Ca) and magnesium (Mg). Leaf necrosis occurs when high levels of boron are present in irrigation water. Other potential irrigation water contaminants that may affect suitability for agricultural use include heavy metals and microbial contaminants (Bauder *et al.*, 2007).

Ground Water Effect on Crop Production

Ayers and Westcot (1994) found that the quality of well water may vary with the season and/or climate. For example, solutes tend to be dilute in rainy years, and concentrated in dry years. The environment also impacts the quality of pond water, during dry periods, the concentration of the solutes increased as water evaporated. Also WHO (1974) reported that groundwater is slightly acidic to slightly alkaline with pH values from 6.5 to 8.3.

Bicarbonate is an important ion in the evaluation of irrigation water quality. Bicarbonate is responsible for alkalinity of the groundwater. According to Eaton (1950), irrigation water having residual sodium carbonate (RSC) values greater than 5 meq/L are considered harmful to the growth of plant, while irrigation waters with RSC value around 2.5 meq/L is safe for irrigation, a value between 1.25 and 2.5 meq/L is of marginal and a value of more than 2.5 meq/L is unsuitable for irrigation (Hem, 1970). When sodium concentration is high in irrigation water, sodium ion is absorbed by the clay particles and the soil reduces the permeability and this results in soil with poor internal drainage and therefore the air and water circulation is restricted during the wet condition and such a soil is usually hard when dry (Collins and Jenkins, 1996)

Effect Surface Water Quality for Crop Production

For irrigation, the quality of water determines if optimum return from the soil can be obtained as the quality affects soil, crop and water management. Nearly all water contains dissolved salts and trace elements, many of which result from the nature weathering of the earth's surface. In most irrigating situations, the primary water quality concern is salinity levels, since salt can affect both soil structure and crop yield. Surface water contributes the major share of irrigation coverage (Nahid *et al.*, 2008). In classifying water for irrigation, Sodium Adsorption Ratio (SAR) is an important parameter in determining the suitability of irrigation water, which is found normal in surface water (Raghunath, 1990). Good proportion of $Ca^{2+}$and Mg^{2+} is favourable for good permeability problem. Raghunath, (1990) and Wilcox, (1955) classifying water for irrigation is determined considering the combined effects of SSP, EC and boron contents.

The surface water is fresh and good and moderately hard in respect with the classification of TDS, permeability Index (PI) and Total Hardness (Ht) (Freeze and Cherry, 1979). According to Michael (1992), the range of pH in surface water is found slightly alkaline to practically neutral. Surface water is also suitable for most plants provided that moderate amount of leaching takes place or that plants with moderate salinity tolerance are grown. Shaki and Adeloye (2006) using both surface and sub-surface water for irrigation, concluded that surface water has no salinity or toxicity problem and thus, is suitable or almost excellent for being used for irrigation.

Soil Salinity Effect on Crops Production

The salinity effects are generally evidenced by reducing transpiration rates and proportionally related growth, and producing smaller plants. The salinity also alters the soil ability to retain nutrients, thus suppressing plant growth (Goudie, 1992). Alan (1994) reported that plants vary in their response to soil salinity. Salt tolerant plants (plants less affected by salinity) are better able to adjust internally to the osmotic effects of high salt concentrations than salt-sensitive plants. Salt-tolerant plants are more able to absorb water from saline soils, while salt-sensitive plants have limited ability to adjust and are injured at relatively low salt concentrations. Many horticultural and field crops are classified as sensitive or moderately sensitive to soil salinity as shown in Table 3.3.

Table 3.3: Relative Tolerance of Selected Crops to Salinity of Irrigation Water and Salt Tolerance

High (8-12 mmhos/cm)	Medium (3-8 mmhos/cm)	Low (1-3 mmhos/cm)
Field crops		
Cotton	Rye, wheat, oats, sorghum, corn, and soybeans	Field beans, peanuts
Forage crops		
Bermudagrass	Sweet clover, dallisgrass, sudan grass, alfalfa, fescue, wheat and oats for hay, vetch	White clover and landino clover
Vegetable crops		
Garden beets, kale, asparagus, and spinach	Tomato, broccoli, cabbage, peppers, cauliflower, lettuce, sweet corn, potatoes, carrots, onion, peas, squash, and cucumbers	Radishes, celery, and green beans

(Bauder *et al.*, 2007)

Whereas Table 3.3 shows relative tolerance of selected crops to salinity, Table 3.4 shows yield potential of salt-tolerance classes of horticultural and landscape plants to soil salinity levels as formulated by Alan (1994). Bauder *et al.*, (2007) reported that quality of water for plants in soil solution decreases dramatically as EC increases.

Table 3.4: Soil Salinity Levels and Yield Potential of Salt-tolerance Crops

Relative salt	Expected loss of relative growth yield (%)			
Tolerant class	0	25	50	100
	Soil salinity (ECedS/m			
Sensitive	<1.3	1.4 - 2.7	2.6 - 4.2	> 8.0
Moderately sensitive	<3.0	2.7-6.3	4.2 - 9.5	>16.0
Moderately tolerant	<6.0	6.3-10.5	9.5-15.0	>24.0
Tolerant	<10.0	10.5-15.5	15.0-21.0	>32.0

Alan (1994)

Effect of Salts and Individual Ion Toxicities in Soils on Crop Production

(*a*) Salinity hazard: Ayers, (1997) reported that most water quality guidelines on crop productivity are mainly on the water salinity hazard as measured by electrical conductivity (ECw). The primary effect of high ECw on crop productivity is the inability of the plant to compete with ions in the soil solution for water. This is usually referred as physiological drought for plants. The higher the EC, the less water is available to plants, even though the soil may appear wet. Because plants can only transpire "pure" water, usable plant water in the soil solution decreases dramatically as EC increases. A soil high in exchangeable sodium is very undesirable for agriculture as it causes flocculation resulting in impermeable crust. Table 3.5 shows the criteria for irrigation water use based upon conductivity.

Table 3.5: Criteria for Irrigation Water Use Based Upon Electrical Conductivity

Classes of water	Electrical conductivity (dS/m)*
Class 1, Excellent	≤0.25
Class 2, Good	0.25 - 0.75
Class 3, Permissible[1]	0.76 - 2.00
Class 4, Doubtful[2]	2.01 - 3.00
Class 5, Unsuitable[2]	≥3.00

*dS/m at 25°C = mmhos/cm. 1 Leaching needed if used. 2 Good drainage needed and sensitive plants will have difficulty obtaining stands.

The amount of water transpired through a crop is directly related to yield. Therefore, irrigation water with high ECw reduces yield potential (Tables 3.4 and 3.6). Water with an ECw of only 1.15 dS/m contains approximately 2,400 kilograms of salt for every 30 cm depth of water. Crop growth reductions because of dissolved substances in the soil are similar to drought-stressed effects. An osmotic gradient on salty soils is formed. Water uptake by plant roots is increasingly restricted as the concentration of soil salts increases. Because of this, as soil salts build up in the soil, more frequent irrigation is necessary to help flush out salts and reduce water stress. Crop species differ in their abilities to withstand salt stress (Bauder *et al.*, 2007).

Table 3.6: Potential Yield Reduction from Saline Water for Selected Irrigated Crop

Crop	% yield reduction			
	0%	10%	25%	50%
ECw2				
Barley	5.3	6.7	8.7	12
Wheat	4.0	4.9	6.4	8.7
Sugarbeet3	4.7	5.8	7.5	10
Alfalfa	1.3	2.2	3.6	5.9
Potato	1.1	1.7	2.5	3.9
Corn (grain)	1.1	1.7	2.5	3.9
Corn (silage)	1.2	2.1	3.5	5.7
Onion	0.8	1.2	1.8	2.9
Beans	0.7	1.0	1.5	2.4

2ECw = electrical conductivity of the irrigation water in dS/m at 25°C. 3. Sensitive during germination. ECw should not exceed 3 dS/m for garden beets and sugarbeets

***(b)* Sodium hazard:** Sodium hazard (or alkalinity hazard) in the use of water for irrigation is determined by the absolute and relative concentration of sodium (Na^+) to calcium (Ca^{++}) and magnesium (Mg^{++}) ions in a water sample and it is expressed as Sodium Adsorbed Ratio (SAR) which is the measure of sodium hazard in irrigation water (Siamak and Srikantaswamy, 2008; Silva, 2004). Excess sodium in water produces undesirable effects on soil properties and reduces soil permeability (Dhirendra *et al.*, 2009).Sodium when replacing adsorbed calcium and magnesium, becomes hazardous as it causes damage to the soil, making it to be compact and impervious, especially the soil structure, resulting in the formation of crusts,water-logging, reduced aeration and infiltration rate. Excess of Na^+ ions in soil may be also toxic to certain types of crops (Tiwari and Manzoor, 1988; Nata *et al.*, 2009; Ogunfowokan *et al.*, 2009 and 2013).

***(c)* Chlorides:** Although chloride is an essential element to plants in very low amounts, it can cause toxicity to sensitive crops at high concentrations. Like sodium, high chloride concentrations cause more problems when applied with sprinkler irrigation (Mass,1990). Table 3.7 shows the effect of chlorides on plants and its classification in irrigation water. Leaf burn under sprinkler from both sodium and chloride can be reduced by night time irrigation or application on cool, cloudy days. Drop nozzles and drag hoses are also recommended when applying any saline irrigation water through a sprinkler system to avoid direct contact with leaf surfaces (Mass, 1990). Working with faba bean (*Viciafaba*), Ehsan *et al.* (2010) reported reduced growth of faba bean at high concentrations of

Cl^- than that of Na^+. They observed that increasing the concentrations of NaCl in the soil increased the concentrations of Cl-more than that of Na^+ probably due to Na^+ ions interaction with bicarbonates.

Table 3.7: Chloride Classification of Irrigation Water and Its Effect on Plants

Chloride (ppm)	Effect on Crops
Below 70	Generally safe for all plants.
70-140	Sensitive plants show injury.
141-350	Moderately tolerant plants show injury.
Above 350	Can cause severe problems.

Mass (1990)

***(d)* Boron:** Boron is another element that is essential in low amounts, but toxic at higher concentrations as shown in Table 3.8. According to Mass, (1990) Boron toxicity can occur on sensitive crops at concentrations less than 1.0 ppm and it is advised that irrigation water specifically from ground water should be analyzed of boron before used to crops (Mass, 1990).

Table 3.8: Boron Sensitivity of Selected Plants in mg/L

Sensitive		Moderately Sensitive	Moderately Tolerant	Tolerant
0.5 - 0.75	0.76 - 1.0	1.1 - 2.0	2.1 – 4.0	4.1 – 6.0
Peach	Wheat	Carrot	Lettuce	Alfalfa
Onion	Barley	Potato	Cabbage	Sugar beet
	Sunflower	Cucumber	Corn	Tomato
	Dry Bean		Oats	

***(e)* Sulphate:** The sulphate ion is a major contributor to salinity. However, toxicity is rarely a problem, except at very high concentrations where high sulphate may interfere with uptake of other nutrients. Exceptions are sandy fields with less than1 percent organic matter and less than 10 ppm SO_4-S in irrigation water (Mass, 1990).

***(f)* Nitrogen:** Nitrogen (N) in irrigation water is largely a fertility issue. The nitrate ion often occurs at higher concentrations than ammonium in irrigation water. Waters high in N can cause quality problems in crops such as barley and sugar beets and excessive vegetative growth in some vegetables. However, these problems can usually be overcome by good fertilizer and irrigation management.

Water Salinity

Water salinity is the amount of salt contained in the water. It is also called the "salt concentration" and may be expressed in grams of salt per litre of water (grams/litre or g/l), or in milligrams per litre (which is the same as parts per million, ppm). However, the salinity of both water and soil is easily measured by means of an electrical device. It is then expressed in termsof electrical conductivity: millimhos/cm or micromhos/cm. A salt concentration of 1 gram per litre is about 1.5 millimhos/cm. Thus a concentration of 3 grams per litre will be about the same as 4.5 millimhos/cm.

Irrigation Water Quality

The suitability of water for irrigation depends on the amount and the type of salt the irrigation water contains. If the higher the salt concentration of the irrigation water, the greater the risk of salinization (Table 3.9).

Table 3.9: Salt Concentration of the Irrigation Water on Soil Salinization Risk

Salt concentration of the irrigation water (g/litre)	Soil salinization risk	Restriction on use
Less than 0.5 g/litre	No risk	No restriction on its use
0.5-2 g/litre	slight to moderate risk	Should be used with appropriate water management practices. Not generally advised for use unless consulted with specialists.

More than 2 g/litre high risk

Higher the concentration of sodium present in the irrigation water (particularly compared to other soils), the higher the risk.

Toxicity to Specific Elements

Unlike most annual crops, tree and vine crops are generally susceptible to boron and chloride toxicity. Tolerances vary among species and root stocks. Tolerant varieties and root stocks restrict the uptake and accumulation of boron and chloride in leaf tissue. Boron concentrations in the irrigation water exceeding 0.5 to 0.75 mg/L can reduce plant growth and yield. Climatic effects are also important. In the cool moist coastal climates, irrigation waters with boron concentrations exceeding 1 mg/L are used successfully on tree and vine crops.

Chloride moves readily with the soil water, is taken up by the plant roots, translocates to the shoot and accumulates in the leaves. Table 3.2 contains maximum permissible concentrations of chloride in the irrigation water (assuming a 15% leaching fraction) that various root stocks or cultivars can tolerate without experiencing leaf injury. Injury does not necessarily mean a reduction in yield or vice-versa. Chloride injury usually begins with a chlorosis (yellowing) in the leaf tip and margins and progresses to leaf burn or drying of the tissue as injury becomes more acute. Chloride injury can also result from direct leaf absorption during overhead sprinkler irrigation.

Short-term versus Long-term Use of Water

These guidelines are based on the long-term use of the given water quality. Poorer quality water can be tolerated if used on a short-term basis. If good quality water is used for one-third of the irrigation season, saline water with an ECw that would cause a 25 to 50% yield reduction if used continuously (Table 3.10) may be used for the remaining season with little or no yield reduction. Caution is advised in using this irrigation strategy since reduced growth and increased levels of chloride and boron in the soil and plant tissue could reduce yields in future years. Sufficient rainfall or good quality water is needed the subsequent year to leach most of the salts from the upper two or three feet of the root zone. In some soils, good quality water following saline water could cause reduced soil-water infiltration, creating an ideal environment for root diseases.

Table 3.10: Estimated Crop Yield using Irrigation Water of Various Qualities Over the Long-term (Potential Yields are Based on a 15% Leaching Fraction)

Tree and vine crop	Yield potential %*	Rating**			
	100	90	75	50	
	ECw (mmhos/cm)				
Almond***	1.0	1.4	1.9	2.8	S
Apricot***	1.1	1.3	1.8	2.5	S
Blackberry	1.0	1.3	1.8	2.5	S
Boysenberry	1.0	1.3	1.8	2.5	S
Date Palm	2.7	4.5	7.3	12.0	T
Grape	1.0	1.7	2.7	4.5	MS
Grapefruit	1.2	1.6	2.2	3.3	S
Orange	1.1	1.6	2.2	3.2	S
Peach	1.1	1.5	1.9	2.7	S
Plum	1.0	1.4	1.9	2.9	S

*Based on data from E.V Maas, 1990, "Crop Salt Tolerance." In: Agricultural Salinity Assessment and management, ed. K.K. Tanji. ASCE Manual No. 71.ASCE.

**Sensitive (S), moderately sensitive (MS), moderately tolerant (MT), and tolerant (T), to soil salinity.

***Tolerance is based on growth rather than yield.

Table 3.11: Estimated Yield of Vegetable Crops with Long term use of Irrigation Water of Different Qualities Over the Long-term (Potential Yields are Based on a 15% Leaching Fraction)

Vegetable crops	Yield potential %[1]				Rating[2]	
	100	90	75	50	Salt	Boron
	ECw (mmhos/cm)					
Tomato	1.7	2.3	3.4	5.0	MS	T

Brinjal	0.7	1.7	3.1	5.6	MS	-
Onion	0.8	1.2	1.8	2.9	S	S
Radish	0.8	1.3	2.1	3.4	MS	-
Potato	1.1	1.7	2.5	3.9	MS	MS
Cucumber	1.7	2.2	2.9	4.2	MS	MS
Carrot	0.7	1.1	1.9	3.0	S	MS
Cabbage	1.2	1.9	2.9	4.6	M	MT
Cauliflower	1.9	2.6	3.7	5.5	MS	MT
Turnip	0.6	1.3	2.5	4.3	MS	MT
Asparagus	2.7	6.1	11.1	19.4	T	VT

- Data not available. 1. Based on data from Maas and Grattan (1999). 2.Sensitive (S), Moderately sensitive (MS), Moderately tolerant (MT), Tolerant (T) and Very tolerant (VT)

Table 3.12: Maximum Chloride Concentrations that Various Tree and Vine Crops can Tolerate without Developing Leaf Burn (Assumes long-term effects and a 15% leaching fraction)

Crop	Rootstock or Cultivar	Maximum recommended chloride concentration* in the Irrigation Water	
		ppm	meq/L
Avocado	West Indian	180	5
(Persea Americana)	Guatemalan	140	4
Citrus	Sunki Mandarin, Grapefruit, Cleopatra Mandarin, Rangpur lime	590	10
Citrus	Sampson tangelo, rough lemon**, sour orange, Ponkan mandarin	350	10
Citrus	Citrumelo 4475, trifoliate orange, Cuban shaddock, Calamondin, sweet orange, Savage citrange, Rush citrange, Troyer citrange	240	7
Grape (Vitis spp.)	Salt Creek, 1613-3	950	26
	Dog ridge	710	20
Stone fruit (Prunus spp.)	Marianna	590	17
	Lovell, Shalil	240	7
	Yunnan	180	5
	Cultivars		
Berries*** (Rubus spp.)	Boysenberry	240	7
	Olallie blackberry	240	7
	Indian Summer raspberry	120	3

Grape(Vitis spp.)	Thomas seedless, Perlette	470	13
	Cardinal, black rose	240	7
Strawberry(Fragaria spp.)	Lassen	180	5
	Shasta	120	3

*These concentrations may exceed the salinity threshold and cause yield reduction in some crops.
**Data from Australia indicates that rough lemon is more sensitive to Cl than sweet orange.
***Data available for one variety of each species only.

Crop Response to Saline Water

Crops differ significantly in salt and alkali tolerance, Relative salt tolerance of a crop, as judged by its gross yield as well as relative reduction in yield, is significantly influenced by several factors, e.g., soil and water salinity, crop variety and growth stage, climate, irrigation frequency and discharge rate and their interactions by Mass, 1987). Permissible limits of water salinity by drip irrigation for vegetable, fruits and held crops and trees have been summarized in Table 3.13.

Table 3.13: Permissible Limits of Salinity in Water for Vegetable, Fruit, Field Crops Arid Trees by Drip Irrigation

Crops	*Soil type	Location	Salinity level (EC: dsm^{-1})	References
Vegetable crops				
Tomato	Sandy	Israel	3.6	Gormat *et al.* (1973)
	Sandy	Israel	5.6	Goldberg *et al.* (1970)
	Sandy	Israel	5.0	Shumeli (1974)
	SL	Panama	3.71	Bernar (1974)
	SL	Delhi	5.0	Ramadevi (1980)
	SL	Hawaii	5.8	Bower *et al. (1975)*
Cucumber	Sandy	Israel	4.0	Shumeli & Goldberg (1971)
Cucumber	Sandy	Jodhpur	3.0	Singh & Mann (1979)
Potato	Sandy	Jodhpur	3.0	Singh & Mann (1979)
Onion	CL	New Mexico	1.22	Swamis *et al.* (1979
Lettuce	CL	New Mexico	1.22	Swamis *et al.* (1979
Onion	SL	Montana	2.4	Melsted & Deboeri (1977)
Lettuce	SL	Montana	2.4	Melsted & Deboeri (1977)

Radish	SL	Hissar	6.5	Dixit *et al.* (1971)
Sweet corn	Sandy	Israel	4.5	Goldberg & Shumeli (1969)
Bell pepper	SL	Florida	245 (ppm)	Bernstein and Francois (1973)
Chilli	SL	New Mexico	3.5	Horton *et at.* (1979)
Fruit crops				
Grapevine	SL	Australia	1.75	Smart *et al.* (1974)
	Sandy	California	2.0	*Chavez* & Andrew (1974)
Grope fruit	Sandy	Israel	2.0	Bielorai *et al.* (1978)
Strawberry	SL	Egypt	1.75	Tousset (1975)
Peach	Sandy	Australia	3.01	Taylor (1974)
Date palm	SL		1000 (ppm)	Ruoveni (1974)

*SL=Sandy loam, *CL=Clay loam

Table 3.14: Effect of Furrow and Drip Methods of Irrigation at Different ET Levels and Water Salinity on the Yield of Potato

Treatment	Water use (cm)	Yield (t/ha)	Tubers (No/m^2)	Tuber wt(g)
Drip ETioo	28.8	27.5	55	59
Drip ET7s	21.4	21.1	40	53
Drip ETso	14.3	14.7	42	36.3
Drip ETioo(St)	36.6	26.4	36	89.0
Drip ET1oo(S2)	28.6	14.4	42	39.0
Furr. ETtoo	34.0	18.1	32	65.8
CD (0.05)	-	1.8	6.7	10.1

(Singh *et al.* 1978)

Yield reduction is more on applying water less than the crop water requirement (Table 3.14) or with low discharge rate (Table 3.15).

Table 3.15: Mean Per Cent Reduction of Tomato Yield as Influenced by Water Salinity and Discharge Rate

Water	Discharge rate (1/hr)		
Salinity (ds/m)	3.38	1.69	1.13
0.5	0	0	0
5.0	4.6	6.5	0
10.0	12.9	22.2	30.5
15.0	29.0	37.3	44.8

(Ramadevi, 1980)

Water Quality on Fruit Crops

Most fruit trees are relatively sensitive to salinity (Bernstein, 1980; Francois and Maas, 1994; Maas, 1987) and deciduous fruit trees will be amongst the first crops to suffer yield reductions if irrigation water becomes more saline (Hoffman *et al.*, 1989). Prunus species are generally considered to be more sensitive to salinity than most other fruit crops (Maas, 1987) and apricot considered to be less tolerant compared to other Prunus species (Bernstein *et al.*,1956). The effect of salinity on crops is influenced by several factors: ion concentrations and relations in the substrate, duration of exposure, plant species, cultivar and rootstock, stage of plant development, plant organ (e.g. leaves vs. fruit) and environmental conditions (Marschner, 1995). The specific combination of the above-mentioned factors will determine the main mechanisms of salt injury that operate and the relative contribution to growth inhibition and decreased yield.

The damaging effects of salinity on perennial crops are cumulative and it might take several years before the real effects become visible. Such cumulative effects of salinity have been reported for plums after three (Hoffman *et al.*, 1989) and six (Catlin *et al.*, 1993), pears after seven (Myers *et al.*, 1995) and for vines after four (Moolman *et al.*, 1999) years of saline irrigation under field conditions. Shoot growth may be an earlier, or more sensitive indicator of salt stress and as was found for plum trees (Hoffman *et al.*, 1989). However, the effects of salinity on vegetative growth have only an indirect effect on reduced yield in cultivars where fruit are borne primarily on the spur branches (Catlin *et al.*, 1993), as the shoot growth of plum trees was significantly reduced at low salinity levels (1 and 2 dS m^{-1} treatments) without any detrimental effect on yield. Indicators of the detrimental effects of salinity on vegetative growth in several perennial fruit crops and in vines have been identified in previous studies to include: root length, shoot growth, trunk growth, top growth, trunk cross sectional area, pruning mass, unit leaf area, total leaf area, leaf area index, new leaf production, leaf number per plant, individual leaf weight or petiole fresh weight and individual leaf dry weight or petiole dry weight (Boland *et al.*, 1993; Catlin *et al.*, 1993; Francois & Maas, 1994; Hoffman *et al.*, 1989; Lloyd *et al.*, 1990; Myers *et al.*, 1995; Moolman *et al.*, 1999). For grapevines (cultivar Columbar) irrigated with water of between 0.25 and 5 dS m^{-1}, shoot length, the length and number of nodes per shoot, as well as fresh and dry mass per internode decreased with increasing salinity during the second to fourth seasons of saline irrigation (Moolman *et al.*, 1999).

Salinity resulted in significantly smaller individual leaf area and reduced lateral shoot growth, measured during the seventh season of irrigation, of 40-year-old Williams Bon Cretien pear trees irrigated with 2.1 dS m^{-1} irrigation water compared to that of trees receiving irrigation water with an EC of 0.2 dS m^{-1} (Myers *et al.*, 1995). Salinity likewise reduced individual leaf area of 24-year-old Washington Navel citrus trees on sweet orange (*C. sinensis*) rootstock that was irrigated for 5 years with water containing either 5 (control treatment) or 20 mol NaCl m^{-3} prior to measurements (Lloyd *et al.*, 1990). Prior to imposition of the salinity treatments the orchard was irrigated with water drawn from the River Murray which contained on average 5 mol NaCl m^{-3}. However, salinisation did not affect the number of leaves per unit canopy volume of these trees. In contrast, significant decreases in leaf number per plant and leaf dry weight was observed for citrus rootstock Citrus macrophylla Wester seedlings grown for two months in nutrient solutions containing 40 mMNaCl (Ruiz*et al.*, 1999). Shoot length of these plants were reduced by 29% compared to that of the control treatment. Leaf area index of 3-year-old peach trees (cultivar Golden Queen) in drainage lysimeters subjected to irrigation water salinity levels of 0.1, 0.25, 0.5 and 1 dS m^{-1} in combination with regulated deficit irrigation (RDI), decreased with increasing water salinity during the second year of saline irrigation (Boland *et al.*, 1993). In Murray valley (Southeaster Australia), with appropriate irrigation management, soil and root stocks, orange trees can maintain productivity at salinity levels of 2.0 dS/m or more, but fresh fruit profitability is likely to be lower because of a reduction in average fruit size(Grieve *et al.*, 2007).

Citrus is regarded as a salt-sensitive crop, but its yield response to salinity is affected by variety, rootstock, duration of salt exposure, irrigation management, soil type, and climate. This study quantified the yield response of mature Valencia [*Citrus sinensis* (L. Osbeck)] orange trees on sweet orange (*C. sinensis*) rootstock to increased levels of sodium chloride in irrigation water in the Sunraysia area of the Murray Valley in south-eastern Australia. The orchard was planted on loamy sand and trees were irrigated and fertilized with a well-managed under-tree micro sprinkler system. Four levels of salt, ranging from the river-water control (0.44 dS/m) to 2.50dS/m, were applied over a 9-year period. Overall yield effects were smaller than expected, and did not conform well to the often used bent-stick model. Relative to the control, yield was initially higher (by up to 9%) in the intermediate salt treatments, and 3% lower in the highest treatment. However, relative yields of salinized trees decreased with time, and in the final year of the experiment, yield of the highest salt treatment was 9% lower than the control. Yield increases in the intermediate treatments resulted from increases in fruit number. All 3 salt treatments decreased average fruit weight by 4% and decreased juice content but increased juice sugar and acid content. Salt treatment strongly reduced trunk growth, and the effect increased with time. Our results show that with appropriate irrigation management, soils, and rootstocks, citrus trees can maintain productivity at salinity levels of 2.0 dS/m or more, but fresh fruit profitability is likely to be lower because of a reduction in average fruit size (Grieve *et al.*, 2007).

Results are reported from a long-term field experiment designed to determine the effect of irrigation water salinity on the yield and water uptake of mature grapefruit trees. Treatments were started in 1970 and consisted of chloride concentrations in the irrigation water of 7.1, 11.4 and 17.1 meq/1 added as NaCl + $CaCl_2$ at a 1 : 1 weight ratio. For the last four years of the experiment, 1973 to 1976, yield was linearly related to the mean chloride concentration in the soil saturation extract weighted according to the distribution of water uptake with depth and time. There was a 1.45% (1.68 Mg/ha) yield reduction for each 1 meq/1 increase in chloride concentration above a threshold value of 4.5 meq/1. This corresponded to a 13.5% (14.7 Mg/ha) decrease per 1 mmho/cm increase in the electrical conductivity of the soil saturation extract above a threshold value of 1.2 mmho/cm. Total water uptake was reduced as salt concentration in the soil increased. In the high salinity treatment, root concentration in, and water uptake from, the lower portion of the root zone were decreased. The maximum electrical conductivity (ECe) measured at the bottom of the root zone was 7.90 mmho/cm similar to the values of EC, obtained by linear extrapolation to zero yield and also to zero water uptake. Salt accumulation in the soil depended on the quantity and salt concentration of the irrigation water, rainfall, and on the amount of leaching. SAR and the Na^+ concentration of the soil remained low throughout the experiment. No leaf symptoms of Cl^- or Na^+ injury were observed. The results indicate an osmotic - rather than a specific ion effect - of salinity on grapefruit yield (Bielorai *et al.*, 1978).

Fruit production and tree growth characteristics of a Valencia orange orchard are related to equilibrium distribution of salts throughout the root profile in response to uniform applications of irrigation waters varying in salinity and sodicity hazards. Eight years of differential irrigation treatments consisting of basin irrigation with four waters representing low to moderately high salinity, and also with Cl and SO_4 waters, resulted in soil salinity profiles specific for each water. Both the quantity and quality of oranges have declined under irrigation treatments producing accumulation of soluble salts within the root zone. Specific ion, osmotic, and soil suction effects are discussed in relation to salinity stress (Bingham *et al.*, 1974).

A field experiment was conducted for five years to study the response of 6-year old lemon trees cv. Verna on three different rootstock (sour orange, Cleopatra mandarin and macrophylla) to uniform applications of four irrigation waters having Cl^- concentrations of 4 (control), 11, 26.5 and 42.5 mol m^{-3}, respectively.Fruit yield and the growth in trunk circumference were significantly reduced by increasing salinity in the rootzone, although this effect varied with the rootstock. The threshold values for response were 1.53, 2.08 and 1.02 dS m^{-1} for sour orange, Cleopatra mandarin and macrophylla respectively. The corresponding yield reduction for each unit increase in salinity above those values was 10.5, 13.7 and 14.2%, respectively. Trees on macrophylla accumulated higher Cl^- concentrations in the leaves than those from the other two root stocks (Cerdá *et al.*, 1990).

An irrigation experiment with water of different salinities (2.8, 7.6 and 12.7 mol Cl m^{-3}) was carried out from 1982 to 1988 in a mature "Shamouti" orange grove in the coastal plain of Israel. Seasonal accumulation of salts in the soil solution of the root zone (EC of more than 4.0 dS m^{-1} at the end of the irrigation season) was almost totally leached during the winter. The average annual rainfall of 550 mm reduced EC values below 1.0 dS m^{-1}. Tree growth, as measured by the increase in cross sectional area of main branches, was retarded by saline irrigation water (123, 107 and 99 cm^2 growth per tree during six years for the 2.8, 7.6 and 12.7 mol Cl m^{-3} treatments, respectively). Potassium fertilization (360 kg K_2O ha^{-1}) increased yield at all salinity levels during the last three years of the experiment, mainly by increasing fruit size. Saline irrigation water slightly increased sucrose and C1 concentrations in the fruit juice. Salinity decreased transpiration, increased soil water potential before irrigation and decreased leaf water potential. However, the changes in leaf water potential were small. Leaf Cl and Na concentrations increased gradually during the experimental period, but did not reach toxic levels up to the end of the experiment (4.4 g Cl kg^{-1} dry matter in the high salt treatment vs. 1.7 in the control). Relatively more leaf shedding occurred in the salinized trees as compared to the control. The sour orange root-stock apparently provided an effective barrier to NaCl uptake; therefore, the main effect of salinity was probably osmotic in nature. No interactions were found between N or K fertilization and salinity. Additional N fertilization (160 kg N ha^{-1} over and above the 200 kg in the control) did not reduce Cl absorption nor did it affect yield or fruit quality. Additional K had no effect on Na absorption but yield and fruit size were increased at all salinity levels. No significant differences were obtained between partial and complete soil surface wetting (30% and 90% of the total soil area resp.) with the same amounts of irrigation water. The effect of salinity on yield over the six years of the experiment was relatively small and occurred only after some years. But, in the last three years salinity significantly reduced average yields to 74.6, 67.1, and 64.2 Mg ha^{-1} for the three levels of salinity, respectively. Saline waters of up to 13 mol Cl m^{-3} primarily influenced the tree water uptake and growth response of "Shamouti" orange trees, whereas yield was only slightly reduced during six years(Dasberg *et al.*, 1991).

The effect of irrigation water quantity and salinity on fruit yield, fruit quality and leaf mineral composition were studied in a field experiment with 6-year-old lemon trees, cv. Fino 49, on the Macrophylla (*Citrus Macrophylla* Wester) rootstock during 1998–2000. Trees were irrigated with three different qualities of water, having an electrical conductivity 1, 2.5 and 4 dS/m, respectively. For each salinity treatment, trees were irrigated with two different quantities of water, 100 and 125% crop evapotranspiration. Lemon fruit yield significantly decreased with increasing salinity, due to a decrease in the number of fruits per tree. This reduction was caused by an increase in fruitlet drop off induced by salinity.

A significant increase of lemon fruit yield was observed in the last year by increasing the quantity of water. Salinity and amount of water applied affected fruit quality. The percentage of fruit juice, with respect to the total fruit weight, was greater in fruits from the control than for those in the salinity treatments. The opposite effect was observed for peel and pulp contents. Titratable acidity (TA) and total soluble solids (TSS) decreased with salinity, although the ratio TSS: TA was similar in all treatments. Chloride and sodium concentrations in leaves were raised by salinity and amounts of water applied(*García et al.*, 2003).

At Dareton, New South Wale, effects of salinity of irrigation water on the productivity of mature grape vines was studied. NaCl solution was injected into River Murray water to generate five salinity levels ranging from 0.37 to 3.47 dSm^{-1} with Sodium Absorption Ratios of between 2 and 37. These treatments were applied through a trickle irrigation system for 6 years to own rooted sultana grape vines growing in a vineyard. The effect of irrigation water salinity was most severe on vines growing in the most heavily textured soil and increased with time. The yield (Y) response was well described by the Y = D [1 + (ECi/ECih)B]-1 where ECi is salinity of irrigation water, D is theoretical yield at ECi = 0, ECih is half effect ECi and B is shape parameter. Soil texture affected the response via an effect on ECih and to a lesser extent on B. These parameters were related to % (silt and clay) in the final model, which was fitted for each of years 2 to 6 and accounted for 76.2% of the variance in yield. The yield response on the lightest soil most closely resembled the Maas-Hoffman 'bent – stick' model, being relatively flat at low levels of ECi and becoming steeper at moderate salinity levels. Yield losses for heavy soils were much greater than predicted by the Maas-Hoffman model. Bunch number was primary determinant of yield, while a lower berry weight also contributed to the reduction in yield in salinized vines. Effects on dried fruit quality were apparent only when yield was severely reduced (Prior *et al.*, 1992).

Fruit, fruit set and fruit growth of 'Washington Navel' orange fruit was monitored on 24-year-old Citrus sinensis trees on sweet orange root stocks that had been irrigated with either 5 or 20 mol m-3 NaCl for 5 years preceding measurements. Trees irrigated with high salinity water had reduced flowering intensities and lower rates of fruit set. This resulted in final fruit numbers for trees irrigated with 20 $molm^{-3}$ being 38 % those of trees irrigated with 5 $molm^{-3}$ NaCl. Fruit numbers were quantitatively related to canopy leaf area for both salinity treatments. Despite little difference between trees in terms of leaf area/fruit number ratio, slower rates of fruit growth were initially observed on high salinity trees. This effect was not apparent during the latter stages of fruit development. Consequently, fruit on trees irrigated with 20 $molm^{-3}$ NaCl grew to the same size as fruit on trees irrigated with 5 $molm^{-3}$ NaCl, but achieved this size at a later date. Measurements of brix/acid ratios showed that fruit on high salinity trees reached maturity standards 25 days after fruit on low salinity trees. Unimpaired growth of fruit on high salinity trees during summer and autumn occurred, despite appreciable leaf abscission, suggesting that reserve carbohydrate was utilized for growth during this period. Twigs on high salinity trees had much reduced starch content at the time of floral differentiation in winter. Twig starch content and extent of floral differentiation varied in similar way when examined as a function of leaf abscission. Reduced flowering and fruit set in salinized citrus trees is due to low levels of reserve starch, most of which has been utilized to support fruit growth in the absence of carbohydrate production during summer and autumn.

Water Quality on Vegetable Crops

Zhai *et al.*(2015) indicated as yield decreased with increased salinity and recommended that salinity of irrigation water should be controlled under 4 dS/m for tomato crop. In addition, Rahil *et al.*(2013) and Magan *et al.* (2008) reported that total and marketable fruit yield reduced with increasing salinity level. Similarly according to Noshadi *et al.* (2013) tomato yield was increased and then with increasing salinity yield was decreased. Unitary increase of water salinity above 1 dS m^{-1} reduced the commercial and total yield by 11.9 and 11.0%, respectively, and increased the concentration of soluble solids and the titratable acidity of the fruits by 13.9 and 9.4%, respectively in tomato crop (Campos *et al.*, 2006). Total yield, marketable yield, number of marketable fruits and pulp yield reduced with increase in proportion of sodium. Hence, water of moderate salinity with low concentration of sodium has to be used for production of industrial tomato to minimize the significant of yield losses. On the other hand, Under moderate saline irrigation (3 dS/m) the tomato yield production was not significantly affected by irrigation intervals, while under highly saline irrigation (5, 7 dS/m), the yield production significantly affected by irrigation intervals as a result it was recommended to use short irrigation interval (one day interval) instead of applying irrigation every three or four day (Zhai *et al.*, 2015).In Riyadh (Saudi Arabia), decreases in tomato yields due to using low quality water (saline water with EC of 3.6 dS m^{-1}) were 39.2% and 17.6% as compared to fresh water (0.86 dS m^{-1}) for the first and second season, respectively (Abdulrasoul *et al.*, 2010).

Water Quality in Greenhouse Cultivation

Greenhouse cultivation is a widely used farming system to provide a controlled environment suitable for optimal crop production (Yazgan *et al.*, 2008). For this reason, greenhouse crop production is now a steadily growing agricultural sector throughout the world with an estimated 405,000 ha of greenhouses spread all over the world (FAO, 2013). In addition, the groundwater used for irrigating greenhouses near the coastal areas is frequently saline (*Lee et al.*, 2008). The use of saline irrigation water has an adverse effect on soil–water–plant relations, occasionally severely restricting the normal physiological activity and productive capacity of the crops (De Pascale *et al.*, 2013; Plaut *et al.*, 2013). Under high salinity level, the crop growth, leaf surface expansion, and primary carbon metabolism of many crops are negatively affected due to osmotic effect, water deficit, nutritional imbalance, and oxidative stress (Kim *et al.*, 2008). Several crops are sensitive to salinity and the negative effect on growth leads to the decrease in potential profits. For this reason, salinity has been considered as one of the most important factors of irrigation water (Beltran, 1999). Irrigating saline water can also result in salt accumulation in soil, leading to the decrease in yield and deterioration in soil resource (Ould Ahmed *et al.*, 2007; Feizi *et al.*, 2010). In particular, under greenhouse conditions, the salinity problem is a critical constraint to vegetable production due to rapid accumulation of salts in soil (Shannon and Grieve, 1998; Rameshwaran *et al.*, 2015). There have been several studies on the effects of saline irrigation water on plant systems in greenhouses (Andriolo *et al.*, 2005; Ünlükara*et al.*, 2008). In the study by Reina-Sanchez *et al.* (2005), effects of salinity on tomato fruit yield have been quantified in experiments under greenhouse and soil-less cultivation with four salinity levels in Malaga, Spain. Lee *et al.* (2008) quantified the impact of saline irrigation water on chrysanthemums in a greenhouse in Athens, Georgia. Rameshwaran*et al.* (2015) investigated effects of different irrigation regimes with salinity treatments using a drip irrigation system for two pepper varieties in the greenhouse in Antalya, Turkey. Feigin *et al.* (1991) tested the response of lettuce and Chinese cabbage to the combination of a wide range of salinity and potassium nitrate levels in the greenhouse using an aero-hydroponic system. Garrido *et al.* (2008) evaluated physiological, phytochemical, and structural changes in lettuce by salt stress in a soilless system.

Management of Poor Quality Waters

The poor quality water when used continuously the following management points areconsidered for a sustained crop production.

- Dilution with good quality water.
- Flooding with good quality water once or twice to flush out salts beyond root zone.
- Gypsum mixing with water to reduce sodium hazards and also to improve soil structure.
- Providing drainage to remove salts.
- Using poor quality water in sandy soils.
- Growing salt tolerant crops.
- Adopting drip irrigation method for poor quality water.

Conclusion

Dissolved salts in irrigation water forms ions. The most common salts in irrigation water are table salt (NaCl), gypsum ($CaSO_4$), epsom salt ($MgSO_4$) and baking soda ($NaHCO_3$). Salts dissolve in water and form positive ions (cations) and negative ions (anions). The most common cations are calcium (Ca^{2+}), magnesium (Mg^{2+}), and sodicum (Na^+) while most common anions are chloride (Cl^-), sulphate (SO_4^{2-}) and bicarbonate (HCO_3^-). The ratios of these ions vary from one water supply to another. Potassium (K^+), carbonate (CO_3^-) and nitrate (NO_3^-) also exist in water supplies but the concentrations of these constituents are comparatively low. In addition, some irrigation waters, particularly from groundwater sources, contain boron at levels that may detrimental to crop plants. In regions where good quality water is either insufficient or not available, saline water irrigation is inevitable. Continuous use of saline water deteriorates chemical and physical properties of the irrigated soils and ultimately influences crop growth. The use of saline irrigation water has an adverse effect on soil–water–plant relations, occasionally severely restricting the normal physiological activity and productive capacity of the crops. Under high salinity level, the crop growth, leaf surface expansion, and primary carbon metabolism of many crops are negatively affected due to osmotic effect, water deficit, nutritional imbalance, and oxidative stress. Several crops are sensitive to salinity and the negative effect on growth leads to the decrease in potential profits. For this reason, salinity has been considered as one of the most important factors of irrigation water. Irrigating saline water can also result in salt accumulation in soil, leading to the decrease in yield and deterioration in soil resource. In particular, under greenhouse conditions the salinity problem is a critical constraint to vegetable production due to rapid accumulation of salts in soil. Sensitivity and tolerance of crops to salinity level may vary depending on meteorological and soil conditions in the region, as well as the irrigation method. More quantitative data are needed under varying conditions of soil and water, salinity, irrigation frequency, discharge rate, salt distribution, climatic conditions, crop variety, salt fertilizer interaction, and finally the economic feasibility of different irrigation methods.

REFERENCES

Abdulrasoul M. A., A. R. Al-Harbi, M. A. Wahb-Allah (2010). Impact of Irrigation Water Quality, Irrigation Systems, Irrigation Rates and Soil Amendments on Tomato Production in Sandy Calcareous Soil. Turk J. Agric. and Forestry, 34: 59-73.

Alan, D. B. (1994).Soil Salinity, Salt Tolerance and Growth Potential of Horticultural and Landscape Plants, Department of Soil and Plant and Insect Science, University of Wyoming. http://ces.uwyo.edu/PUBs/Wy988.PDF.

Andriolo, J.L., G.L. Da Luz, M.H. Witter, R.S. Godori, G.T. Barros and O.C. Bortolotto (2005). Growth and Yield of Lettuce Plants under Salinity.Hortic. Braz., 23: 931–934.

APHA (2005).Standard Methods for Examination of Water and Wastewater.21st ed. American Public Health Association, Washington DC, USA.

Ayers, R. S. and D.W. Westcot (1994).Water Quality for Agriculture, University of California FAO, California, USA.

Ayers, R.S. (1997).Quality of Water for Irrigation. *Journal of the Irrigation and Drainage,* 103 (2): 140 -142.

Ayres, R. S. and D. W. Westcot (1985).Water Quality for Agriculture. FAO Irrigation and Drainage Paper No. 29. Food and Agriculture Organization of the United Nations, Rome. pp. 1-117.

Bauder, T. A., R. M. Waskom and J. G. Davis (2007).Irrigation Water Quality Criteria. Colorado State University, US Department of Agriculture. Research Report No. 7/03.

Beltran, J.M. (1999). Irrigation with Saline Water: Benefits and Environmental Impact. Agric. Water Manag., 40: 183–194.

Bernar, J.H. (1974). Spring Cucumber-Drip Versus Furrow Irrigation. In: *Proc. 2nd Drip Irrig. Congr. Sand Deigo,* Calif, USA.

Bernstein, L. (1980). Salt Tolerance of Fruit Crops. *USDA Agric. Inf. Bull.,* 292: 1-8.

Bernstein, L. and L.E. Francois (1973). Comparison of Drip, Furrow and Sprinkler Irrigation. *Sod Sci.,* 115: 73-86.

Bernstein, L., J.W. Brown and H.E. Hayward (1956). The Influence of Rootstock on Growth and Salt Accumulation in Stone Fruit Trees and Almonds. In: *Proc. Am. Soc. Hort. Sci.,* 68: 86 - 95.

Bielorai, H., J. Shalhavet and Y. Levy (1978) Grapefruit Response to Variable Salinity in Irrigation Water and Soil. *Irrigation Science,* 1: 61- 71.

Bielorai, H., J. Shalhevet and Y. Levy (1980).Grape Fruit Response to Variable Salinity in Irrigation Water and Soil. *Irri. Sci.* 1(1): 61-70.

Biernbaum, J. A. (1994). Water Quality. In: H. K. Tayama, T. J. Roll and M. L. Gaston (eds.), Tips on Growing Bedding Plants. 3rd ed. Ohio Florist Assoc., Columbus, Ohio. pp. 65–76.

Bingham, F.T., R.J. Mahler, J. Parra and L.H. Stolzy (1974).Long-term Effects of Irrigation-Salinity Management on a Valencia Orange Orchard. *Soil Science,* 117: 369 - 377.

Boland, A.M., P.D. Mitchell and P.H. Jerie (1993). Effect of Saline Water Combined With Restricted Irrigation on Peach Tree Growth and Water use. *Aust. J. Agric. Res.,* 44: 799-816.

Bower, C.A., B.A. Kralhi and N. Ikeda (1975).Growth of Tomato on a Typical Soil as Influenced by Drip Irrigation and Soil Salinity. *J. Amer. Soc. Hort. Sci.,* 100: 519 - 521.

Breckle, S.W. (1995). The Significance of Salinity in Water, Desertification and Development, Dryland Ecology in Social Perspective, Academic Press, London, and New York, pp: 277-292

Campos, C.A.B., P.D. Fernandes, H.R. Gheyi, F.F. Blanco and C.B. Onçalves (2006). Yield and Fruit Quality of Industrial Tomato under Saline Irrigation. Sci. Agric, 63: 146-152.

Catlin, P.B., G.J. Hoffman, R.M. Mead and R.S. Johnson (1993). Long Term Response of Mature Plum Trees to Salinity. *Irrig. Sci.,* 13: 171-176.

Cerdá, A., M. Nieves and M.G. Guillen (1990). Salt Tolerance of Lemon Trees as Affected by Rootstock. *Irrigation Science,* 11: 245 - 249.

Chavez, H. and F. Andrew (1974). Drip Irrigation Increases Yields, Lowers Water Costs. *Citrus &Vegetable Mag,* 38:6-18.

Collins, R. and A. Jenkins. (1996). The Impact of Agriculture and Land use on Stream Chemistry in the Middle Hills of The HImalayes. *Nepal J. Hydro.,* 185:71-86

Dasberg, S., H. Bielorai, A. Haimowitz and Y. Erner (1991). The Effect of Saline Irrigation Water on *Shamouti* orange Trees. *Irrigation Science,* 12: 205–211.

De Pascale, S., F. Orsini and A. Pardossi (2013).Irrigation Water Quality for Greenhouse Horticulture. In: Good Agricultural Practices for Greenhouse Vegetable Crops; FAO Plant Production and Protection Paper 217; Food and Agriculture Organization of the United Nations: Rome, Italy, pp. 169–204.

Dewis J. and F. Freitas (1970).Physical and Chemical Methods of Soil and Water Analysis. FAO Soils Bulletin 10. FAO, Rome. 275 p.

Dhirendra, M. J., A. Kumar, N. Agrawal (2009). Assessment of the Irrigation Water Quality of River Ganga in Haridwar District, Rasayan. J. Chem., 2: 285-292.

Dixit, S.P., M.C. Agarwal and J. Nath (1971). Performance of Sub-surface Drip Method of Irrigation under Two Different Qualities of Irrigation Water. In: *Proc. All India Symp. Soil Salinity*, Kanpur, Uttar Pradesh. P: 199-122.

Eaton, F.M. (1950). Significance of Carbonates in Irrigation Water. *Soil Sci.*, 69:123-133.

Ehsan, T., R. Pichu and K. M. Glenn (2010). High Concentrations of Na^+ and Cl Ions in soil Solution have Simultaneous Detrimental Effects on Growth of Faba bean under Salinity Stress. Journal of Experimental Botany, 25 (2): 131-134.

FAO (2013). Good Agricultural Practices for Greenhouse Vegetable Crops; FAO Plant Production and Protection Paper 217; Food and Agriculture Organization of the United Nations: Rome, Italy.

Feigin, E.; Pressman, E.; Imas, O.; Miltau, O. 1991. Combined Effects of KNO_3 and Salinity on Yield and Chemical Composition of Lettce and Chiness Cabbage. Irrig. Sci. 12, 223–230.

Feizi, M., M.A. Hajabbasi and B. Mostafazadeh-fard (2010). Saline Irrigation Water Management Strategies for Better Yield of Safflower (Carthamustinctorius L.) in an Arid Region. Aust. J. Crop Sci., 4: 408–414.

Francois, L.E. and E.V. Maas (1994). Crop Response and Management on Salt-Affected Soils. *In*: M. Pessarkli (ed.). Handbook of Plant and Crop Stress. New York: Marcel Dekker: 149 - 181.

Freeze, R. A. and J. A. Cherry (1979).Ground Water. Prentice Hall Inc., N. J. USA. pp. 383-456.

García, S.F., M. Carvajal, I. Porras, P. Botia and V. Martinez (2003).Effects of Salinity and Rate of Irrigation on Yield, Fruit Quality and Mineral Composition of 'Fino 49' Lemon. *European Journal of Agronomy*, 19: 427–437.

Garrido, Y., J.A. Tudela, A. Marín, T. Mestre, V. Martínez and M.I. Gil (2008). Physiological, Phytochemical and Structural Changes of Multi-leaf Lettuce Caused by Salt Stress. J. Sci. Food Agric. 2014, 94, 1592–1599.

Goldberg, D. and M. Shmueli (1970). Drip Irrigation a Method used under Arid and Desert Conditions of High Water and Soil Salinity. *Trans. ASAE*, 13: 38 - 41.

Goldberg, D. and M. Shumeli (1969). Trickle Irrigation-A Method for Increased Agricultural Production under Conditions of Saline Water and Adverse Soils. In: *Proc. Intern. Arid Land Cong.*, Tuscon, Arizona.

Gormat, D., D. Goldberg, D.Rimon, and J. Benasher (1973).Physiological Effects of Water Quality and Method of Application on Tomato, Cucumber and Pepper. In: *Proc. American Soc. Hort. Sci.*, 98: 202-205.

Grieve, A. M., L. D. Prior and K. B. Bevington (2007). Long-term Effects of Saline Irrigation Water on Growth, Yield and Fruit Quality of 'Valencia' Orange Trees. *Australian Journal of Agricultural Research* 58(4) 342-348.

Grieve, A.M., L. D. Prior and K. B. Bevington (2007). Long-term Effects of Saline Irrigation Water on Growth, Yield and Fruit Quality of 'Valencia' Orange Trees. Australian Journal of Agricultural Research, 58(4) 342-348.

Guodie, A. S. (1992). The Human Impact: Man's Role in Environmental Change. Black Well Publishing Press, Oxford, England.

Hem, J.D. (1970). Study and Interpretation of The Chemical Characteristics of Nature Water. U.S. Geological Survey Water Supply, 2254, pp. 263.

Hesse, P. R. (1971). A Textbook of Soil Chemical Analysis. John Murray Ltd., London.

Hoffman, G.J., P.B. Catlin, R.M. Mead, R.S. Johnson, L.E. Francois and D. Goldhamer (1989). Yield and Foliar Injury Responses of Mature Plum Trees to Salinity. *Irrig. Sci.*, 10: 215-229.

Horton, R. *et al.* (1979). Chilli-pepper Growth as Affected by High Frequency Deficit Irrigation. *Annual Meeting Soil Sci. Soc. Ann.* p. 204.

Howie, H. and J. Lloyd (1989). Response of Orchard 'Washington Navel' Orange, *Citrussinensis* (L.) Osbeck to Saline Irrigation Water. II. Flowering, Fruit Set and Fruit Growth. *Australian Journal of Agricultural Research*, 40: 371 – 380.

Islam, M. S. and S.Z.K.M. Shamsad (2009). Assessment of Irrigation Water Quality of Bogra District in Bangladesh. Bangladesh J. Agric. Res., 34 (4) 597-608.

James. J. Riley (1982). Western Sudan Agriculture Research Project. Agriculture Research Corporation, The Sudan Government, United State for International Development.

Kim, H., J.M. Fonseca, J. Choi, C. Kubota, D.Y. Kwon (2008). Salt in Irrigation Water Affects The Nutritional and Visual Properties of Romaine Lettuce (*Lactuca sativa* L.). J. Agric. Food Chem., 56: 3772 – 3776.

Lee, S.B., C.O. Hong, J.G. Oh, J. Gutierrez and P.J. Kim (2008). Effect of Irrigation Water Salinization on Salt Accumulation of Plastic Film House Soil Around Sumjin River Estuary. Korean J. Environ. Agric., 27: 349–355.

Lloyd, J., P. Kriedemann and D. Aspinall (1990). Contrasts Between *Citrus* Species in Response to Salinisation: An Analysis of Photosynthesis and Water Relations for Different Rootstock Scion Combinations. *Physiol. Plant*, 78: 236 - 246.

Maas, E.V. (1985). Crop Tolerance to Saline Sprinkling. *Plant Soil*, 89: 273-284.

Maas, E.V. (1987). Salt Tolerance of Plants. *In*: B.R. Christie (ed.). CRC Handbook of Plant Science in Agriculture – CRC Series in Agriculture Vol. II. Boca Raton, Fla: CRC Press, p. 57 - 75.

Maas, E.V. and G.L. Hoffman (1977). Crop Salt Tolerance Current Assessment. *J. Irr. and Dr. Divi. ASCE*, 103: 115-134.

Maas, E.V. and S.R. Grattan (1999). Crop Yields as Influenced by Salinity. In: R.W. Skaggs and J.V. Schilfgaarde, eds. Agricultural Drainage. Agronomy Monograph 38. ASA, CSSA, SSSA, Madison, USA.

Magan, J.J., M. Gallardo, R.B. Thompson and P. Lorenzo (2008). Effects of Salinity on Fruit Yield and Quality of Tomato Grown in Soil-less Culture in Greenhouses in Mediterranean Climatic Conditions. Agricultural Water Management, 95: 1041-1055.

Malash, N., T.J. Flowers and R. Ragab (2005). Effect of Irrigation Systems and Water Management Practices using Saline and Non-saline Water on Tomato Production. Agric. Water Management, 78: 25-38.

Marschner, H. (1995). Mineral Nutrition of Higher Plants, 2nd Ed. New York: Academic Press.

Mass, E.V. (1990). Crop Salt Tolerance. In: Agricultural Assessment and Management Manual. K.K. Tanji (ed.). ASCE, New York. pp. 262-304.

Melsted J.D. and D. Deboeri (1977).Drip and Sprinkler Irrigation of Carrots and Onions. *Trans. ASAE*, 77:20-13.

Michael., A. M. (1992). Irrigation Theory and Practice.Vikas Publishing House Pvt. Ltd., New Delhi. pp. 686-740.

Moolman, J.H., W.P. De Clercq, W.P.J. Wessels, A. Meiri and C.G. Moolman (1999). The use of Saline Water for Irrigation of Grapevines and The Development of Crop Salt Tolerance Indices. WRC Report No. 303/1/98. Pretoria: Water Research Commission.

Myers, B.A., West, D.W. Callinan and C.C. Hunter (1995). Long Term Effects of Saline Irrigation on Yield and Growth of Mature Williams Pear Trees. *Irrig. Sci.,* 16: 35-46.

Nahid, S., Haque, M. and S.F.Elahi (2009).Evaluation of Surface Irrigation Water Quality in MuktagachaUpazila of Bangladesh.Songklanakarin J. Sci. Technol., 31(2): 229-235.

Nahid, S., M. H. Aminul and S. F. Elahi (2008).Evaluation of Surface Irrigation Water Quality in Muktagacha Upazila of Bangladesh. Dept. of Soil, Water and Envi., University of Dhaka, Dhaka-100, Bangladesh.

Nata, T., K. Bheemalingeswara and A. Berhane (2009). Groundwater Suitability for Irrigation: A case Study from Debre Kidane Watershed, Eastern Tigray, Ethiopia. Ethiopia MEJS, 1(1): 36-358.

Noshadi, M., S. Fahandej and A.R. Sepaskhah (2013). Effects of Salinity and Irrigation Water Management on Soil and Tomato in Drip Irrigation. International Journal of Plant Production, 7: 295-312.

Ogunfowokan, A. O., J. F. Obisanya and O.O. Ogunkoya (2009).Assessment of Chemical Quality of three Streams under Different Agricultural Land use Systems in Obafemi Awolowo University, Ile-Ife, Nigeria. Toxicol. Environ. Chem., 91(5): 847-872.

Ogunfowokan, A. O., J. F. Obisanya, and O. O. Ogunkoya (2013).Salinity and Sodium Hazards of three Streams of Different Agricultural Land use Systems in Ile-Ife, Nigeria. Appl. Water Sci., 3:19-28.

Ould Ahmed, B.A., T. Yamamoto and M. Inoue (2007). Response of Drip Irrigated Sorghum Varieties Growing in Dune Sand to Salinity Levels in Irrigation Water. J. Appl. Sci., 7: 1061– 1066.

Peterson, H.G. (1999). Water Quality and Micro-irrigation for Horticulture http://www.safewater.org/PDFS/resourceswaterqualityinfo/Resource_Water_Qual_Facts.pdf

Plaut, Z., M. Edelstein and M.Ben-Hur (2013).Overcoming Salinity Barriers to Crop Production using Traditional Methods. Crit. Rev. Plant Sci., 32: 250–291

Prior, L.D., A.M. Grieve and B.R. Cullis (1992). Sodium Chloride and Soil Texture Interactions in Irrigated Field Grown Sultana Grapevines. I. Yield and Fruit Quality. *Australian Journal of Agricultural Research,* **43:** 1051–1066.

Raghunath, H. M. (1990). Ground Water. New Delhi, India. pp. 563.

Rahil, M., H. Hajjeh and A. Qanadillo (2013). Effect of Saline Water Application through Different Irrigation Intervals on Tomato Yield and Soil Properties. Open Journal of Soil Science, 3: 143-147.

Ramadevi, A.N. (1980). Ph. D. Thesis, IARI, New Delhi.

Rameshwaran, P., A. Tepe, A. Yazar and R.Ragab (2015). The Effect of Saline Irrigation Water on the Yield of Pepper: Experimental and Modelling Study. Irrig.Drain., 64: 41–49.

Reina-Sanchez, A., R. Romero-Aranda and J. Cuartero (2005). Plant Water Uptake and Water use Efficiency of Greenhouse Tomato Cultivars Irrigated with Saline Water. Agric. Water Manag., 78: 54–66.

Rhoades, J. D. (1982). Reclamation and Management of Salt-affected Soils After Drainage. In: Proc. First Annual Western Provincial Conference on Rationalization of Water and Soil Research and Management, Alberta, Canada. pp. 123–197.

Richards, L. A. (1954). Diagnosis and Improvement of Saline and Alkali soils.USDA Agricultural Handbook No. 60, US Department of Agriculture, Washington DC. 160p.

Rowe, D. R. and I.M. Abel-Magid (1995). Handbook of Waste Water Reclamation and Reuse. CRC Press Inc., p. 550.

Ruiz-Sánchez, M.C., J. Egea, R. Galego and A. Torrecillas (1999). Floral Biology of 'Búlida' Apricot Trees Subjected to Postharvest drought Stress. *Ann. Appl. Biol.*, 135: 523-528.

Ruoveni, O. (1974). Drip vs. Sprinkler Irrigation of Datepalm. *Annual Rept. Date Growers Institute*, 51:3-5.

Shahimasi, E. and V. Kashuta., (2008).Irrigation Water Quality and its Effects upon Soil. Tirana Agricultural University, Tirana, Republic of Macedonia.

Shaki, A. A. and A. J. Adeloye (2006).Evaluation of Quantity and Quality of Irrigation Water at Gadowa Irrigation Project in Murzuq Basin, Southwest Libya. Journal of Agricultural Water Management, 84: 193-201.

Shannon, M.C. and C.M. Grieve (1998). Tolerance of Vegetable Crops to Salinity. Sci. Hortic., 78: 5–38.

Shumeli, M. (1974). Drip Irrigation with Saline Water. *Citrograph*, 59: 291-294.

Shumeli, M. and D. Goldberg (1971). Emergence, Early Growth and Salinity of Vegetable Crops Germinated by Sprinkler and Trickier Irrigated in *an Arid* Zone. *Hort. Sci.*, 6 (6) : 563 - 565.

Siamak,G. and S. Srikantaswamy (2008). Assessment of Seasonal Variation and Drinking Water Quality in Mysore City. Asian Journal of Environmental science, 3 (2): 104 -110.

Silva, E. (2004).Quality of Irrigation Water in Sri Lanka: Status and Trends. Asian J. Water Environ. Pollut., 1(1&2): 5-12.

Singh, S.D. and H.S. Mann (1979).Optimization of Water use and Crop Production in an Arid Zone. Res. Bull. No. 1, CAZRI, Jodhpur.

Singh, S.D., J.P. Gupta and P. Singh (1978). Water Economy and Saline Water use by Drip Irrigation *Agron. J.*, 70: 948-951.

Smart, R.E., C.R. Tushingston and J.C. Evans (1974). Grapevine Response to Furrow and Drip Irrigation *American J. Enology and Viticulture*, 25: 62-66.

Swammis, T.W., D.L. Weeks and E.G. Hanson (1979). Influence of Irrigation Method on Salt Accumulation in Row Crops. *Trans. ASAE*, 22: 691-696.

Talyor, A. (1974). Trickle Irrigation Experiments in Goulburn Valley. *Victoria Hort. Digest*, 4: 4-8.

Tiwari, T. N. and A. Manzoor (1988).River Pollution in athmandu Valley, Nepal: Suitability of River Water for Irrigation. Indiana J. Environ. Prot., 8 (4): 269 - 274.

Tousset, C.G. (1975). Effect of Drip Irrigation on Growth and Yield of Strawberries on Sandy Soils. *Victoria Hort. Digest*, 45: 45 - 50.

Ünlükara, A., B. Cemek, S. Karaman and S. Ersahin (2008). Response of Lettuce (*Lactuca Sativa Var. Crispa*) to Salinity of Irrigation Water.New Zealand J. Crop Hortic. Sci., 36: 263–271.

WHO, (1971). International Standards of Drinking Water. World Health Organization, Geneva.

Wilcox, L.V. (1955). Classification and use of Irrigation water. USD Circular No 969. Washington DC.

Yazgan, S., S. Ayas, C. Demirtas, H. Büyükcangaz and B.N. Candogan (2008). Deficit Irrigation Effects on Lettuce (*Lactuca Sativavar. Olenka*) Yield in Unheated Greenhouse Condition. J. Food Agric. Environ., 6: 357–361.

Zhai, Y., Q. Yang and M. Hou (2015). Effects of Saline Water Drip Irrigation on Tomato Yield, Quality, and Blossom-end Rot Incidence – 3a Case Study in The South of China. PLOS ONE, 10: 1-17.

Horticulture and Ecology - *Studies & Management* **Pages 61-85**
Edited by: **Dr. Alka Chauhan and Dr. Pawan Kumar 'Bharti'**
ISBN: 978-93-88854-09-2
Edition: **2019**
Published by: **Discovery Publishing House Pvt. Ltd., New Delhi (India)**

4 Effect of Foliar Spray of Organic and Inorganic Nutrients on the Growth and Yield of Black Gram (*Vigna mungo* L.)

[1]Dr. V. Aravinth

ABSTRACT

Field Experiment was conducted during February – April, 2017 at Thanthai Roever Institute of Agriculture and Rural Development, Perambalur, Tamil Nadu to study the effect foliar spray of organic and inorganic nutrients on the growth and yield of black gram. The experiment was laid out in Randomized Block Design with twelve treatments replicated thrice. The growth and yield components of black gram viz., plant height, leaf area index, dry matter production, length of the pod, number of pods plant^{-1}, number of seeds pod^{-1} and test weight were favourably influenced by RDF +3% Panchagavya + 10% Vermiwash. It was followed by application of RDF +Pulse wonder + 10% Vermiwash. RDF +3% Panchagavya + 10% Vermiwash recorded the highest yield of 953 kg ha^{-1} as compared to other treatments. This treatment also gave the highest return per rupee invested of ₹ 2.64 in black gram raised during February – April 2017.

Introduction

Pulse crop plays an important role in Indian agriculture and India is the large producer and consumer of pulses in the world. Pulses contain high percentage of quality protein nearly three times as much as cereals (Upadhayay *et al.*, 1999). Thus, they are source to overcome protein malnutrition among human being. For vegetarian diet, pulses form the major source of protein. Pulses are wonderful gift of nature with unique ability of biological nitrogen fixation, deep root system, mobilization of insoluble soil nutrients and bringing qualitative changes in soil properties - which make them known as soil fertility restorers.

Black gram *Vignamungo* L. is one of the most important pulses of rainfed areas grown thorough out the country. This crop is grown in different cropping systems as a mixed crop, catch crop and sequential crop in the country. Black gram seed contains 25-26 per cent protein, 56.6 per cent carbohydrates, 1.5 per cent fat and minerals combination, amino acid and essential vitamins . It is used

1 Assistant Professor of Agronomy, Thanthai Roever Institute of Agriculture and Rural Development, Perambalur, Tamil Nadu 621 115, India

as nutritive fodder specially for milch cattle. It is also used as a green manuring crop. Black gram is native of India and in India total black gram production was estimated as 1.61 million tonnes from 3.19 million hectare area with a productivity of 505 $kgha^{-1}$, whereas in Tamil Nadu it occupies an area of about 3.65 lakh hectares with a production of about 3.1 lakh tonnes and productivity of 851 kg ha^{-1} (Anon., 2014).

The yield potential of black gram is very low because of the fact that the crop is mainly grown in rainfed condition with poor management practices and also due to various physiological, biochemical as well as inherent factors associated with the crop. Apart from the genetic makeup, the physiological factors viz., in sufficient partitioning assimilates, poor pod setting due to the flower abscission and lack of nutrients during critical stage of crop growth, coupled with a number of disease and pest (Mahala *et al.*, 2001) constitute the major constraints for the poor yield. The productivity of black gram in our country is very low. Hence, there is a need for enhancement of the productivity of black gram by proper agronomic practices. One among them is foliar application of organic and inorganic sources of nutrients for exploiting genetic potential of the crop. This is considered to be an efficient and economic method of supplementing part of nutrient requirements at critical stages. Foliar application is credited with the advantage of quick and efficient utilization of nutrients, elimination of losses through leaching, fixation and regulating the uptake of nutrients by plant (Manonmani and Srimathi, 2009).

Since foliar nutrients usually penetrate the leaf cuticle or stomata and enter the cells facilitating easy and rapid utilization of nutrients. Foliar spray of organic and inorganic nutrients such as Panchagavya,Vermiwash, Pulse wonder and DAP was found to be beneficial in enhancing the yield of pulses.

Keeping the above in view the present investigation was under taken to study the-Effect of foliar application of organic and inorganic nutrients on the growth and yield of black gram [*Vignamungo*(L.)]with the following objectives :

- To study the effect of foliar spray of organic and inorganic nutrients on the growth of black gram
- To assess the effect of foliar spray of organic and inorganic nutrients on yield parameters and yield of black gram.
- To workout the economics.

Review of Literature

System approach to plant nutrition is gaining importance as evidenced by the recent research findings. Improved management of organic matter is considered to be a pre-requisite for sustaining soil health and crop productivity. Application of organic and inorganic nutrients maintains the soil nutrient supply in an optimum amount for sustaining soil health and crop productivity through optimization of benefits from all possible sources of plant nutrients. Foliar application of organic fertilizers improves the quality of crop and also it will improve the soil health and its productivity. Thus, the most logical way to manage long-term fertility of soil is to apply organic nutrients to plants, which will also take care of environmental pollution including soil, water and air.

The literature pertaining to influence of organic and inorganic nutrients on the growth, yield parameters and yield and economics attributes in black gram are presented in this chapter.

Effect of Foliar Spray of Organic and Inorganic Nutrients on the Growth of Blackgram

Rajendran *et al.*, (2006) reported that application of Vermicompost @ 5 t/ha with foliar spray of 3% Panchagavya 10 DAS enhanced the yield and quality of grains in chickpea. Senthilkumar *et al.* (2008) observed significant increase in growth characters like plant height(97.5 cm) , increased number of plants and straw yield due to application of 15% Vermiwash in greengram. Jayakumar *et al.*, (2008) stated that application of 2% DAP at pre-flowering stage significantly increased the growth parameters like plant height (30.1 cm), number of branches (3-4) and higher leaf area index in blackgram. Kadambian *et al.*, (2009) observed that application of 3% Panchagavya spray at 10 DAS resulted in the significant increase in the growth of green gram.

Hatti *et al.* (2010) reported that growth of blackgram increased due to the application of Vermiwash which also increased grain yield due to the high level of macro and micronutrients. Tharmaraj *et al.* (2011) revealed that application of 3% Panchagavya recorded rapid changes in the phenotypes of plants and also improved the growth of redgram. Medhi and Roy (2011) revealed that foliar application of 2% DAP significantly influenced the plant height (69.66 cm), leaf area index (3.055) and leaf chlorophyll content of blackgram.

Patil *et al.* (2012) concluded that application of 1/3 rd enriched compost + 1/3rd vermicompost + 1/3rd Glyricidia leaf manures and foliar spray of Panchagavya @ 3% at flower initiation and 15 DAF recorded significantly higher grain yield (2400 kg per hectare) in chickpea. Doss *et al.* (2013) reported that application of 1% K + 2% DAP significantly increased the growth, yield and grain yield in blackgram. Rekha *et al.* (2013) observed that application of 15% Vermiwash recorded higher leaf area, number of pods per plant and also increased grain yield of greengram. Vimalendranloganathan and Wahab (2014) reported that application of 100% recommended dose of fertilizers and 4 sprays of 3% Panchagavy are corded the highest growth attributes and yield of fresh baby corn. Mamathashree *et al.*, (2016) reported that foliar spray of 19:19:19 @ 2% recorded higher plant height (185.7 cm) and also improved growth and yield of blackgram.

Effect of Organic and Inorganic Nutrients on Yield Parameters and Yield of Blackgram.

Behera and Elamathi (2007) reported that 2% foliar spray of DAP and NAA 40 ppm twice at 25 and 35 days after sowing recorded significant improvement in yield and yield parameters in chickpea. Swaminathan *et al.*, (2007) concluded that application of 3% Panchagavya as foliar spray on 15, 25 and 40 days after sowing in black gram recorded the highest grain yield of 1195 kg per hectare. Sritharan *et al.* (2007) stated that foliar application of 2% urea recorded highest grain yield of 955.20 kg per hectare and subsequently improved the total chlorophyll content and soluble protein content in blackgram.

Ghosh and Joseph (2008) reported that application of Vermiwash along with 2% DAP spray recorded significantly higher number of pods per plant (21.77), number of seeds per pod (8.57) and 1000 g test weight (31.67 g) in green gram. Jaykumar *et al.*, (2008) observed that foliar spray of 3% DAP at flowering significantly increased the number of pods per plant, grain weight and ultimately grain yield in blackgram.

Manonmani and Srimathi (2009) concluded that application of 2% DAP followed by urea 1% recorded higher 100 seed weight (5.6 and 5.5 g), seed yield (1240 and 1040 kg per hectare) and germination per cent (92 and 88%, respectively) in blackgram. Rajavel and Vincent (2009) stated that foliar sprays of 2% DAP recorded the highest yield of 955 kg ha^{-1} in blackgram. Suresh kumar *et al.* (2011) reported that foliar spray of 3% Panchagavya recorded higher yield in blackgram. Tripathi *et al.* (2011) reported that application of 15% Vermiwash significantly increased the yield of black gram (824 kg per hectare and 842 kg per hectare). Choudhary and Yadhav (2011) reported that application of 2% DAP recorded the highest dry matter accumulation per metre row length (114.9 g) in blackgram. Amutha *et al.* (2012) reported that foliar spray of nutrient mixture with 3% Panchagavya with 10% Vermiwash proved to be the best treatment to improve leaf area index, total dry matter accumulation and seed yield in black gram.

Singh and Guriqbal (2013) reported that application of 25 and 37.5 kg P_2O_5 per hectare increased the grain yield in greengram. Rahman *et al.* (2014) concluded that the foliar spray of N, P and K significantly increased the yield in greengram. Saravanan and Panneerselvam (2014) reported that application of enriched compost 1/3 + Vermicompost 1/3 + Daincha leaf manure 1/3 and foliar spray of 3% Panchagavya at flower initiation and 15 DAF recorded significantly higher grain yield in blackgram. Das and Jana (2015) stated that higher yield of greengram were recorded with the application of 2% urea spray. Shyamraokulkarni *et al.* (2015) reported that foliar spray of 3% Panchagavya at flower initiation stage recorded significantly higher yield of greengram.

Economics

Dixit and Elamathi (2007) concluded that application of foliar spray of 400 ppm NAA +0.5 % chelated micronutrient + 2% DAP recorded higher gross returns, net returns and B:C ratio due to higher productivity in terms of yield in black gram. Shashikumar *et al.* (2013) stated that application of foliar spray of 40 ppm NAA + 0.5% chelated micronutrient +2% DAP given at 35 and 50 DAS recorded significantly higher growth components and also higher grain yield (1298 kg per hectare) and B:C ratio (3.03) in black gram. Vinothkumar *et al.* (2013) revealed that application of foliar spray of 2% DAP twice at flower initiation and pod formation stages recorded significantly higher net return of Rs.20,090 with B:C ratio of 2.22 in soybean. Marimuthu and Surendran (2015) reported that application of 100% recommended dose of NPK +2% DAP + TNAU pulse wonder (5 kg per hectare) was statistically significant and recorded higher plant growth (37.62 cm), grain yield (1162 kg ha^{-1}) and BC ratio of 2.98 in black gram.

Materials and Methods

Field experiment was conducted at Thanthai Roever Institute of Agriculture and Rural Development, Perambalur, Tamil Nadu, during February to April 2017 to study the effect of foliar spray of organic and inorganic nutrients on the growth and yield of black gram. The materials used and the methods followed are presented in this chapter.

Materials

Location of the Experiment Farm

The field experiment was conducted at Thanthai Roever Institute of Agriculture and Rural Development, Perambalur. The Experimental farm is geographically situated at 11.8° N latitude, 78.8°E longitude and an altitude of 150 m above mean sea level.

Weather and Climate

The average rainfall of Perambalur is 908 mm per annum. The weather data during cropping period are presented in Table 4.1.

Soil Characteristics

The soil is clay loam with low in available nitrogen, medium in available phosphorus and high in available potassium. The details of soil analysis are furnished in Table 4.2.

Crop and Variety

Black gram variety VBN 6 was chosen for the study. The morphological characteristics of VBN 6 are furnished in Table 4.3.

Methods

Experimental Design

The experiment was laid out in Randomized Block Design with three replications. The layout of the experimental field is shown in Figure 4.1.

Table 4.1: Weather Data During Cropping Period (February – April, 2017)

Month &Days	Standard week	Mean temperature (°C)		Relative humidity (%)	Rainfall (mm)	No. of rainy days
		Max	Min			
Feb 2017						
04-10	5	31.30	22.45	90	-	-
11-17	6	32.92	23.67	92	-	-
18-24	7	33.66	21.67	93	-	-
25-03	8	31.48	19.16	94	-	-
March 2017						
04-10	9	37.18	21.50	92	-	-
11-17	10	35.25	21.10	93	-	-
18-24	11	36.68	20.67	94	-	-
25-31	12	37.42	25.25	93	-	-
April 2017						
01-07	13	38.99	26.36	89	-	-

Table 4.2: Physico – Chemical Properties of the Experimental Soil

Sl. No	Particulars	
A. Mechanical Analysis (International Pipette method – Piper, 1966)		
1.	Coarse sand (%)	36.62
2.	Fine sand (%)	14.11
3.	Silt (%)	12.37
4.	Clay (%)	36.47
5.	Textural class	Clay loam
B. Chemical Analysis		
1.	Available nitrogen (kg ha^{-1}) (Subbiah and Asija, 1956)	198
2.	Available phosphorus (kg ha^{-1})(Olsen *et al.*, 1954)	18.6
3.	Available potassium (kg ha^{-1})(Jackson, 1973)	287.84
4.	Organic carbon (%) (Walkely and Black, 1934)	0.26
5.	Soil reaction (pH)(Jackson, 1973)	7.38
6.	Electrical conductivity (dSm^{-1}) (Jackson, 1973)	0.32

Table 4.3: Varietal Characteristics of Black Gram

Particulars	Black gram – VBN 6
Duration (days)	65-70
Height (cm)	18.6
Average yield (kg ha^{-1})	850
100 grain wt (g)	3.0-4.5
Special features	Resistant to Yellow Mosaic, synchronized pod maturity

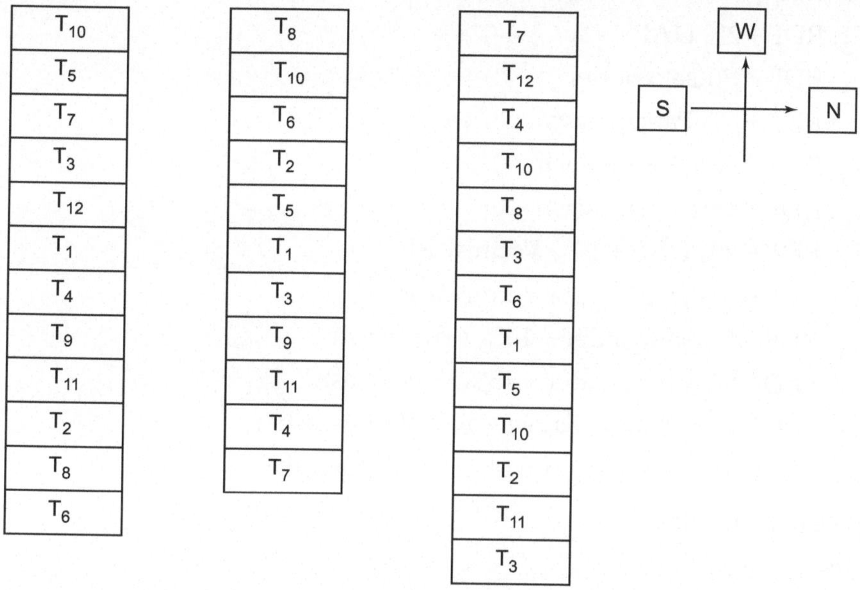

Fig. 4.1: Layout of the Experimental field

Experimental Details

Treatment Details

Particulars	Black gram
Season	February – April
Variety	VBN – 6
Field number	B 6

Experimental design	RBD
Gross plot size	4 m × 3 m
Net plot size	3.4 m × 2.4 m
Replication	3
Date of sowing	04.02.2017
Date of harvesting	07.04.2017

Treatment Details

T_1 : RDF

T_2 : RDF + 2% DAP

T_3 : RDF + Pulse wonder

T_4 : RDF + 3% Panchagavya

T_5 : RDF + 10% Vermiwash

T_6 : RDF + 15% Vermiwash

T_7 : RDF + 2% DAP + 10% Vermiwash

T_8 : RDF + 2% DAP + 15% Vermiwash

T_9 : RDF + Pulse wonder + 10% Vermiwash

T_{10} : RDF + Pulse wonder + 15% Vermiwash

T_{11} : RDF + 3% Panchagavya + 10% Vermiwash

T_{12} : RDF + 3% Panchagavya + 15% Vermiwash

Crop Management

Field Preparation

The experimental field was ploughed with tractor drawn cultivar and rotavator in criss - cross manner, so as to obtain desirable tilth.

Fertilizer Application

Recommended FYM was applied to the field before sowing. Fertilizers were applied plot wise as per the treatment schedule. Nitrogen was applied as urea, phosphorus as Di ammonium phosphate. Full dose of recommended N and full dose of P_2O_5 were applied basally.

Foliar Application of Nutrients

Preparation of 2% DAP

2% DAP was prepared by dissolving 20 g of DAP in 1000 ml of water. For this, 10 kg of DAP was dissolved in 25 litres of water and kept overnight. The supernatant liquid was dissolved in 475 litres of water to make 500 litres required for 1 hectare.

Preparation of Vermiwash

10% Vermiwash was prepared by dissolving100 ml of Vermiwash in 900 ml of water.

15% Vermiwash was prepared by dissolving150 ml of Vermiwash in 850 ml of water.

Preparation of 3% Panchagavya

3% Panchagavya was prepared by dissolving 30 ml of Panchagavya in 1000 ml of water.

Preparation of Pulse wonder

Pulse wonder was sprayed @ 5 kg ha^{-1}.

Seeds and Sowing

Black gram seeds @ 20 kg/ha were sown. Irrigation was given at critical stages depending upon the soil and climate condition.

Gap Filling

Gap filling was done at 10 DAS so as to maintain uniform plant population.

Water Management

Irrigation was given immediately after sowing with due care to avoid excess flooding of water and subsequent irrigations ware given as and when necessary.

After care

Need based plant protection measures were taken to protect the crop from the damage of insects and diseases.

Harvesting

The pods were harvested from the net plot area separately after observing the maturity symptom of pod.

Biometric Observations

Five plants in each replication of individual treatments were selected at random and labeled for recording biometric observations. The observations were recorded at 45 DAS and at harvest.

Growth Components of Black Gram

Plant height

The plant height was measured from ground level to the tip of terminal leaves at 45 DAS and at harvest and recorded in cm.

Leaf area index

Leaf area index was calculated at flowering stage by adopting the procedure suggested by Pattuswamy *et al*. (1976).

$$\text{Leaf area} = L \times B \times K \times \text{number of leaves}$$

Where,

L = Maximum length of the leaf in cm.

B = Maximum breadth of the leaf in cm.

K = Constant factor (0.7)

From this LAI was calculated by using the following formula

$$\text{LAI} = \frac{\text{Total leaf area (cm}^2)}{\text{Ground area (cm}^2)}$$

Dry matter production (DMP)

From each plot five plants were selected at random from outside the net plot area and then oven dried at 65 ± 5°C till it reached a constant weight. The DMP was recorded at harvest stage and expressed in kg ha^{-1}.

Yield Components of Black Gram

Number of pods plant^{-1}

Five plants tagged in each plot were used for counting the pod number/ plant.

Number of seeds pod^{-1}

Number of seeds pod^{-1} was recorded from the sample tagged plants in each plot.

Hundred seed weight

After harvest and adequate drying one hundred seeds from each plot were counted, weighed and expressed in grams.

Yield

Grain yield

The grain yield was recorded from the net plot at 14 percent moisture basis and expressed in kg ha^{-1}.

Haulm yield

The dry weight of the haulm was recorded by subtracting the grain yield from the total DMP at harvest and expressed in kg ha^{-1}.

Soil Analysis

Pre sowing soil samples were taken. The soil samples were shade dried and passed through 2 mm sieve. The samples were analyzed for the nutrient status.

Mechanical Analysis

The mechanical composition of the soil was analyzed following International Pipette Method suggested by Piper (1996).

Soil Reaction (pH)

The pH of the soil was determined in 1:2.5 soil water suspension using pH meter as per procedure described by Jackson (1973).

Electrical Conductivity (EC)

The electrical conductivity (EC) was measured in 1:2 soil water suspension with Elico conductivity bridge (Jackson, 1973).

Organic Carbon

The organic carbon content was determined by the method suggested by Walkley and black (1934).

Available Nitrogen

This was estimated by alkaline permanganate method (Subbiah and Asija, 1956) and expressed in kg ha^{-1}.

Available Phosphorus

This was estimated by the method described by Olsen *et al.,* (1954) and expressed in kg ha^{-1}.

Available Potassium

This was estimated by neutral normal ammonium acetate extract method as suggested by Jackson (1973) and expressed in kg ha^{-1}.

Statistical Analysis

The data on observations and characters studied were statistically analyzed and whenever the results were found significant, the critical differences were arrived at 5 percent level to draw statistical conclusions (Panse and Sukhatme, 1978).

Economics

The economic parameters such as gross return, net return and return per rupee invested for all the treatment were worked out based on the prevailing market prices. The net return was worked out different treatments by subtracting the cost of cultivation from gross return. The return per rupee was calculated by using the following method,

$$\text{Return rupee}^{-1}\text{ invested} = \frac{\text{Gross return (₹ ha}^{-1})}{\text{Cost of cultivation (₹ ha}^{-1})}$$

Experimental Results

Field experiment was conducted during February – April of 2017 at Thanthai Roever Institute of Agriculture and Rural Development to study the effect of foliar spray of organic and inorganic nutrients on the growth and yield of black gram. The experimental results of the study are presented in this chapter.

Growth Components of Black Gram

Plant Height

The data on the plant height recorded at 45 DAS and harvest are presented in Table 4.4.

The plant height was significantly influenced by the application of organic and inorganic nutrients.

The treatment, T_{11}(RDF + 3% Panchagavya + 10% Vermiwash) recorded the highest plant height of 31.14 cm and 41.31 cm at 45 DAS and at harvest, respectively. This was followed by T_9 (RDF + Pulse wonder +10% Vermiwash), which recorded a plant height of 30.20 cm and 40.43 cm at 45 DAS and at harvest. The treatments, T_7 and T_{12} were next in order. The least plant height of 25.83 and 36.00 cm at 45 DAS and at harvest was recorded in T_1 (RDF).

Leaf Area Index

The data pertaining to leaf area index at flowering stage are presented in Table 4.5.

Among the treatments, T_{11}(RDF + 3% Panchagavya + 10% Vermiwash) recorded the highest leaf area index of 4.3. It was followed by T_9 (RDF + Pulse wonder + 10% Vermiwash). The lowest leaf area index of 2.6 was recorded in T_1, control (Recommended dose of fertilizers).

Dry Matter Production

The data recorded on dry matter production at harvest stage presented in Table 4.6.

The dry matter production was significantly influenced by the application of organic and inorganic nutrients.

Application of RDF + 3% Panchagavya + 10% Vermiwash (T_{11}) recorded the highest dry matter production of 2093.46 kg ha^{-1}. It was followed by the treatment T_9 (RDF + Pulse wonder +10% Vermiwash). The least dry matter production of 704.661 kg ha^{-1} was recorded under T_1 (Recommended dose of fertilizers alone).

Yield Components

Number of Pods Plant^{-1}

The data on number of pods plant^{-1} are furnished in Table 4.7.

The number of pods plant^{-1} were significantly influenced by all the treatments.

The treatment, T_{11} (RDF +3% Panchagavya +10% Vermiwash) recorded the highest pods plant^{-1} 23.80. This was followed by the treatment, T_9 (RDF + Pulse wonder + 10% Vermiwash). The least number of pods plant^{-1} of 17.06 was recorded in RDF(T_1).

Pod Length

The data on pod length are presented in Table 4.8.

The pod length was significantly influenced by all the treatments.

The treatment, T_{11} (RDF +3% Panchagavya +10% Vermiwash) recorded the highest pod length of 4.40 cm. This was followed by T_9(RDF + Pulse wonder + 10% Vermiwash). The least pod length of 3.60 cm was recorded in RDF (T_1).

Number of Seeds Pod^{-1}

The data on number of seeds pod^{-1} are presented in the Table 4.9.

The number of seeds pod^{-1} were significantly influenced by all the treatments.

The highest number of seeds pod^{-1} of 6.06 was recorded in T_{11}(RDF + 3% Panchagavya + 10% Vermiwash). This was followed by T_9 (RDF + Pulse wonder +10% Vermiwash).The least number of seeds pod ^{1} of 5.04 was recorded in RDF (T_1).

Hundred Seed Weight

The data on hundred seed weight are furnished in Table 4.10.

The highest hundred seed weight of 4.51 g was recorded in T_{11}(RDF + 3% Panchagavya + 10% Vermiwash) . This was followed by T_9(RDF + Pulse wonder +10% Vermiwash). The least hundred seed weightof 3.10 g was recorded in RDF (T_1).

Table 4.4: Effect of Foliar Spray on Plant Height in Black Gram (cm)

Treatment	Treatment Schedule	45 Days	Harvest
T_1	RDF (Recommended Dose of Fertilizers)	25.83	36.00
T_2	RDF + 2% DAP	28.06	38.86
T_3	RDF + Pulse wonder	27.93	38.83
T_4	RDF + 3% Panchagavya	26.60	38.11
T_5	RDF + 10% Vermiwash	28.26	38.94
T_6	RDF + 15% Vermiwash	28.13	38.92
T_7	RDF + 2% DAP +10% Vermiwash	29.56	40.14
T_8	RDF + 2% DAP + 15% Vermiwash	28.73	39.64
T_9	RDF + Pulse wonder + 10% Vermiwash	30.20	40.43
T_{10}	RDF + Pulse wonder + 15% Vermiwash	28.46	39.60
T_{11}	RDF + 3% Panchagavya + 10% Vermiwash	31.14	41.31
T_{12}	RDF + 3% Panchagavya + 15% Vermiwash	29.56	40.04
	SEd	0.63	0.05
	CD (p=0.05)	1.31	0.10

Table 4.5: Effect of Foliar Spray on Leaf Area Index in Black Gram

Treatment	Treatment Schedule	Flowering stage
T_1	RDF (Recommended Dose of Fertilizers)	2.8
T_2	RDF + 2% DAP	3.0
T_3	RDF + Pulse wonder	2.6
T_4	RDF + 3% Panchagavya	2.7
T_5	RDF + 10% Vermiwash	3.6
T_6	RDF + 15% Vermiwash	3.5
T_7	RDF + 2% DAP +10% Vermiwash	4.0
T_8	RDF + 2% DAP + 15% Vermiwash	3.4
T_9	RDF + Pulse wonder + 10% Vermiwash	4.1
T_{10}	RDF + Pulse wonder + 15% Vermiwash	3.9
T_{11}	RDF + 3% Panchagavya + 10% Vermiwash	4.3
T_{12}	RDF + 3% Panchagavya + 15% Vermiwash	3.6
	SEd	0.03
	CD (p=0.05)	0.07

Table 4.6: Effect of Foliar Spray on Dry Matter Production in Black Gram (kg ha^{-1})

Treatment	Treatment Schedule	Harvest stage
T_1	RDF (Recommended Dose of Fertilizers)	704.67
T_2	RDF + 2% DAP	1164.80
T_3	RDF + Pulse wonder	1029.46
T_4	RDF + 3% Panchagavya	853.06
T_5	RDF + 10% Vermiwash	1291.73
T_6	RDF + 15% Vermiwash	1278.66
T_7	RDF + 2% DAP +10% Vermiwash	1750.93
T_8	RDF + 2% DAP + 15% Vermiwash	1377.60
T_9	RDF + Pulse wonder + 10% Vermiwash	1974.93
T_{10}	RDF + Pulse wonder + 15% Vermiwash	1350.53
T_{11}	RDF + 3% Panchagavya + 10% Vermiwash	2093.46
T_{12}	RDF + 3% Panchagavya + 15% Vermiwash	1444.80
	SEd	40.89
	CD (p=0.05)	84.79

Table 4.7: Effect of Foliar Spray on Number of Pods Plant^{-1} in Black Gram

Treatment	Treatment Schedule	Pods plant^{-1}
T_1	RDF (Recommended Dose of Fertilizers)	17.06
T_2	RDF + 2% DAP	18.50
T_3	RDF + Pulse wonder	18.40
T_4	RDF + 3% Panchagavya	17.20
T_5	RDF + 10% Vermiwash	21.06
T_6	RDF + 15% Vermiwash	18.70
T_7	RDF + 2% DAP + 10% Vermiwash	22.80
T_8	RDF + 2% DAP + 15% Vermiwash	19.30
T_9	RDF + Pulse wonder + 10% Vermiwash	23.13
T_{10}	RDF + Pulse wonder + 15% Vermiwash	18.93
T_{11}	RDF + 3% Panchagavya + 10% Vermiwash	23.80
T_{12}	RDF + 3% Panchagavya + 15% Vermiwash	21.13
	SEd	0.08
	CD (p=0.05)	0.17

Table 4.8 : Effect of Foliar Spray on Pod Length in Black Gram(cm)

Treatment	Treatment Schedule	Pod length
T_1	RDF (Recommended Dose of Fertilizers)	3.60
T_2	RDF + 2% DAP	3.96
T_3	RDF + Pulse wonder	3.83
T_4	RDF + 3% Panchagavya	3.82
T_5	RDF + 10% Vermiwash	4.16
T_6	RDF + 15% Vermiwash	4.10
T_7	RDF + 2% DAP + 10% Vermiwash	4.30
T_8	RDF + 2% DAP + 15% Vermiwash	4.14
T_9	RDF + Pulse wonder + 10% Vermiwash	4.32
T_{10}	RDF + Pulse wonder + 15% Vermiwash	4.13
T_{11}	RDF + 3% Panchagavya + 10% Vermiwash	4.40
T_{12}	RDF + 3% Panchagavya + 15% Vermiwash	4.28
	SEd	0.09
	CD (p=0.05)	0.19

Table 4.9: Effect of Foliar Spray Number of Seeds Pod^{-1} in Black Gram

Treatment	Treatment Schedule	Seeds pod^{-1}
T_1	RDF (Recommended Dose of Fertilizers)	5.04
T_2	RDF + 2% DAP	5.16
T_3	RDF + Pulse wonder	5.13
T_4	RDF + 3% Panchagavya	5.06
T_5	RDF + 10% Vermiwash	5.40
T_6	RDF + 15% Vermiwash	5.20
T_7	RDF + 2% DAP +10% Vermiwash	5.80
T_8	RDF + 2% DAP + 15% Vermiwash	5.35
T_9	RDF + Pulse wonder + 10% Vermiwash	5.90
T_{10}	RDF + Pulse wonder + 15% Vermiwash	5.30
T_{11}	RDF + 3% Panchagavya + 10% Vermiwash	6.06
T_{12}	RDF + 3% Panchagavya + 15% Vermiwash	5.60
	SEd	0.01
	CD (p=0.05)	0.02

Table 4.10: Effect of Foliar Spray on Hundred Seed Weight in Black Gram (g)

Treatment	Treatment Schedule	Hundred seed weight
T_1	RDF (Recommended Dose of Fertilizers)	3.10
T_2	RDF + 2% DAP	3.40
T_3	RDF + Pulse wonder	3.38
T_4	RDF + 3% Panchagavya	3.21
T_5	RDF + 10% Vermiwash	3.75
T_6	RDF + 15% Vermiwash	3.60
T_7	RDF + 2% DAP + 10% Vermiwash	4.36
T_8	RDF + 2% DAP + 15% Vermiwash	4.11
T_9	RDF + Pulse wonder + 10% Vermiwash	4.42
T_{10}	RDF + Pulse wonder + 15% Vermiwash	3.98
T_{11}	RDF + 3% Panchagavya + 10% Vermiwash	4.51
T_{12}	RDF + 3% Panchagavya + 15% Vermiwash	4.24
	SEd	0.02
	CD(p=0.05)	0.04

Yield

Grain Yield

The data on grain yield are presented in Table 4.11.

The grain yield was significantly influenced by all the treatments.

Among the treatments, RDF+3% Panchagavya + 10% Vermiwash (T_{11}) produced the highest grain yield of 952 kg ha^{-1}. This treatment was followed by T_9(RDF + Pulse wonder + 10% Vermiwash). The least grain yield of 624 kg ha^{-1} was recorded in RDF (T_1).

Haulm yield

The data on haulm yield are presented in Table 4.12.

The haulm yield was significantly influenced by all the treatments.

Among the treatments RDF+3% Panchagavya+10% Vermiwash(T_{11}) produced the highest haulm yield of 1243.22kg ha^{-1}. This treatment was followed by T_9 (RDF + Pulse wonder + 10% Vermiwash). The least haulm yield of 852.70 kg ha^{-1} was recorded in RDF (T_1).

Economics

The data on economics of different treatments are presented in Table 4.13.

The highest net return (₹ 56314.90) and return $rupee^{-1}$ invested (Rs. 2.64) was obtained under T_{11} (RDF + 3% Panchagavya + 10% Vermiwash). It was followed by T_9 (RDF + Pulse wonder+ 10% Vermiwash). The least net return (₹ 28742.85) and return $rupee^{-1}$ (₹ 1.94) was obtained under RDF (T_1).

Table 4.11: Effect of Foliar Spray on Grain Yield of Black Gram (kg ha^{-1})

Treatment	Treatment Schedule	Grain yield
T_1	RDF (Recommended Dose of Fertilizers)	624
T_2	RDF + 2% DAP	696
T_3	RDF + Pulse wonder	673
T_4	RDF + 3% Panchagavya	647
T_5	RDF + 10% Vermiwash	750
T_6	RDF + 15% Vermiwash	728
T_7	RDF + 2% DAP + 10% Vermiwash	876
T_8	RDF + 2% DAP + 15% Vermiwash	810
T_9	RDF + Pulse wonder + 10% Vermiwash	910
T_{10}	RDF + Pulse wonder + 15% Vermiwash	785
T_{11}	RDF + 3% Panchagavya + 10% Vermiwash	953
T_{12}	RDF + 3% Panchagavya + 15% Vermiwash	843
	SEd	13.61
	CD (p=0.05)	28.22

Table 4.12: Effect of Foliar Spray on Haulm Yield of Black Gram (kg ha^{-1})

Treatment	Treatment Schedule	Haulm yield
T_1	RDF (Recommended Dose of Fertilizers)	852.70
T_2	RDF + 2% DAP	952.78
T_3	RDF + Pulse wonder	920.88
T_4	RDF + 3% Panchagavya	886.78
T_5	RDF + 10% Vermiwash	1014.55
T_6	RDF + 15% Vermiwash	986.22
T_7	RDF + 2% DAP +10% Vermiwash	1170.57
T_8	RDF + 2% DAP + 15% Vermiwash	1095.48
T_9	RDF + Pulse wonder + 10% Vermiwash	1208.58
T_{10}	RDF + Pulse wonder + 15% Vermiwash	1045.67
T_{11}	RDF + 3% Panchagavya + 10% Vermiwash	1243.22
T_{12}	RDF + 3% Panchagavya + 15% Vermiwash	1135.47
	SEd	18.99
	CD (p=0.05)	39.39

Table 4.13: Effect of Treatments on Economics in Black Gram

Treatment	Treatment details	Cost of cultivation	Gross return (Rs. ha^{-1})	Net return (Rs.ha^{-1})	BCR
T_1	RDF (Recommended Dose of Fertilizers)	30540	59282.85	28742.85	1.94
T_2	RDF + 2% DAP	30780	66188.40	35408.40	2.15
T_3	RDF + Pulse wonder	31790	63931.20	32141.20	2.01
T_4	RDF + 3% Panchagavya	31665	61527.70	29862.70	1.95
T_5	RDF + 10% Vermiwash	33040	71271.85	38231.85	2.17
T_6	RDF + 15% Vermiwash	34290	69234.10	34944.10	2.16
T_7	RDF + 2% DAP + 10% Vermiwash	33280	83302.65	50022.65	2.50
T_8	RDF + 2% DAP + 15% Vermiwash	34530	77021.25	42491.25	2.23
T_9	RDF + Pulse wonder + 10% Vermiwash	34290	86493.70	52203.70	2.52
T_{10}	RDF + Pulse wonder + 15% Vermiwash	35540	78607.30	43067.30	2.21
T_{11}	RDF + 3% Panchagavya + 10% Vermiwash	34165	90479.90	56314.90	2.64
T_{12}	RDF + 3% Panchagavya + 15% Vermiwash	35415	80140.10	44725.10	2.26

Discussion

Field experiment was conducted during February to April, 2017 at Thanthai Roever Institute of Agriculture and Rural Development to study the effect of foliar spray of organic and inorganic nutrients on the growth and yield of black gram. The results of the field experiments are discussed in this chapter.

Growth Components

The integrated nutrient management greatly influenced the growth characters like plant height, DMP (Figure 4.1.) and leaf area index (Figure 4.2.) in black gram. The growth components (plant height, LAI and DMP) were influenced due to application of recommended dose of fertilizer + foliar spray of 3% Panchagavya and 10 % Vermiwash (T_{11}). This might be due to the combined application of organic and inorganic nutrients which supplied the required amount of nutrients to the plant leading to better growth of crop than the control treatment (RDF alone).

Maheswari *et al.* (2017) reported that the foliar spray of Vermiwash 10% + 3% Panchagavya increased the growth attributes (shoot length, internode length, leaf surface area, number of leaves) in lab lab. Besides the addition of inorganic nutrients, the foliar spray increased the leaf area along with the number of branches as compared to other treatments.

Yield Components and Yield

The yield potential of black gram is determined by the resultant value of yield components which are greatly influenced by the growth parameters. Among the treatments, application of RDF + foliar spray of 3% Panchagavya + 10% Vermiwash (T_{11}) recorded the highest number of pods plant^{-1} (Figure 4.3.), number of seeds pod^{-1} (Figure 4.4.), test weight and grain yield (Figure 4.5). Increased growth of crop due to combined foliar spray of organic and inorganic nutrients helped the crop to enhance the yield components such as number of pods plant^{-1}, seeds pod^{-1} and 100 grain weight. The cumulative effect of all these parameters contributed for higher grain and haulm yield of crop than the control treatment (RDF alone).

Kulkarni *et al.* (2016) reported that the foliar spray of Vermiwash 5% increased the number of pods and 1000 seed weight in green gram which gave significant variance in Vermiwash treatments.

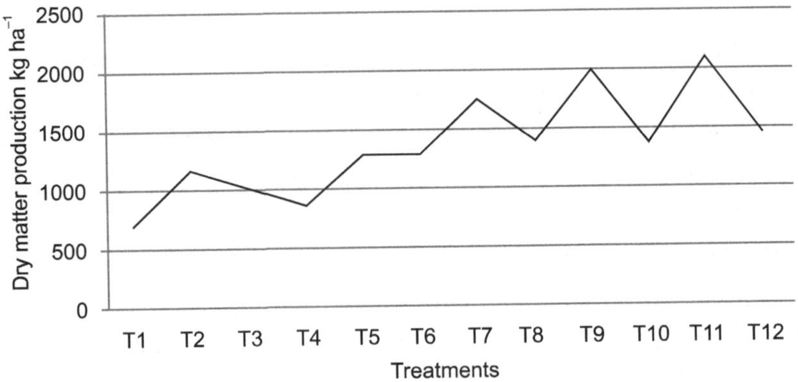

Fig. 4.1: Dry matter production

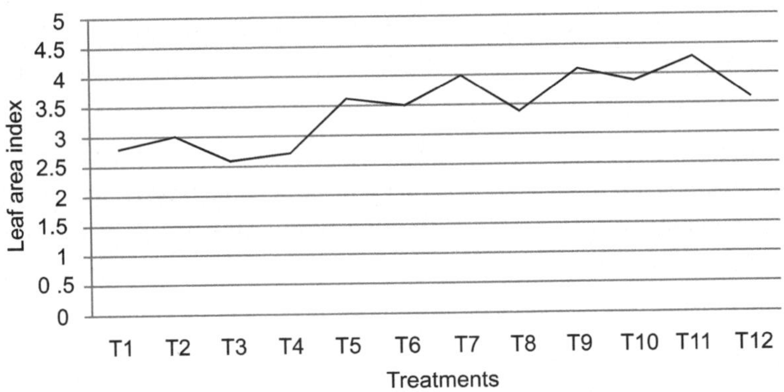

Fig. 4.2: Leaf area index

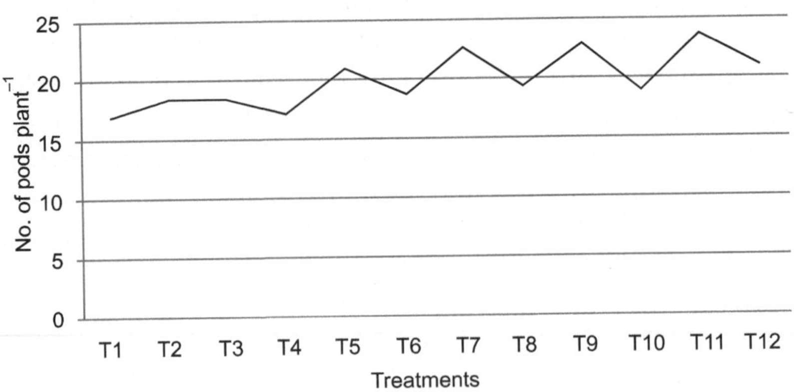

Fig. 4.3: No. of pods plant^{-1}

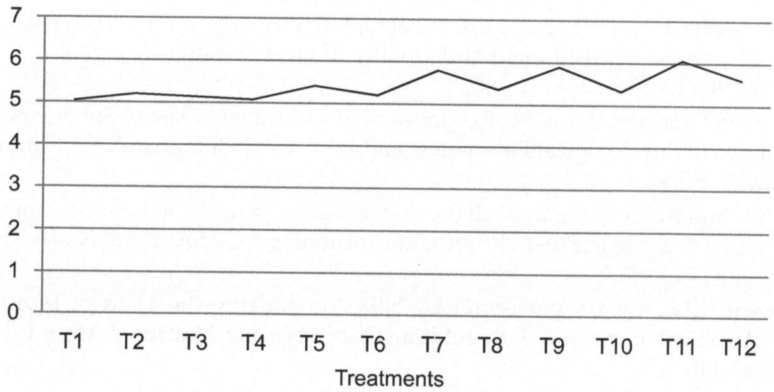

Fig. 4.4: Seeds pod^{-1}

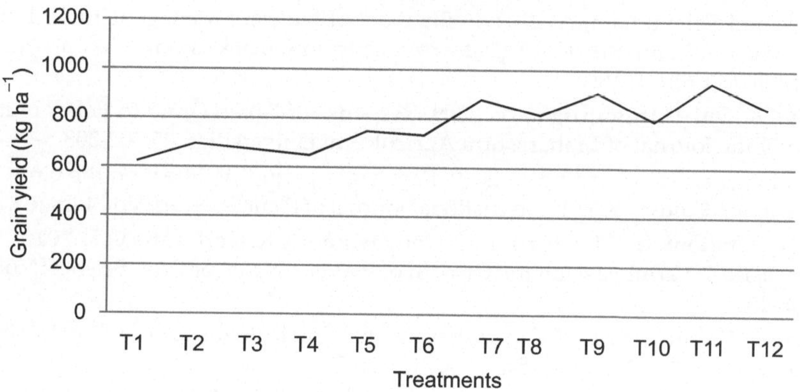

Fig. 4.5: Grain yield (kg ha^{-1})

Conclusion

Based on the results of the experiment, it can be concluded that application of 100% RDF + foliar spray of 3% Panchagavya + 10% Vermiwash will be economical in black gram for realizing higher yield and benefit cost ratio. This practice is economically viable, practically applicable and agronomically efficient technology which paves way for the realization of higher returns from black gram besides improvement in soil fertility. Next to this practice, 100% RDF + foliar spray of Pulse wonder (5 kg ha^{-1}) + 10% Vermiwash (T_9) recorded higher benefit cost ratio.

REFERENCES

Amutha. R., Nithila, S., and Shiva Kumar 2012. Management of Source Limitation by Foliar Spray of Nutrients and Growth Regulators in Black Gram. International J. Plant Sci., 7(1) :65 - 68.

Anadhakrishnaveni S., Palchamy, A. and MahendranS. 2004. Effect of Foliar Spray of Nutrients on Growth and Yield of Green Gram (*Phaseolusradiatus*). Legume Res., 27(2) : 149 - 150.

A. Fazulla Shariff, Ashok S. Sajjan, H.B. Babalad, L.B. Nagaraj and S. Giresh Palankar. 2017. Effect of organics on seed yield and Quality of Green Gram (*Vigna radiata* L.) Legume Research 40 (2) : 388-392.

Baghel M. S. and Yadhav H.S. 1992. Response of Black Gram to Date of Sowing and Growth Regulators to Physiological Parameters and Seed Yield. Bharatiya Krishi Annusandhan Patrika, 9: 38 - 42.

Balusamy M. and Meyyazhagan N. 2000. Foliar Nutrition to Pulse Crop. Training Manual on Recent Advances in Pulses Production Technology, CASA, Tamil Nadu Agricultural University : 113 - 115.

Chandrasekar C.N. and Bangarusamy U. 2003. Maximizing the Yield of Mung Bean by Foliar Application of Growth Regulating Chemicals and Nutrients. Madras Agric. J. 90 (1-3): 142-145.

Ganapathy M., Baradhan G. and Ramesh N. (2008). Effect of Foliar Nutrition on Reproductive Efficiency and Grain Yield of Rice Fallow Pulses. Legume Res., 31(2):142-144.

Geetha, P. and Velayutham, A. 2009. Refinement of Nutrient Management Techniques for Growth, Yield and Nutrient Uptake of Rice Fallow Black Gram. Madras Agricultural Journal; 96(1/6):163-166.

Govindan, K. and Thirumurugan, V. 2000. Response of Green Gram to Foliar Nutrition of Potassium. Journal of Maharashtra Agricultural Universities, 25:302-303.

G. Kumaravelu and D. Kadamban. 2009. Panchagavya and Its Effect on the Growth of the Greengram Cultivar K-851. International Journal of Plant Sciences, Vol. 4 Issue 2 : 409-414.

Hatti S.S., Londonkar R.L., Patil S.B., Gangawane A.K. and Patil C.S. 2010. Effect of *Eiseniafoetida* Vermiwash on the Growth of Plants. Journal of Crop Science, Vol. 1, Issue 1 : 06-10.

Influence of Vermiwash and Panchagavya on Lablab Beans Under Pot Experimental Conditions. Int. J. Adv. Res. Biol. Sci. 4(2): 20-27.

Jayabal, A., Revathy, M. and Saxena, M.G. 1999. Effect of Foliar Nutrition on Nutrient Uptake Pattern in Soybean. Andhra Agric. J., 46: 243 - 244.

Jeyakumar, P., Velu, G., Rajendran, C., Amutha, R. and Chidambaram,S. 2008. Varied Responses of Blackgram (*Vignamungo*) to Certain Foliar Applied Chemicals and Plant Growth Regulators. Legume Res., 31 (2): 110-113.

Kalpana, R. (2001). Effect of Irrigation Layouts and Foliar Spraying of Nutrients and Growth Hormone on Soybean (*Glycine max (L) Merrill*) Ph.D (Ag) Thesis, Tamil Nadu Agricultural University, Coimbatore.

Kuttimani, R. andVelayutham, A. 2011. Foliar Application of Nutrients Enhances the Yield Attributes and Nutrient Uptake of Green Gram. Agric. Sci. Digest., 31 (3) : 202 – 205.

Maheswari V.N., Kaleena P.N, Srikumaran M.P., Rekha G.S. and Elumalai, D. 2017.

Maheswari V.N, Srikumaran V.P, Rekha G.S, Elumalai D. and Kaleena P.K. 2016.

Growth Promoting Effects of Vermiwash and Panchagavya on *Dolichus lablab* under Field Experimental Conditions. Int J ApplSciBiotechnol, Vol. 4(4): 513 -518.

Manivannan, V., Thanunathan, K., Imayavaramban, V. and Ramanathan, N. 2003.Growth and Growth Analysis of Rice-Fallow Black Gram as Influenced by Foliar Application of Nutrients with and Without *Rhizobium* Seed Inoculation. Legume Research; 26(4):296-299.

Muhammad Arsalan, Shoaib Ahmed, Junaid Nawaz Chauhdary, Muhammad Sarwar. 2016. Effect of Vermicompost and Phosphorus on Crop Growth and Nutrient Uptake in Mungbean. Journal of Applied Agriculture and Biotechnology 1(2): 38-47.

Pandian, B. J., S. Anand Kumar, V. Veerabadran and Ravichandran, V.K. 2001. Growth and Yield of Rice Fallow Green Gram as Influenced by Methods of Sowing, Stubble Management and Nutrient Application in Tambiraparani Command Area. Madras Agric. J., 88(7-9): 406 - 409.

PatilS. V., Halikatti S. I., Hiremath S. M., Babalad H. B., Sreenivasa M. N., Hebsur N. S. and Somanagouda.G. 2012. Effect of Organics on Growth and Yield of Chickpea (*Cicer arietinum* L.) in Vertisols. Karnataka J. Agric. Sci., 25 (3) : 326-331.

Pradeep, Mohan Dixit and S. Elamathi. 2007. Effect of Foliar Application of DAP, Micronutrients and NAA on the Growth and Yield of Green Gram. Legume Res., 30(4) : 305-307.

Rajkhowa D.J., Saikia, M. and RajkhowaK. M. 2002. Effect of Vermicompost With and Without Fertilizer on Green Gram. Legume Res., 25: 295-296.

Rekha G.S. Valivittan K. and Kaleena P.K. 2013. Studies on the Influence of Vermicompost and Vermiwash on the Growth and Productivity of Black Gram. Advances in Biological Research 7 (4): 114 - 121.

Rajavel M., Vincent, S. (2009). Influence of Nutrients and Hormones on Yield Maximization of Black Gram. Journal of Ecobiology; 24(4): 387-394.

Ramesh, K. and Thirumurugan,V. 2001. Effect of Seed Pelleting and Foliar Nutrition on Growth of Soybean. Madras Agric. J., 88: 465-468.

Senthil Kumar S., Sriramach M.V. and Haripriya.K. 2004. Effect of Vermicompost and Fertilizer on the Growth and Yield of Rose. J. Interacademicia. 8: 207-210.

Suresh Kumar, R., Ganesh, P., Tharmaraj, K. and Saranraj, P. 2011. Growth and Development of Black Gram (*Vigna mungo*) Under Foliar Application of Panchagavya as Organic Source of Nutrient. Curr. Bot. 2(3) : 09-11.

Siddappa, Rand Hegde N.K. 2011. Effect of Foliar Spray of Vermiwash and Nutritional Treatments on Growth and Yield Performance of Curry Leaf var. *Suvasini*. The Asian Journal of Horticulture; Vol. 6 No. 1 : 68 - 70.

Shashi Kumar, R. Basavarajappa, S.R. Salakinkop, Manjunatha Hebbar, M.P. Basavarajappa and H.Y. Patil. 2013. Influence of Foliar Nutrition on Performance of Black Gram (*Vignamungo*), Nutrient Uptake and Economics Under Dry Land Ecosystems. Legume Res., 36(5) : 422 – 428.

Shashi Kumar, Basavarajappa, R., Salkinkop, S. R., Manjunatha Hebbar., Basavarajappa, M. P., and Patil, H. Y. 2013. Effect of Growth Regulator, Organic and Inorganic Foliar Nutrition on the Growth and Yield of Black Gram (*Vignamungo L.)* Under Rainfed Condition. Karnataka Journal of Agricultural Sciences; 26(2): 311-313.

Shashikumar, Basavarajappa, R., Salakinkop, S. R., Manjunatha Hebbar., Basavarajappa, M. P., and Patil, H. Y. 2013. Influence of Foliar Nutrition on Performance of Black Gram (*Vignamungo L.*), Nutrient Uptake and Economics Under Dry Land Ecosystems. Legume Research; 36 (5):422-428.

Shyamrao Kulkarni, S.N. Upperi and R. L. Jadhav. 2016. Green Gram Productivity Enhancement Through Foliar Spray of Nutrients. Legume Research, 39 (5) : 814 - 816.

Sritharan, N., Anitha, R., and Mallika Vanangamudi, 2007. Foliar Spray of Chemicals and Plant Growth Regulator on Growth Attributes and Yield of Black Gram (*Vignaradiata L.).* Plant Archives; 7(1):353-355.

Srivastava, G.P. and Srivastava,V.C. 1994. Effect of Irrigation and Foliar Spray of Nutrients on Growth and Seed Yield of Bengal Gram (*Cicerarietinum).* Indian J. Agric.Sci., 64(4): 219-222.

Subramani M., Solaimalai, A. and Velayutham, A. 2002. Effect of Plant Population and Methods of Fertilizer Application on Yield Attributes and Yield of Irrigated Black Gram. Madras Agric. J. 89(4-6): 305-306.

Tharmaraj, K., Ganesh, P., Suresh Kumar, R., Anandan. Aand Kolanjinathan. K. 2011. A Critical Review on Panchagavya – A Boon Plant Growth. International Journal of Pharmaceutical & Biological Archives; 2(6): 1611 - 1614.

Tharmaraj, K., Ganesh, P. and Kolanjinathan, K., Suresh Kumar, R., Anandan, A, 2010. Influence of Vermicompost and Vermiwash on Physical and Chemical Properties of Black Gram Cultivated Soil. IJRS: Vol. 3, 077- 083.

Vijayakumari, B., Hiranmai Yadav, R., Gowri, P. and Kandari, L.S 2012. Effect of Panchagavya, Humic Acid and Micro Herbal Fertilizer on the Yield and Post-harvest Soil of Soybean. Asian Journal of Plant Sciences 11(2) : 83 - 86.

Vimalendran Loganathan and Wahab, K. 2014. Influence of Panchagavya Foliar Spray on the Growth Attributes and Yield of Baby Corn (*Zea mays*)cv. COBC 1. Journal of Applied and Natural Science 6 (2): 397 – 401.

Vinoth Kumar, C., K. Vaiyapuri, M. Mohamed Amanullah and G. Gopalaswamy, 2013. Influence of Foliar Spray of Nutrients on Yield and Economics of Soyabean. Journal of Biological Science 13(6) : 563-565.

Yakadri, M. and Thatikunta, R. 2002. Effect of Soil Application of Potassium and DAP Spray in Black Gram. Madras Agric. J. 89(1-3): 147-149.

ABBREVIATIONS

T	-	Treatment
R	-	Replication
pH	-	Potential hydrogen
EC	-	Electrical conductivity
dSm^{-1}	-	deci- Siemen per meter or deci mho per meter
ml	-	milliliter
%	-	percent
g	-	gram
mg/l	-	milligram per liter or ppm
ANOVA	-	analysis of variance
cm	-	centimeter
ht	-	height
g/plant	-	gram per plant
DAS	-	Days after sowing
kg /plot	-	kilogram per plot
mg	-	milligram
RDF	-	Recommended dose of fertilizers
SEd	-	Standard error
CD	-	Critical difference
BCR	-	Benefit cost ratio
ppm	-	parts per million
DAP	-	Diammonium phosphate

Two Leaf Stage

Foliar Application of Dap

Harvesting

Horticulture and Ecology - *Studies & Management* Pages 86-115
Edited by: Dr. Alka Chauhan and Dr. Pawan Kumar 'Bharti'
ISBN: 978-93-88854-09-2
Edition: 2019
Published by: Discovery Publishing House Pvt. Ltd., New Delhi (India)

5 Water Management in Fruit Crops

[1]A. Solaimalai, [2]M. Jayakumar, [3]Dr. A. Rajkumar and [4]S. Irulandi

Introduction

The main concern of productive agriculture is the effective and efficient supply of water to crop fields since irrigation potential is created at huge cost. The investments required for developing surface irrigation for one hectare is estimated at over ₹ 50000. The overall efficiency under this system is only 30-50%. As more and more areas have to be brought under irrigation, it has become necessary to introduce modern irrigation techniques like micro irrigation (drip/micro sprinkler), sprinkler etc. for economizing the water use. The efficiency under drip irrigation has been estimated to be as high as 80-90%.

Water is a major component for sustainable development of fruit crops and an in dispensable resource which needs careful monitoring and management in order to achieve higher water use efficiencies. The irrigated area under horticultural crops in India is likely to increase from 6.0 to 8.1 million ha (Srinivas,1998). In order to utilize the available water efficiently for fruit crops, scientific management of water resources become inevitable. Horticultural crops demand assured irrigation for higher yields. However, these crops provide

a conducive situation for the application of drip irrigation and fertigation. The Government has initiated programmes, as a result of which, substantial area has been covered under drip irrigation in the horticulture sector. The growth has been significant in the states of Maharashtra, Andhra Pradesh, Karnataka and Tamil Nadu.

1 Associate Professor (Agronomy), Department of Fruit Crops, Horticultural College & Research, TNAU, Periyakulam–625 604, Tamil Nadu, India.
2 Corresponding Author: Scientist, Regional Coffee Research Station, Thandikudi, Dindugul-District, Tamil Nadu, India.
3 Assistant Professor (Horticulture), Krishna College of Agriculture & Technology, Sree Rangapuram, Usilampatti (TK), Madurai (Dt), Tamil Nadu, India.
4 Assistant Professor (Agricultural Entomology), Department of Fruit Crops, Horticultural College & Research, TNAU, Periyakulam–625 604, Tamil Nadu, India.

Critical Soil Moisture Periods of Crops

All the stages of growth are equally sensitive to soil moisture stress for crops where vegetative parts are of economic importance. Total growth and yield of perennial plants are the summation of effects of stress at each growth stage (Table 5.1). However, adequate water supply is essential at flower bud initiation, flowering and fruit set. Flower bud formation, however, increase due to restricted water supply prior to flower bud initiation in the case of citrus and mango.

Table 5.1: Critical Soil Moisture Stage of Fruit Crops

Fruit crops	Critical soil moisture stage of crops
Citrus	Flowering, fruit setting, fruit growth
Banana	Early vegetative period flowering and fruit formation
Mango	Start of fruiting to maturity
Pine apple	Vegetative growth
Grape	Vegetative growth. Frequent irrigation during vegetative stage may cause rotting of fruits
Guava	Period of fruit growth
Ber	A drought resistant plant; irrigation is required during fruit growth

Available soil moisture (%): For fruit crops 50% Available soil moisture is taken as critical limit

For realizing maximum benefit from the scarce irrigation water, irrigation is to be scheduled at moisture sensitive periods by withholding irrigations at other periods of lesser sensitivity. Such irrigation schedules along with improved practices increase the water-use efficiency in crop production.

Peak Consumptive Use and Critical Period

These stages do not usually coincide with the periods of peak consumptive use by crops. It is not appropriate to consider the crops, at these critical stages, require more water as their water needs are at the higher. Critical stages of water requirement are usually the turning points in plant life cycle. This can be represented by a sigmoid curve (Figure 5.1). The curve shows two most important points of change in the growth rate,viz., the point of inflection and the point of deflection.

The point of inflection indicates a sudden spurt in vegetative growth and the point of deflection represents the slowing down of vegetative growth and initiation of the reproductive phase. Crops demand adequate water at these stages and cannot afford to stand water stress without serious reduction in growth and yield. These two stages of crop life, therefore, considered as the most critical stages of water requirement (Table 5.2).

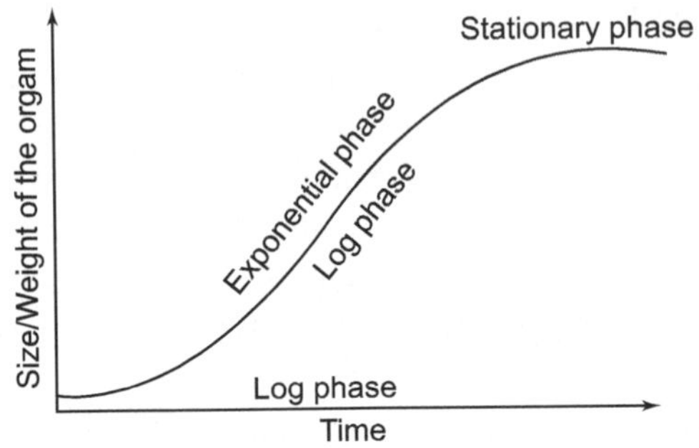

Fig. 5.1: Sigmoid curve of plant growth

Table 5.2: Water Requirement of Fruit Crops

Crop	Water requirement (mm)
Banana	1200-2200
Citrus	900-1200
Grapes	500-1200
Pineapple	700-1000
Coconut	80-100 (lit/plant/day)
Mango	30-40 (lit/plant/day)
Guava	22-30 (lit/plant/day)
Banana	8-12 (lit/plant/day)
Sapota	20-30(lit/plant/day)
Amla	15-25(lit/plant/day)
Papaya	15-25(lit/plant/day)

For the young tree which is in their pre bearing stage, 1/3rd of the recommended dose of water may be given and slowly increased to reach the above level during full bearing.

Crop Stages and Critical Period

When the crop plants are young and delicate, they are not able to stand and demand a liberal supply of water. Again, with the start of grand growth period, crop puts up a faster rate of vegetative growth and transpiration and bio-chemical activities in plants occur at higher rate. This leads to tremendous increase in water need of the crop and the supply of water should be adequate to maintain the normal rate of active growth and evapotranspiration. Water stress at the sensitive stages causes a serious retardation ingrowth process that ultimately depresses the yield. The sensitive stages differ from one crop to the others. Water stress at these stages causes lower branching, tuber bulking, inadequate flowering, flower drops, poor setting of fruits and serious fruit drops.

It is true that crops require adequate water supply throughout their life cycle for best growth and yield. Only in the later stages of crop maturity, water supply is reduced or stopped to obtain uniform and quicker crop maturity. Crops may be allowed to stand water stress to some extent during certain periods of life excepting at the critical stages to save some water under situations of water scarcity.

Determination of Critical Periods of Water Need

It assumes importance to use irrigation water judiciously when water supply is limiting. For this purpose, a crop is subjected to pre-determined water stress at different stages of growth and then the corresponding yield reductions are considered. It is then related to the crop that has not been subjected to any water stress and irrigated according the normal schedule. Another way to decide the critical periods is to miss irrigation at different stages of the crop and then relating the corresponding the yield reductions with the yield from control plot which is irrigated normally. Periods at which yield reductions are significant are considered as the critical periods of water need in the life of the crop.

Managing the Available Irrigation Water

Irrigation is in short supply in most locations and therefore demands a careful and economic use. Economy of water helps to bring more areas under protective irrigation and leads to a greater crop production in areas of limited water supply. On areas where water is scarce, farmers are not able to apply normal irrigation to crops and are forced to skip some irrigation.

It is therefore necessary to decide a priority of stages of crops when irrigations are to be applied and the stages when one or more irrigations can be skipped. The critical stages of water need of crops receive the foremost attention. It is necessary to simultaneously consider and weigh the relative importance of the various stages for irrigation and the availability of water. A preferential status of crop stages according to their relative importance to yield should be considered for irrigation in areas of water scarcity.

Drip Irrigation for Fruit Crops

Drip irrigation offers scope for enormous savings in water usage and it is the most useful system to boost horticultural production in areas with limited water resources. Research work carried out at TNAU indicates the saving in irrigation water ranges from nearly 40 to 68 per cent with an additional yield benefit of 14-98 per cent over the conventional irrigation methods. Drip irrigation can be thought of in rainfed areas with meager water resources available during the periods other than the rainy seasons. Most of the fruit crops require drip irrigation during the period of flowering to fruit development in order to increase the fruit set and improve the fruit size reflecting on final yield. However, the drip irrigation has to be dispensed 10 – 15 days before the expected harvesting period in order to improve the sweetness of the fruits.

Micro irrigation is suitable for all row crops and especially for wide-spaced high- value crops. The required quantity of water is provided to each plant at the root zone through a pipe net work. Hence, there is little loss of water from the soil surface. Micro irrigation is well adapted for undulating terrain, shallow soils,porous soils and water scarce areas. Saline/brackish water can also be used since water is applied daily, which keeps the moisture and salt stress at a minimum.

Micro-irrigation, which includes drip and micro sprinklers, is an effective tool for conserving water resources and studies have revealed significant water saving, ranging between 40 and 70% by drip irrigation compared with surface irrigation, and increases as high as 100% in some crops in specific locations (Table 5.3). Micro irrigation is very popular in wide-spaced fruit crops like mango, guava, sapota, pomegranate, lime, oranges, grapes, banana etc.

Table 5.3: Water Used and Yield of Crops in Micro Irrigation and Conventional Methods

Crop	Methods of irrigation	Water require-ment (cm)	% water saving	Yield(kg / ha)	% increase in yield	Water use efficiency (kg / hamm)
Banana	Drip	97.00	45.00	87,500	52.00	90.20
	Surface	176.00	-	57,500	-	32.67
Grapes	Drip	27.80	48.00	32,500	23.00	116.90
	Surface	53.20	-	26,400	-	49.62
Papaya	Drip	73.88	67.89	23,490	69.47	0.32
	Surface	225.80	-	13,860	-	0.06

(WTC Annual Reports 1985-2003)

Mango

Mango flourishes equally well under low and heavy rainfall of 250-2500 mm annually. With the rainfall of around 750mm and above, irrigation is not essential. Irrigation, however, improves the yield and quality of fruits. For an adult tree, the water requirement is 40-60 litres per day. Quality of irrigation water especially concentration of CO_3 and HCO_3 ions, influence the availability and mobility of nutrients and hence mineral composition of the foliage. Like Na and Ca, concentrations of P, Mn and Fe whose availability is sensitive to quality, especially CO_3 and HCO_3 concentration of irrigation water were also high in old as compared to young leaves. Soil E_C should be less than 1 for better growth and productivity.

The carbohydrate accumulation in mango is accompanied by fruit bud differentiation and at this time there is no active growth. So little or no carbohydrate is utilized by the plant. Irrigation promotes vegetative growth under favourable climatic conditions. It is, therefore, suggested that during fruit bud differentiation period, irrigation of mango plants should be stopped. Otherwise irrigation during this period converts fruit or flower bud into vegetative bud, which ultimately adversely affects the fruit yield. During fruit development period, under hot and dry climate, irrigation checks the drop of immature fruits. The moisture deficit in soil brings early maturity to fruits. So regular and normal irrigation to plants during fruit development and maturity period improves the quality of fruits. For cultivation under irrigated conditions, adopt drip system of irrigation.

Fruit quality of mango also showed significant improvement over conventional and regulated deficit irrigation regimes. Application of PRD at 50 % of the full crop water requirement (ETc) resulted in higher fraction of fruit. Differences were consistently significant as compared to the control. When mango fruits are produced for processing, a higher fraction of mesocarp is advantageous-provided that differences prove to be consistent over an extended period (Table 5.4).

Table 5.4: Effect of Irrigation on Mesocarp Volume of Mango Fruit

Treatments	2004	2005
CO (100% of ETc)	71.1 a	76.1 a
PRD (50% of ETc)	78.0 b	78.5 b
RDI (50% of ETc)	77.3 b	76.3 a
NI (no irrigation)	71.1 a	76.3 a

Table 5.5: Effect of Irrigation Levels on the Yield and Yield Parameters of Mango

Treatments	Water applied (cm)	Fruits/ plant	Fruit weight (g)	Yield (q/ha)	Water use efficiency (q/ha-cm)	Emission Uniformity (%)
Basin irrigation with 1.0 IWR of crop	27.50	194	138	26.95	0.98	85.10
Basin irrigation with 1.0 IWR of crop + polythenemulch	27.28	222	142	31.65	1.16	85.25
Drip irrigation with 1.0 IWR of crop	26.32	360	125	45.27	1.72	87.24
Drip irrigation with 1.0 IWR of crop + polythenemulch	25.67	293.14	153	44.92	1.75	90.25
Drip irrigation with 0.8 IWR of crop	23.95	278.71	146	40.72	1.70	90.80

Drip irrigation with 0.8 IWR of crop + polythenemulch	23.12	328.53	161	52.95	2.29	93.12
Drip irrigation with 0.6 IWR of crop	23.32	239	148	35.46	1.52	92.72
Drip irrigation with 0.6 IWR of crop + polythenemulch	18.67	366	163	59.92	3.21	95.35
Drip irrigation with 0.4 IWR of crop	25.70	225	141	31.88	1.24	91.43
Drip irrigation with 0.4 IWR of crop + polythenemulch	23.09	262	145	38.10	1.65	93.40
CD (5 %)	0.95	27	4	1.12	0.102	0.962

(Hemant Kumar *et al.*, 2010). IWR: irrigation water requirement

At Raipur (Chhattisgarh), fruits characters, yield and yield attributing parameter were higher under drip irrigation with 0.6 of irrigation water requirement + polythene mulch and the same characters were lower under control (Basin irrigation with 1.0 irrigation water requirement)(Table 5.5). Application of black plastic mulch with drip irrigation system can conserve moisture, check the growth of weeds and improve the fruit yield and quality. Water use efficiency was higher under drip irrigation with 0.6 irrigation water requirement + polythene mulch and low under basin irrigation with 1.0 irrigation water requirement (Hemant Kumar *et al.*, 2010).

Sujatha *et al.*, (2006) studied that the drip irrigation in mango cv. Kesar at 0.75 Ep registered higher fruit weight during first year and number of fruits in second year than control (without irrigation). Prakash *et al.*, (2015) studies revealed that the irrigation treatments 13 – 24 L day-1 plant-1 recorded the highest percentage of fruit set, fruit weight, number of fruits per tree, fruit yield per tree and quality characters like, TSS, ascorbic acid, sugar, carotenoids were also the highest in the same treatment.

Banana

Banana being a succulent, evergreen and shallow rooted crop requires large quantity of water for increasing productivity. Water requirement of banana has been worked out to be 1,800 – 2,000 mm per annum. Irrigate immediately after planting; give life irrigation after 4 days; subsequent irrigations are to be given once in a week for irrigated plantations of garden lands and once in 10 – 15 days for wet lands. Irrigate the fields copiously after every manuring. In winter, irrigation is provided at an interval of 7-8 days while in summer it should be given at an interval of 4-5 days. However, during rainy season irrigation is provided if required as excess irrigation will lead to root zone congestion due to removal of air from soil pores, thereby affecting plant establishment and growth. In all, about 70-75 irrigations are provided to the crop.

Banana production should be supported by an efficient irrigation system like drip irrigation. Normal furrows, basin and trench systems are followed. Application of drip irrigation and mulching technology has reported to improve water use efficiency. There is saving of 58% of water and increasing yield by 23 – 32% under drip. Besides, the system also enables efficient fertilizer application through the fertigation technique.

Application of irrigation through drip system helps to maintain the proportion of soil air and soil water which results in early and vigorous growth of bunches (Table 5.6). Raw bunch gets matured earlier by 30-45 days and yield is increased by 15-30% and 58-60% of water is saved on irrigation, weed is less, cost on inter cultural operations is saved and water soluble fertilizers can be applied.

Drip irrigation may be given @ 15 litres /plant /day from planting to 4th month, 20litres /plant/day from 5th month till shooting stage and 25 litres/plant/day from shooting till 15 days prior to harvest. Two methods are followed in case of drip irrigation:

(*i*) **Single line system:** The spacing between the plants is 1.5 × 1.5 m. One lateral line and one dripper per plant are used.

(*ii*) **Double line system:** The distance between the lines is 1 m., between two plants is 1.5 m and between two double lines is 1.8m each. One lateral and one dripper for two plants are arranged. The distance between the two lines may also be 2.1 × 2.4 m.

Table 5.6: Impact of Irrigation Methods in Banana

Particulars	Furrow irrigation	Drip irrigation
Height of plant (cm)	153	169
Girth of plant (cm)	60.39	71.28
Number of leaves	34.11	35.29
Flowering period (days)	342	310
Harvesting period (days)	433	397
Bunch weight (kg)	14	17
Fruit yield (t/ha)	46.40	69.72

(Anonymous, 2000)

Saving in irrigation water and greater net profit due to drip irrigation in banana production has been reported by Kanannavar *et al.* (2009) and Pawar *et al.* (2010). Pramanik and Patra (2016) reported that drip irrigation resulted in significantly the highest yield in both plant (39.87t/ha) and ratoon crop (36.85 t/ha) over conventional method of irrigation. Shashidhara *et al.* (2007) reported that drip irrigation increased yield of banana to the extent of 5.94% and 3.54%, respectively as compared to surface irrigation. Thadchayini and Thiruchelvam (2005) reported 31% higher banana yield in drip irrigation compared to surface irrigation. Sharma and Kispotta (2014) reported that yield is 21.95% more. 38.82% water is being saved by drip system.Pramanik and Biswas (2012) showed that drip fertigation method resulted in considerably higher yield inplant (39.87 t/ha) and ratoon crop (36.85 t/ha) as compared with those obtained by conventional method of irrigation(37.09 and 34.84 t/ha for plant and ratoon crop respectively).

Hegde and Srinivas (1990) indicated an increase in the banana yield under drip irrigation compared to the basin irrigation. Young *et al.*, (1985) stated that drip irrigation of banana crop produced double the yield obtained from a well-managed sprinkler irrigation system in Hawaii. The yield improvement under drip irrigation was mainly due to the maintenance of soil near field capacity throughout the growth period in the active root zone, leading to low soil suction, which there by facilitated better water utilization, higher nutrients uptake and excellent maintenance of soil-water-air relationship with a higher oxygen concentration in the root zone (Kumar and Pandey, 2008). Pramanik *et al.* (2014)observed that under this drip fertigation treatment yield of both plant and ratoon crop was also higher (32.5%and 26.4% for plant and ratoon crop, respectively) as compared to in the conventional method of irrigation.

Khalifa (2006) observed that the quantities of water applied to banana plants were 15964 m^3/ha, 20201 m^3/ha, 27642 m^3/ha, 30635 m^3/ha and 32928 m^3/ha under drip irrigation regimes 40%, 6%, 80%, 100% and 120% of (ETc), respectively compared to116905 m^3/ha for surface irrigation. Pramanik and Biswas (2012) evaluated that irrigation water use was found to be the higher under conventional method of irrigation (57.00 cm and 33.00 cm for plant crop and ratoon crop respectively) for the entire lifecycle of the crop.

Pramanik *et al.* (2014) observed that the irrigation water-use was found to be higher under the conventional method of irrigation (57.0 cm for plant crop and 33.0 cm for ratoon crop) for the life cycle of the crop. The irrigation requirement of the crop was found to be lower in plants under drip fertigation. Considerable saving in water (41.7% in plant and 40.4% in ratoon crop) was observed in drip fertigation under 60 per cent CPE and 80 per cent RDF. The water-saving was about 29 per cent in banana due to adoption of drip irrigation over flood irrigation (Narayanamoorthy, 2003). They have further added that water required to produce one quintal of banana under drip method is only 1.33 horse power (HP) hours of water against the requirement of 3.17 HP hours of water under flood irrigation.

But in case of drip irrigation water is made available in the root zone there by reducing the water stress pressure directly near (Bankar *et al*, 1993; Sivanappan, 1993; Srinivas and Hedge, 1990). Srivastava *et al.* (1999) reported that with the higher water application it recorded lower water use efficiency.

More *et al.* (1999) reported that plant height, pseudostem girth and flowering percentage were higher under drip irrigation as compared to basin irrigation. At Jorhat (Assam), Salvin *et el.* (2000) indicated that there was improved growth and early shooting of banana cv. Barjahaji under trickle irrigation compared to basin irrigation. Among different levels of irrigation (at different levels of evaporation replenishment viz. 50, 75, 100 and 125 per cent of USWB class pan evaporation), 75% evaporation replenishment was found better. At Raipur (Chhattisgarh), Agrawal and Agrawal (2005) recorded maximum plant height, growth of pseudostem and number of functional leaves under the treatment of irrigation at 0.6 PEF through drip with plastic mulch as compared to other irrigation levels and basin irrigation in banana cv. Dwarf Cavendish.

Shelke *et al.* (1998) studied the effect of different irrigation system (surface and drip) on banana production in Marathawada, Maharashtra. They compared three irrigation levels (0.6, 0.8 and 1.0 PEF) for drip system based on IW/CPE and recorded maximum yield at higher level of irrigation as compared to lower level of irrigation. Parikh *et al.* (2002 a) found that to achieve optimum growth and fruit yield of banana, drip irrigation at 0.75 PEF at alternate day with minimum two emitters of 4 lph capacities need to be placed at 30 cm distance from pseudostem in black cotton soil. At Jalgaon (Maharashtra), Anonymous (2009 b) reported that yield and yield attributes were adversely influenced by reduced levels of 50 to 60 PER. Maximum number of hands per bunch, number of fingers per bunch, bunch weight and yield were recorded under application of irrigation at 80 PER. At Rahuri (Maharashtra), drip irrigation was efficient with 48 % saving in water and 30-35 % saving in labour compared to surface irrigation with cv. Basrai banana (Berad *et al.*, 1998). In banana, Anonymous (2009 d) concluded that 44.4 and 22.2 % water saving under 50 and 70 per cent ER, respectively as compared to 90 per cent ER.

Acid Lime

Like mandarin and sweet orange, the acid lime is also sensitive to moisture deficit. Citrus plants are also affected by poor water quality and improper and often insufficient irrigation. Poor water management practices compound the problems faced by the plants. Irrigation scheduling based on pan evaporation can save upto 23% water. Irrigation at 0.8 of open pan evaporation through drips is ideal to increase growth, yield and quality of Nagpur Mandarin. Water containing chlorides less than 200 ppm, EC less than 0.25 mmhos/cm and RSC less than 2.5 me/l and SAR less than 8 is considered safe for irrigation. Microirrigation practices can help to save upto 40% water and simultaneously improve plant performance.Irrigate copiously after planting. After establishment, irrigation may be given at 7 – 10 days interval. Avoid water stagnation. Adopt drip system for new plantations.

At Akola, Maharashtra, plant growth in respect of plant height and plant spread was found maximum in 100% micro irrigation at Evpwhich was at par with 90% micro irrigation at Evp (Goramnagar *et al.*, 2017) (Table 5.7).

Table 5.7: Effect of Micro-irrigation and Fertigation on Height, Plant Spread, Number of Fruits Per Plant of Acid Lime

Irrigation	Plant height (m)	Plant spread (m)	Fruits /plant
100% Evp	3.76	4.41	596.9
90% Evp	3.77	4.39	664.2
80% Evp	3.63	4.26	676.7
CD (5 %)	0.13	0.10	21.85

(Goramnagar *et al.*, 2017)

Shirgure *et al.* (2003) observed a significant response of irrigation and fertigation on acid lime plant height and the response was more in 30 per cent depletion of available water with 500:140:70 g NPK g per tree through fertigation in acid lime.

Shirgure *et al.*, (2003) studied the effect of irrigation scheduling and fertigation through drip irrigation on 6-8 year old acid lime which shows that TSS, fruit yield average fruit weight, juice percent and acidity (42.5% and 7.0%) was more in irrigation scheduled at 30 % depletion of available water content with 500:140:70 fertigation.

Sweet Orange

Immediately after planting irrigate copiously. Irrigations may be given once in 10 days. Avoid water stagnation near the plant. Significantly higher fruits per plant at 75 per cent irrigation and fertigation individually and in combination in Nagpur Mandarin (Shirgure *et al.*, 2001; Panigrahi and Srivastava, 2011a; Kumar *et al.*, 2013; Shirgure *et al.*, 2014). Shirgure (2013) observed that while comparing with plant height and girth the only canopy volume was found significant among the various scheduling irrigation treatments and the highest fruit was observed under irrigation at 80 % ER in stages I-V and 30% ER in stage VI during the study period in Nagpur mandarin. Kumari *et al.*, (2013) reported that the irrigation was applied at 75 % ETC and percentage water saving for drip fertigation treatment was 33.94% over the conventional irrigation in sweet orange.

Grapes

The field trials on irrigation requirement of guava have indicated that the higher TSS content was determined at the lowest soil moisture content (1.23%) while the lowest amounts were obtained at the highest moisture content. The lowest amount of ascorbic acid content was obtained at 1.23% soil moisture.

The expectation from PRD is that any yield reduction will be insignificant compared with the benefits gained through diverting the saved water to irrigate other crops. If deficit irrigation is properly practiced, it may increase crop quality. PRD has been found to be promising in several crops. For example, the protein content and baking quality of wheat, the length and strength of cotton fibers, and the sucrose concentration of sugar beet and grape all increase under deficit irrigation. When the two halves of a maize root system were alternately exposed to drying and wetting, water use was reduced by 34.4–36.8% and total biomass production was reduced by only 6–11%, as compared with well-watered plants.

Performance of table grapes was assessed under conventional drip irrigation (CDI), irrigated on both sides of the root system, alternate partial root-zone drip irrigation (ADI), irrigated with 50% of the control, alternatively on the two sides of the root system during consecutive watering and fixed partial root-zone drip irrigation (FDI), irrigated with 50% of the control on only one side of the root system. Fruit yield and yield components under different irrigation treatments in 2005 and 2006 are shown in Table 5.8. ADI gained 44.8% more bunch number per tree than FDI in 2005 and it also improved bunch number per tree significantly as compared to CDI in 2006. Berry number per bunch was at the same level under the three irrigation treatments in 2005 but ADI gained

Table 5.8: Yield Attributes of Table Grape Under Different Irrigation Methods

Parameters	Year	ADI	CDI	FDI
Bunch number per tree	2005	5.89 a	5.75 ab	3.25 c
	2006	25.30 a	19.75 b	23.50 ab
Berry No. per bunch	2005	102.30 a	116.00 a	112.00 a
	2006	66.08 a	57.80 ab	50.56 b
Bunch weight (g)	2005	486.80 a	519.47 a	442.69 a
	2006	355.82 b	445.83 a	360.22 b
Bunch volume (cm^3)	2005	427.16 a	473.69 a	362.41 a
	2006	339.88 b	415.82 a	323.23 b
Berry weight (g)	2005	4.07 a	4.08 a	3.95 b
	2006	5.38 b	7.71 a	7.13 a
% of edible grape	2005	93.36 a	87.58 b	95.47 a
	2006	94.25 a	90.37 b	93.23 a
Yield per tree (kg)	2005	5.18a	5.06 ab	2.66 c
	2006	17.30 a	17.08 ab	16.25 b
WUEET (kg/m^3)	2005	3.28a	2.24	1.69c
	2006	7.11a	5.61	5.61

30.7% more berry number per bunch than FDI at the same irrigation level in 2006. Bunch weight and volume of ADI was kept at the same level with CDI in 2005 but it was reduced significantly in 2006. Furthermore, ADI increased the percentage of edible grape by 3.88–5.78% significantly at the same fruit yield level in both years.

Under ADI, the vitamin C (Vc) content of fruit is increased by 15.3–42.2% in both years, but decreased the fruit titrated acid (TA) by 13.2% at the same level of TSSC compared to CDI, therefore increased TSSC/TA by 22.5% at post-veraison in 2005 presented in Table 5.9. ADI also increased TSSC at the similar level of TA with highest TSSC/TA significantly at harvest in 2006. During both the year higher Vc was observed under ADI indicating the, indicating a higher nutrition value in the berries produced unfer ADI. Higher TSSC/TA ratio under ADI indicates higher total soluble solids concentration and medium titrated acid of grape, indicating sweeter and more delicious fruit in both years.

Table 5.9: Fruit Quality of Table Grape Under Different Irrigation Regimes

Year	Treatments	Vc(mg/100 FWg)	TSSC(%)	TA(mg/100 FWg)	TSSC/TA
2005	CDI	0.268 b	13.56 b	5.16 a	26.28 c
	ADI	0.309 a	13.68 b	4.48 b	32.19 b
	FDI	0.162 c	15.00 a	4.25 c	33.48 a
2006	CDI	0.090 b	13.17 b	2.33 a	56.52 b
	ADI	0.128 a	13.65 a	2.33 a	58.58 a
	FDI	0.108 ab	13.10 b	2.47 a	53.04 c

Irrigate immediately after planting and on the 3rd day and then once in a week. Withheld irrigation 15 days before pruning and also 15 days before harvest. Grigorov *et al.* (2000) irrigated grape vines at 60-65, 70-75 or 80-85 per cent depletion of soil moisture from field capacity with drip method of irrigation and found that yield increased with increasing frequency of irrigation, and the highest average yield (9,130 kg/ha) was obtained in vines irrigated at 80-85 per cent of field capacity with drip method.

Guava

Irrigate copiously immediately after planting, again on third day and afterwards once in 10 days or as and when necessary. In guava, increase in plant height with increasing levels of irrigation and fertigation (Ramni was *et al.*, 2012). In Lucknow (Uttar Pradesh), higher fruit number (27.3), fruit weight (107.3 g) and fruit yield (16.92 kg m^{-3}) were recorded by application of irrigation at 80% PE (T3) per day per plant coupled with black polyethylene mulching. Maximum water saving (47.52%) was recorded through drip irrigation and polyethylene mulching as compared to control (unmulched basin irrigation). Fruit yield varied from a maximum value of 16.92 kg m^{-3} canopy volume in drip irrigation 80% PE level with black polyethylene mulching as compared to minimum in control (8.21 kg m^{-3}). Drip irrigation coupled with polyethylene mulching resulted in better quality of fruits in terms of increased TSS (12.1°Brix), total sugars (6.61%), ascorbic acid (169.2 mg 100 g^{-1}) and reduced acidity (0.27%) as compared to the minimum TSS (10.1° Brix), total sugars (6.12%), ascorbic acid (159.6 mg/100 g) and increased acidity (0.34%) in control under ultra-high density planting (2.0 m × 1.0 m) of guava (Singh *et al.*, 2015).

Ramniwas *et al.*, (2012) reported that "Shwetha" cultivar of guava shows 75% RDF and 75% irrigation of IW/CPE through drip resulted in notably greater number of flowers per shoot (32.02), fruit set (45.88%), fruit retention (47.83%) and fruit yield of 29.33 t/ha. Junaid *et al.*, (2013) studied in guava that the controlling Soil moisture potential between –40 kPa to –45 kPa at 0.2 m depth immediately under the drip emitter and fertilizer dose of 80% recommended dose of fertilizer can be used as an indicator for drip irrigation scheduling in semi-arid region of India.

Mandal *et al.*, (2007) concluded that the guava plants planted at 5 × 5 m had higher irrigation production efficiency (6.79 kg m^{-3}) than 6 × 6 m (4.70 kg m^{-3}), fruit weight (161.3 g), TSS (11.7oB) and total sugars (10.71%) and vitamin C contents were superior in fruits obtained from drip-irrigated plants as compared to flood-irrigated ones. Kumar *et al.*, (2013) reported that the Safeda under drip irrigation 0.75EpR at 120% RDF and the highest plant canopy (38.86 cm) was recorded in L-49 under drip irrigation 0.75EpR at 120% RDF. Pramanikand Patra (2014) proved that the guava fruits yield increased significantly with increase in application of irrigation water and nitrogen fertilizer. However, maximum fruit yield, higher water use efficiency, net return and B: C ratio was registered from drip irrigation at 1.00.

Kumar *et al.*, (2013) reported that the maximum growth of plants was recorded with 1.0 volume of water through drip along with fertigation of 125 per cent RDF. As well as the maximum yield and economics were observed with 0.8 volume of water through drip along with fertigation of 100 per RDF. Singh *et al.*, (2007) reported that drip irrigation at 80% evapo-transpiration (ET) crop based on pan evaporation applied gave significantly higher fruit yield (45.57 t/ha) compared with the surface irrigation (29.43 t/ha. Ramniwas *et al.*(2012) showed that 100% irrigation of cumulative pan evaporation + 100% water soluble fertilizers gave maximum yield/plant (6.59 kg). However, maximum B: C ratio (2.91) was obtained at 75% irrigation of cumulative pan evaporation + 75% water soluble fertilizers.

Table 5.10: Effect of Drip Fertigation on Yield Parameters and Yield of Guava

Treatments	Fruits/ branch (no)	Fruitlength (cm)	Fruitvolume (cc)	Fruit weight (g)	Fruit yield / plant(kg)	B:Cratio
1.00 EpR	87.25	8.91	126.88	138.08	25.75	2. 40
0.75 EpR	91.75	9.10	155.57	139.19	27.17	3.51
0.50 EpR	82.50	8.62	108.23	132.83	25.04	1.84
CD (5 %)	2.45	0.43	2.75	2.58	0.73	-

(Harendra Kumar *et al.,* 2015).

At Jorhat (Assam), drip irrigation at 0.75 EpR recorded higher fruit / branch, fruit length, fruit volume, fruit weight, fruit yield and B: C ratio than drip irrigation either 1.00 or 0.50 EpR in guava (Table 10) (Harendra Kumar *et al.,* 2015). A distinct dry spell starts from November and extends to March and sometimes up to April-May. The limited water resource is a constraint in increasing area under guava (Sharma, 2009).

Table 5.11: Yield Attributes and Quality Components of Guava cv. "Sardar" as Influenced by Various Levels of Drip Irrigation

Treatments	Fruit weight (g)	Yield /plant (kg)	TSS (%)	Ascorbic acid(mg/100g)
2 drippers /plant daily	115.00	10.05	12.0	160.00
3 drippers /plant daily	105.00	14.50	12.0	155.00
4 drippers /plant daily	135.50	14.89	12.5	172.33
2 drippers /plant alternate day	96.00	9.89	12.0	156..67
3 drippers /plant alternate	110.50	10.0	11.0	148.33
4 drippers /plant alternate	122.50	13.89	9.5	176.67
conventional flow irrigation at 0.75 CPE	123.00	10.18	10.0	180.00
CD 5 %	14.01	1.26	0.83	14.36

(Shukla *et al.,* 2017)

At Udaipur (Rajasthan),irrigation at 75% ET through 4 dippers per plant per day exhibited significantly higher plant height (350 cm), canopy volume (24.83 cubic metre), fruit weight (135 g) and fruit yield (14.89 kg/ plant) (Table 5.11). While, in quality wise higher TSS in irrigation at 75% ET through 4 drippers/ plant daily and vitamin C content in control (conventional flow irrigation at 0.75 CPE) (Shukla *et al.,* 2017).

Higher yield obtained under drip irrigation over conventional method due to lesser amount of water application may be attributed to better moisture conditions in the rhizosphere throughout the growing periods in guava (Ramniwas *et al.,* 2012 & 2013). Reduced growth parameters under conventional system might be due to poor aeration in root zone (Sarolia *et al.,* 2005).

Sapota

Excess irrigation may cause flower and fruit shedding and increase the number of mis-shapened fruits. Young plants should be watered regularly during dry season and at an interval of 6-12 days during winter. The optimum level of irrigation lies around 0.5/1W/CPE ratio. Drip irrigation at the rate 20-30l/day/tree is recommended by Tamil Nadu Agricultural University. For the young trees which are in the pre bearing stage, 1/3 of the recommended dose of water may be given and slowly increased reaching the above level during full bearing stage. Irrigate copiously immediately after planting and on the third day and once in 10 days afterwards till the graft establishes.

At Kharagpur (W.B),water requirement of sapota crop varies between 2.14 mm (10.71 litres) per day per plant in winter season and 6.89 mm (34.44 L) per day per plant in summer season for 100% water requirement treatment at peak growth stage. The biometric observations (canopy, height, girth, no. of branches) of sapota plants showed positive influence of the irrigation and plastic mulch treatments on growth of sapota crop. Due to mulch alone the increase in Sapota yield varied from 7.62 to 41% in different treatments. Yield of sapota crop was found to increase by 21.05% due to drip in comparison to ring basin irrigation (Tiwari *et al.,* 2014).

Tiwari *et al.,* (2014) reported that the water requirement of sapota crop varies between 2.14 mm (10.71 litres) per day per plant in winter season and 6.89 mm (34.44 litres) per day per plant in summer season for 100% water requirement treatment at peak growth stage and maximum yield of sapota was obtained under 100% drip with plastic mulch was found to increase by 21.05% in comparison to ring basin irrigation (Table 5.12).

Table 5.12: Effect of Plastic Mulch and Drip Irrigation on Biometric Attributes and Sapota Yield

Treatments	Plant height (m)	Girth (cm)	Branches (Nos)	Canopy (E-W) (m)	Yield (t/ha)
100 % of irrigation requirement met through drip irrigation	4.55	37.30	13.40	4.12	11.50
100% of irrigation requirement met through drip irrigation with plastic mulch	4.82	39.10	14.00	4.34	16.10
80% of irrigation requirement met through drip irrigation	3.90	38.30	11.00	3.85	11.20
80% of irrigation requirement met through drip irrigation with plastic mulch	4.00	39.00	12.60	3.85	15.60
60% of irrigation requirement met through drip irrigation	4.81	36.20	10.80	3.83	9.20

60% of irrigation requirement met through drip with plastic mulch	3.95	37.40	11.20	3.89	11.04
100% of irrigation requirement met through ring basin irrigation with plastic mulch	3.92	30.90	11.60	3.98	11.04
100% of irrigation requirement met through ring basin	3.75	30.00	11.20	3.65	9.50
CD (5 %)	0.60	5.12	1.75	NS	2.25

(Tiwari *et al.*, 2014)

Papaya

Adequate moisture supply is essential at all stages of crop growth. While water stress induces maleness and poor fruit set, excess moisture can cause carpellody. Trials taken up at TNAU have revealed that conventional irrigation at 60-80 % available soil moisture depletion is found to be optimum for papaya. Conventionally, papaya plants are irrigated at 10-12 days interval in winter and weekly once in summer if there are no rains. Plants also perform well under drip irrigation when supplied with 20 to 25 l/day for bearing trees.

Irrigate copiously after planting. Irrigate the field once in a week. Apply 10 litres of water per day + 13.5 g urea and 10.5 g muriate of potash / week through drip irrigation and soil application of super phosphate 300 g per plant at bimonthly intervals starting from 3-4 months after planting immediately after thinning of plants is recommended.

Tank and Patel (2013) proved that the papaya under drip irrigation revealed that 0.8 PEF with 100% recommended dose of N&K shows the maximum yield and greater individual fruit weight and they are at par with treatment drip irrigation @ 0.8 PEF with 80% recommended dose of N and K.At Bangalore (Karnataka), Srinivas (1996 a) recorded that plant height and stem girth were significantly higher with daily irrigation at 0.6 PFE compared to alternate irrigation. Providing two emitters per plant gave maximum plant height and stem girth. Number of fruit per plant (36.0), average fruit weight (1.320 kg) and fruit yield (116.5 t/ha) were significantly higher with daily drip irrigation as compared to alternate day drip irrigation. Maximum number of fruits, fruit weight and yield with two emitters per plant as compared to one emitter per plant for papaya (cv. Coorg Honey Dew). At Bangalore (Karnataka), Srinivas (1996 b) revealed that increasing evaporation replenishment rates from 20 to 120 per cent of USWB class A pan evaporation under drip irrigation, subsurface drip (at 250 mm depth in soil) and surface drip irrigation proportionately increased plant height and stem girth, fruit number (88.3 per cent) and fruit yield (34.6 per cent). Fruit yield differences above 60 per cent evaporation-replenishment rates were not significant. Higher fruit yield in subsurface drip irrigation was observed as compared to surface drip irrigation of papaya.

At Navsari (Gujarat), maximum plant girth (45.43 cm), height (1.81 m) and number of leaves per plant (31.74) were recorded with drip irrigation at 0.6 PEF on alternate day + black plastic mulch (50 micron, 20 per cent coverage) which was at par with drip alone in papaya (cv. Taiwan 786) (Anonymous, 2010 b). In new alluvium agro climatic zone of West Bengal, Biswas *et al.* (1999) concluded that daily drip irrigation at 0.8 PEF gave higher yield as compared to higher and lower drip irrigation levels while the lower yield was obtained under conventional irrigation method at 1.0 PEF with papaya cv. Honey Dew.

In calcareous soil of North Bihar, Suresh and Saha (2004) observed that number of fruits per plant was higher (24.1) with the application of 0.8 PEF level of irrigation with drip while fruit weight (0.970 kg) and yield (23.2 kg/plant) of papaya were found to be maximum with application of 1.0 PEF of water through drip and mulch in papaya cv. Pusa Dwarf. At 0.8 PEF level of irrigation by drip system produced significantly maximum number of fruits per plant and yield as compared to 0.6 and 1.0 PEF level of irrigation by drip. However average fruit weight was not affected by different irrigation treatments in papaya cv. Madhu Bindu (Anonymous, 2008 a).

Pomegranate

Regular irrigation is necessary for newly planted pomegranate plants till their establishment. Later irrigation is essential during flowering and fruit development as irregular moisture availability would result in dropping of flowers as small fruits. It may also cause fruit cracking on mature fruits. Though bed or basin system of irrigation is followed, nowadays, drip irrigation is practiced as a water saving technique. Copious irrigation is essential during fruiting season. Patel and Patel (1998) reported that the increase in yield was mainly because of better growth, bigger size and more juice content in the fruits under drip-irrigated plants.

Water requirement of 5 years old pomegranate tree varied from 5.62 to 48.81 litres/day at different stages such as initial, crop development, mid and late season in the western parts of Maharashtra, India specifically 8.24, 26.16, 39.53 and 41.96 litres/day / tree respectively. The seasonal water requirement of pomegranate tree was 14057.33 litres/year/tree. The reference crop evapotranspiration (Etc) values ranged from 24.4 to 56.0 mm/week and crop coefficient (Kc) values at initial, crop development, mid and late stages were 0.15 – 0.20, 0.20 – 1.18, 1.18 and 1.18 – 0.55 respectively. Water use by pomegranate started from the bud break (initial) stage. It increased gradually as the canopy developed and as evaporative demand increased. The canopy was fully developed by mid-August and peak water use occurred at crop development (September – October), mid-season (November – December), late season (January – mid April) and rest period (mid-April – July) (Meshram *et al.*, 2009). Meti *et al.*, (2008) reported that water requirement of matured pomegranate Cv. Jyothi tree for three seasons (kharif, rabi and summer) to be 11, 17 and 22 litres/day/ tree in vertisols of Malaprabha command area (Karnataka). However, Baner and Kadam (200) estimated age-wise water requirement of pomegranate that ranged from 1.33 –3.4 litres/day/tree in 1st year, 5.13 – 12.13 litres/day/tree in 2nd year, 14.63 – 35.70 litres/day/tree in 3rd year, 2.90 – 51.00 litres/day/tree in 4th year and 27.4 – 66.30litres/day/tree in 5th year.

Table 5.13: Effect of Wetted Area and Pan Fraction on Yield and Water Use Efficiency of Pomegranate

Treatments		Total water applied (litres/tree/ year)	Water applied (litres/ tree/day)	Fruit yield /tree (kg)	WUE (kg/ ha-cm)
Wetted area (%)	Pan fraction				
20	0.25	5983	25	7.2	120
40	0.25	6640	27	9.4	142
60	0.25	7276	30	11.18	154
40	0.50	7922	33	13.67	173
40	0.75	9213	38	15.28	166
80	0.50	10507	43	16.29	155
60	0.75	11150	46	17.06	153
80	0.75	13088	54	17.88	137
Surface irrigation 0.6 IW/CPE ratio		13047	54	10.43	80
Control		5337	22	4.02	75
CD 5 %		-	2.30	1.46	6.44

Meti *et al.* (2008)

Higher fruit yield of 17.88 kg/tree was obtained in 80% wetted area + 0.75 pan fraction treatment. Higher WUE of 173 kg/ha-cm and water saving of 39% were over surface irrigation (Table 5.13) (Meti *et al.*, 2008).

Table 5.14: Fruit Yield of Pomegranate and WUE as Influenced by Irrigation Methods and Quality of Water

Treatments	Good quality water		Saline water	
	Fruit yield (t/ha)	WUE (t/ha-cm)	Fruit yield (t/ha)	WUE (t/ha-cm)
Sub surface drip irrigation	26.8	3.0	23.6	2.6
Surface drip irrigation	17.5	1.9	15.7	1.8
Surface irrigation at 35 mm CPE	16.4	1.4	9.9	0.9
Surface irrigation at 60 mm CPE	13.9	1.2	6.7	0.6

(Aggarwal and Khanna, 1983)

At Hissar (Haryana), Aggarwal and Khanna (1983) reported that significant difference in fruit yield and water use efficiency using both the water sources in pomegranate (Table 5.14).

Ber

The budded plants are to be irrigated immediately after planting and within an interval of 3 - 4 days for two months. Thereafter in the interval of irrigation can be extended as 7 to 10 days till to the establishment of new plants though ber is considered as an arid crop. For adult grown up trees, irrigation during fruit development in November to February is essential than any other period of growth for production of quality fruits. In desertic conditions where soils are very coarse textured and irrigation is scares, a double walled earthern pot called as Jaltripti is used to irrigate the plants with less moisture evaporation loss which also reduces the mortality. Irrigate the plants initially for establishment. Provide 5% slope towards the base of the tree for *in situ* water harvesting.

Apple

Performance of apple was assessed under three irrigation treatments, conventional irrigation (CI) irrigated on both sides of the tree; a partial root-zone drying treatment (PRD) which received 50% of CI on alternating sides of the tree and (3) a deficit treatment (DI) which received 50% of conventional irrigation on a fixed (east) side of the tree. Compared to the CI regime, reduced fruit weight and higher total soluble solids was observed in the fruits under PRD. No significant difference in flesh firmness or starch score due to irrigation treatment was evident in either season. The development of red fruit skin colour, assessed by the percentage of green skin was similar between irrigation regimes and seasons, although fruit in Year 2 were rated as having greater intensity of redness (Table 5.15).

Table 5.15: Fruit Quality Attributes of Apple cv. Fuji Under Different Irrigation Regimes

Days after harvest	Treatments	Firmness (N)	Soluble solids (Brix)
1	Control irrigation (CI)	69.1	13.50
	Deficit irrigation (DI)	73.2	15.08
	Partial root zone drying (PRD)	74.3	15.55
	LSD (a=0.05)	3.3	0.75
7	Control irrigation (CI)	73.3	14.40
	Deficit irrigation (DI)	75.0	15.75
	Partial root zone drying (PRD)	75.4	16.60
	LSD (a=0.05)	NS	0.68

Kumar (2004) observed higher flowering intensity, fruit set and yield of apple with drip irrigation at 100 per cent ETc. Rzekanowski and Rolbiecki (2000) conducted a study on drip irrigation in different cvs. of apple and observed that drip irrigation resulted in an increased yield of 9 per cent in cv. Melba, 22 per cent in McIntosh and 25 per cent in Spartan to that of control.

Litchi

In eastern plateau region, a field experiment was conducted to study the efficacy of deficit irrigation of litchi crop under quantitative (60, 40 and 20 % of ETc) and temporal deficit (skipping irrigations at different phenological stages from flowering to fruiting) irrigation strategies under basin and drip irrigation systems of water application. Although the effect of DI on fruit yields was insignificant, drip irrigation system recorded highest fruit weight (22.6 g) at 60% ETc and irrigation starting from flowering stage. The prolonged moisture stress between two irrigations under basin system resulted in lower fruit length and diameter and higher fruit cracking percentage. Deficit water application under drip system resulted in higher reducing sugar content (7.5%) of litchi fruits. Higher irrigation water use efficiency (57.1 g/m^3) was observed in case of drip irrigation having irrigation at 20% of ETc and irrigation starting from fruit development stage. Deficit irrigation showed great potential to increase the irrigation water use efficiency of litchi production without affecting the fruit quality and with slight deviation in potential yield.

Mali *et al.,* (2015) studied that in litchi highest fruit weight at 60% ETc with irrigation starting from flowering stage and the prolonged moisture stress between two irrigations under basin system resulted in lowest fruit length, fruit diameter and higher fruit cracking percentage (10.2%) and maximum irrigation water use efficiency (57.1 g/m^3) was observed in case of drip irrigation having irrigation at 20% ETc with irrigation.

Drip irrigation in mango

Drip irrigation in papaya

Peach

Growth and production of peach trees were monitored under furrow,surface and subsurface drip and micro jet irrigation systems for different irrigation scheduling. Higher water use efficiency, yield and larger trees growth were reported under surface and subsurface drip as compare to micro jet irrigation systems and furrow irrigation (Bryla *et al.*, 2003). Gunduz *et al.* (2011) investigated the effect of amount of irrigation, irrigation interval using drip irrigation on yield and quality of peach. Amount of irrigation water application to peach crop was estimated using pan evaporation data with different pan coefficient. The amount of irrigation water application had significant influence on peach yield.

Strawberry

Minami *et al.* (1982) reported that drip irrigated strawberry with Class A pan evaporation factor of 0.8 produced higher yield than plants irrigated to a lower (0.4-0.7) factor. Similarly, Rajput (1983) observed that with 6 cm irrigation depth, strawberry yield was 5.8 times higher (27.6 q/ha) than under rainfed conditions (4.75 q/ha). Non-irrigated strawberry plants have markedly lower yields compared to irrigated plants (Dwyer *et al.*, 1987). Tekinel *et al.* (1989) studied the effects of drip and other conventional irrigation methods on the yields of strawberry and obtained highest yield and fruit quality in the drip irrigation treatments.

Fahad and Hagemann (1992), while working on irrigation scheduling in container grown and open field grown strawberry plants recorded 37 per cent higher yield in drip irrigation as compared to furrow method of irrigation. Serrano *et al.* (1992) studied the performance of four irrigation treatments in strawberry by watering the plants when soil water potential reached –0.01, –0.03, –0.05 and –0.07 MPa. The maximum yield was obtained in plots irrigated at 0.01 MPa soil water potential. Further they observed that yield reduction was associated with reduction in total assimilation rate resulting from the decreased assimilatory surface area in plants irrigated at lower soil water potentials. Demir *et al.* (1995) studied the effect of drip and furrow irrigation methods under Bursa condition and found that fruit yield in strawberry increased significantly in drip irrigation (15,080 kg/ha) as compared to furrow irrigation (13,720 kg/ha).

Kruger *et al.* (1999) also obtained higher yield in more frequently irrigated plants as compared to stressed plants. They also reported that fruit yield in strawberry reduced when water stress conditions occur during flowering and fruit development stages. Evenhu is and Alblas (2002) studied the effect of irrigation on strawberries with the use of decision support systems and found that crop productivity increased at field capacity (100 hPa). Similarly, Ostrowska and Chepinski (2003) reported that drip irrigation increased the yield of cultivars Elsanta, Senga Sengana and Elkat. Sharma *et al.* (2005), while working on drip irrigation in strawberry reported that fruit yield was significantly higher in drip irrigation at 100% evaporation (78.6 q/ha) as compared to non-irrigated treatment (12.13 q/ha).

Yuan *et al.* (2004) studied the effect of drip irrigation on the growth and yield of strawberries under greenhouse conditions. The amounts of irrigation water applied were 0.75, 1.00 and 1.25 times water surface evaporation (Ep) measured by a standard 200 mm diameter pan and the corresponding regimes were denoted Ep 0.75, Ep 1.00 and Ep 1.25. Higher berry yield was recorded in more frequently irrigated plots and concluded that frequent irrigation increased strawberry yields not only by increasing the number of berries, but by increasing the size and weight of the berries.

Higher yield was produced in –150 hPa irrigation level (750 g/plant), which was significantly higher than other treatments *viz.* –300 hPa to –600 hPa (663 g/plant) and –300 hPa (660 g/plant) (Hoppula and Salo, 2007). Similarly, fruit yield of the strawberry cultivars decreased in water stress conditions (126.44 g, 106.38 g and 85.15 g per plant as compared to control 169.77 g, 150.36 g and 136.31 g per plant for cultivar Elsanta, Salut and Elkat, respectively) under greenhouse conditions (Klamkowski and Treder, 2008)

Kim *et al.* (2009) evaluated quality characteristics and yield of 'Maehyang' and 'Seolhyang' strawberry cultivars under different irrigation regimes. They found that the yield of cv. 'Seolhyang' in the drip irrigated treatment and the water stress treatment were 7.8 and 6.7 kg m^{-2}, respectively, while those in 'Maehyang' were 5.4 and 4.7 kg m^{-2}, respectively. The yield of both cultivars decreased in the water stress treatments by 13.1 and 13.6 per cent, respectively compared with drip irrigation treatments. Similarly, Kumar *et al.* (2012) studied the influence of irrigation levels on yield of strawberry cv. Chandler. They reported that the fruit yield (175.15 g/plant) was highest in I1 level (1.0 Irrigation Water/Cumulative Pan Evaporation ratio) of irrigation as compared to other levels of irrigation.

Economics of Irrigation Methods

Suresh and Saha (2004) estimated maximum B: C ratio i.e. 10.96 with 1.0 PEF of irrigation water through drip with mulch and lowest 4.56 with 1.0 PEF of water through traditional method of irrigation. Muhammad *et al.* (2005) at PFDC, Tavanur reported that higher benefit cost ratio 1.76 was observed under drip irrigation treatment as compared to normal practices (1.42) with a saving of '22,000/hectare. Anon. (2008 a) revealed that 0.6 PEF level of irrigation through drip recorded maximum CBR i.e. 1:3.33 with a maximum 40 per cent water saving as compared to others levels.

Do's and Don'ts for Fruit Crops

- In situ soil moisture conservation by trenching, contour/field bunding, Gully Plugging, Loose boulder check dams may be taken up.
- Use locally available organic mulches to conserve moisture in situ in the basin. Adopt to drip/trickle irrigation for judicious use of water. In situ grafting on drought resistant root stocks for better establishment of saplings. Practicing conservation horticulture such as inter crops and soil moisture conservation.

- Avoid soil application of fertilizers till sufficient soil moisture is available.
- Adopting to foliar nutrition of major nutrients under water stress conditions to enhance the nutrient uptake and use efficiency.
- Provide protective irrigation through pitcher and protective shade to young plants to reduce the high evaporative demand.
- In addition to drip irrigation and mulching for production of fruit crops under water limiting conditions, novel irrigation methods, like partial root zone drying (PRD), could be adapted in grapes, mango and citrus. The partial root zone drying method helps in development of a deeper root system.
- For all fruit crops, basin mulching with locally available plant material and plastic mulch may be taken up.
- Try to compost all the available plant waste materials and use it as organic manure to fruit and vegetable crops.
- For all the horticultural crops, drip Irrigation may be followed. Pitcher irrigation wherever drip is unavailable, is suitable for protective maintenance.

Conclusion

Methods of irrigation affect water consumption, which is a critical issue in many parts of the world including the Pacific Northwest region of the United States. Irrigation methods and injection of nutrients, particularly nitrogen, through water (fertigation) also play major roles in apple fruit quality and production. Irrigation with a drip system uses less water than sprinkler irrigation. However, irrigation through sprinkler systems can improve the establishment and maintenance of orchard floor vegetation. Sprinklers also create a cooler environment in the orchards under fruit-growing conditions. Management of irrigation is an important practice in fruit production regions of the world, particularly in arid and semi-arid climates. It draws attention to the principles of irrigating fruit crops, and identifies the critical factors for measuring crop requirements and the control of irrigation, both to optimize cropping and minimize waste. Frequency of irrigation and amount of water applied to fruit crops is a common concern among the fruit producers of India. Insufficient water supply may result in reduced tree growth, yield and fruit quality due to water stress. Excessive irrigation, on the other hand, may increase nutrient leaching, water-logging problems, incidence of pests and diseases and the associated cost of frequent operation and maintenance of the irrigation system. Optimizing water applications by scheduling irrigation to fruit orchards may increase water productivity, reduce production costs, and increase tree growth and fruit yield. Irrigation plays an important role in raising and stabilizing yield and maintaining quality of fruit crops.

Traditionally, agricultural research has focused primarily on maximizing total production. In recent years, focus has shifted to the limiting factors in production systems, notably the availability of either land or water. Within this context, deficit irrigation (DI) has been widely investigated as a valuable strategy. Deficit irrigation is an optimization strategy in which irrigation is applied during drought-sensitive growth stages of a crop. Outside these periods, irrigation is limited or even unnecessary if rainfall provides a minimum supply of water. Water restriction is limited to drought-tolerant phenological stages, often the vegetative stages and the late ripening period. Total irrigation application is therefore not proportional to irrigation requirements throughout the crop cycle. While this inevitably results in plant drought stress and consequently in production loss, DI maximizes water productivity, which is the main limiting factor (English, 1990). In other words, DI aims at stabilizing yields and at obtaining maximum WP rather than maximum yields.

The deficit irrigation can be obtained by increasing the interval between two irrigations, by reducing the amount of water applied during each of the irrigation or by combination of these two strategies. While scheduling the deficit irrigation for a particular crop, the stress should not become severe that the plant suffers permanently; instead, it should be moderate beneficial stress to which plant is subjected during non-critical phonological stages. To avoid the severe water stress, accurate assessment of plant water stress is essential. As mentioned earlier plant is the best indicator of its water stress and plant based indicators can be used for deficit irrigation scheduling.

REFERENCES

Aggarwal, M.C. and S.S. Khanna (1983).Efficient Soil and Water Management in Haryana. Bulletin of the Haryana Agricultural University, Hissar, Haryana, India. P: 118.

Agrawal, N. and S. Agrawal (2005). Effect of Drip Irrigation and Mulches on the Growth and Yield of Banana Cv. Dwarf Cavendish. *Indian J. Hort.*,62(3): 238 - 240.

Anonymous (2000). MPKV Extension Publication No. 298, Mahtma Phule Krishi Vidyapeeth, Rahuri, Maharashtra.

Anonymous (2008 a). Nutrient and Water Management through Fertigation in Papaya. 4th Meeting of Crop Production Sub Committee of Research Council, April, 9-10, 2008, pp. 9 - 14.

Anonymous (2009 b). Standardization of Stage Wise Water Requirement in Banana. Biennial Research Report, Indian Institute of Horticultural Research, Bangalore held at Thrissur 16th to 19th November, 2009, p. 149.

Anonymous (2009 d). Studies on Irrigation and Nutrient Interaction in Banana. Biennial Research Report, Indian Institute of Horticultural Research, Bangalore held at Thrissur 16th to 19th November, 2009, pp. 194-195.

Anonymous (2010 b). Large Scale Testing of Precision Farming Technologies in Papaya. Report of 6th Meeting of Natural Resources Management Joint Sub Committee, April 6-7, pp. 85-89.

Banker, M.C., M.C. Mane, K.K. Khade and S.T. Kanjle (1993).Comparative Performance of Drip vs Conventional Method of Irrigation on Banana. In: *Procs. All India Symposium on Sprinkler and Drip Irrigation,* 9-10 IEI: 89-92.

Berad, S. M., S. H. Shinde and S. D. Dahiwalkar (1998).Effect of Drip Fertigation and Paired Planting on Productivity and Economics of Banana. *J. Maharashtra Agric. Univ.,* 23(3): 288-290.

Biswas, R. K., S.K. Rana and S. Mallick (1999). Performance of Drip Irrigation in Papaya Cultivation in New Alluvium Agro-Climatic Zone of West Bengal. *Ann. Agric. Res.,* 20(1): 116-117.

Bryla, D.R., J.T. Thomas, E.A. James and R.S. Johnson (2003). Growth and Production of Young Peach Trees Irrigation by Furrow, Microjet, Surface Drip or Subsurface Drip Systems. Hort Science, 38: 1112-1116.

Demir, A.O., A. Korukcu and I. Arici (1995). Yield and Irrigation Water Requirement of Strawberry Irrigated with Furrow and Drip Irrigation Methods under Bursa Conditions. *Ulusal Kulturteknik Kongresi.* pp. 423-436.

Dwyer, L.M., D.W. Stewart, L. Houwing and M. Balchin (1987).Response of Strawberries to Irrigation Scheduling. *Horticulture Science,* 22: 42-44.

Evenhuis, A. and J. Alblas (2002). Irrigation of Strawberries by the use of Decision Support Systems. *Acta Horticulturae,* 567 (2): 475-478.

Fahad, A.H. and N. Hagemann (1992). Differences in Water Requirement with Sprinkler and Drip Irrigation. *Gartenbau Magazine,* 1(4): 64-65.

Goramnagar, H.B., P.K. Nagre, S.G. Bharad and D. Paithankar (2017).Effect of Micro-irrigation and Fertigation on Growth Parameter and Fruit Yield of Acid Lime. International J. Chemical Studies, 5 (6): 15-18

Grigorov, M.S., N.V. Kurapina and A.V. Malyuga (2000). Drip Irrigation of Vineyards in The Volga/Don Interfluve. *Sadovodstvo-i-Vinoqradarstvo,* 2: 19- 20.

Gunduz, M., N. Korkmaz, S. Asik, H.B. Unal and M. Avci (2011). Effects of Various Irrigation Regimes on Soil Water Balance, Yield and Fruit Quality of Drip-irrigated Peach Trees. J Irrig Drain Eng 137: 426-434.

Harendra Kumar, U. Kotoky, N. Lal, J. Kumar, K. Sinha and A. K. D. Anal (2015).Effect of Drip Fertigation on Yield and Productivity of Guava (PsidiumguajavaL.).Trends in Biosciences 8(2): 555-558.

Hedge, D.M. and K. Srinivas (1990).Growth, Productivity and Water use of Banana under Drip and Basin Irrigation in Relation to Evaporation Replenishment. Indian J. Agron., 35 (1-2): 106-112.

Hemant Kumar, P., N. Agrawal, R. Agrawal, S. Dubey and S.P. Tiwari (2010).Effect of Drip Irrigation and Polythene Mulch on the Fruit Yield and Quality Parameters of Mango (*Mangiferaindica* L.).*J. Hortl. Sci.,* 5 (2): 140-143,

Hoppula, R.I. and T.J. Salo (2007).Tensiometer Based Irrigation Scheduling in Perennial Strawberry Cultivation. *Irrigation Science,,*25: 401-409.

Junaid, N., Khan, A.K. Jain, R. Sharda, N. Singh, P.S.S. Gill and S. Kaur (2013). Growth, Yield and Nutrient Uptake of Guava (Psidium Guavaja L..affected by Soil Matric Potential, Fertigation and Mulching under Drip Irrigation. AgricEng International *CIGR J.,* 12:15-17.

Kanannavar, P.S., S.S. Kumathe, B.D. Premanand and N. Kawale (2009).Water Saving and Economics of Banana Production under Drip Irrigation in North Eastern Dry Zone of Karnataka. J. Birsa Agricultural University, 12: 39-42.

Khalifa, A.B.A. (2006). Comparison of Surface and Drip Irrigation Regimes for Banana (*Musa AAA*) cv. Grand Nain in Gezira, Sudan ((Master Degree Dissertation). Retrieved from https://ruforum.org/system/tdf/Ahmed%20Babiker%20Ahmed%20Khalifa%20%20 thesis.pdf?file=1&type=node&id=31642&force=

Kim, S.K., H.Y. Na, J.H. Song and M.J. Kim (2009). Influence of Water Stress on Fruit Quality and Yield of Strawberry cvs. 'Maehyang' and 'Seolhyang'. *ActaHorticulturae,* 842: 177-180.

Klamkowski, K. and W. Treder (2008).Response to Drought Stress of three Strawberry Cultivars Grown under Greenhouse Conditions.*Journal of Fruit and Ornamental Plant Research,* 16: 179-188.

Kruger, E., G. Schmidta and U.Bruckner (1999). Scheduling Strawberry Irrigation Based upon Tensiometer Measurement and a Climatic Water Balance Model. *Scientia Horticulturae,* 81: 409-424.

Kumar, D. and V. Pandey (2008).Effect of NPK Fertigation on Growth, Yield and Quality of Banana 'Rasthali' (AABPathkapoora) in Coastal Agro-climatic Conditions of Eastern India. Indian Journal of Agricultural Sciences, 78 (9): 798 - 800.

Kumar, H., U. Kotoky, and A. Devee (2013). Effect of Drip Fertigation on Growth of Guava (Psidiumguajava L.). *Asian J. Hort.,* 8 (2): 534 - 536.

Kumar, P.S., V.K. Chaudhary and R. Bhagawati (2012). Influence of Mulching and Irrigation Level on Water-use Efficiency, Plant Growth and Quality of Strawberry (*Fragariax Ananassa*). *Indian Journal of Agricultural Sciences,* 82(2): 127- 133.

Kumar, S. (2004).Effect of Drip Irrigation, Fertigation and Root Stocks on Apple Under High Density Planting. Ph.D. Thesis, Dr .Y.S. Parmar University of Horticulture and Forestry Nauni, Solan (H.P.) India.

Kumari, H., P.K. Yadav, A.K. Singh and S.K. Sharma (2013).Evaluation of Water Regime and Fertigation on Growth, Yield and Economics of Sweet Orange (Citrus Sinensis Osbeck. Cv. Mosambi. *Asian J. Hort.,* 8(2): 709 - 713.

Mali, S., B. Das, A.K. Singh, and A. Bhatnagar (2015).Effect of Fruit Stage Based Irrigation Scheduling on Yield, Quality and Irrigation Water use Efficiency of Litchi (Litchi Chinensis Sonn.)Cv. Shahi. *J. Bioscan,* 10 (1): 397 - 401.

Mandal, G., S. Kumar, R. Kumar and R. Singh (2007).Effect of Drip Irrigation and Plant Spacing on Yield, Quality and Economic Return of Guava (Psidium Guajava L)Grown in Saline Soil. *ActaHortic.,*60: 735 - 742.

Meshram, D.T., S.D. Gurantiwar, H.K. Mittal and R.C. Purohit (2009).Water Requirement of Pomegranate for Solapur District of Maharashtra State. In: Proc. of 2nd International Symposium on Pomegranate and Minor Including Mediterranean Fruits. USA, Dharward, India, pp: 1-169.

Meti, C.B., Y.R.Aladakatti, A.B. Patil, D.H. Mudkavi, B.M. Radder and G.Patil (2008). Studies on Optimum Wetted area and Pan Fraction for Higher Yield and Water use Efficiency of Pomegranate in Vertisols of Malaprabha Command Area. Karnataka J. of Agric. Sciences, 21 (3): 469 - 470.

Minami, K, A.F. Olitta, D. Barbin and C.G.B. Demetrio (1982).Study of Drip Irrigation in Strawberry (*Fragaria sp.*) Culture. In: Proceedings of the Tropical Region. *American Society for Horticultural Science,* 25: 363-370.

More, M. R., R. K. Patil, D. B. Tekale and G.V. Vaishnav (1999).Growth, Productivity, Water use and Economics of Banana Cultivation under Drip and Basin Irrigation System.*J. Soils and Crops*, 9(1): 23-25.

Muhammad, C. P., M.Joseph, R. F. Mary, S. Sajeena and V. Varughese (2005). Crop Geometry in Nendran Banana under Drip Irrigation.International Conference on Plasticulture and Precision Farming.17- 21 Nov, 2005, New Delhi, p. 197.

Narayanamoorthy A. (2003). Averting Water Crisis by Drip Method of Irrigation: A Study of two Water Intensive Crops. Indian Journal of Agricultural Economics, 58 (3): 427-437.

Ostrowska, K. and P. Chepinski (2003). The Effect of Drip Irrigation on the Yield and Content of Organic Compounds in Fruits of Three Strawberry Cultivars. *Folia Horticulturae,* 15 (2): 159-166.

Panigrahi, P and A.K. Srivastava (2011a). Integrated use of Water and Nutrients through Drip Irrigation in Nagpur Mandarin. J Agri. Eng., 48 (3): 44-51.

Parikh, M. M., N. G. Savani, P. K. Shrivastava and S. Raman (2002 a). Number and Spacing of Emitters Requirement for Drip Irrigated Banana. Global Conference on Banana and Plaintain, 28-31 October 2002, Bangalore, India, p. 113.

Patel, N.M. and M.M. Patel (1998). Water Requirement of Pomegranate (*Punicagranatum L.*) cv. Ganesh for Better Yield under Resources Limited Situations.In: Proc. of *National Seminar on New Horizons in Production and Post Harvest Management of Tropical and Subtropical Fruits*, Delhi, Dec. 8-9.

Pawar, B.R., V.V. Landge, D.S. Deshmukh and P.P. Yeware (2010). Economics of Banana Production in Drip Irrigated and Flood Irrigated Gardens. International Journal of Commerce and Business Management, 3: 88-91.

Prakash, K., R.M. Vijayakumar, T.M., Balamohan and S.D. Sundhar Singh, (2015). Effect of Drip Irrigation Regimes and Fertigation Levels on Yield and Quality of Mango Cultivar 'Alphonso' under Ultra High Density Planting. *ActaHortic,* 17:1066.

Pramanik, S.and R.K. Biswas (2012). Effect of Drip-Fertigation on Soil Moisture Distribution and Irrigation Water use Efficiency of Banana in West Bengal. Journal of Soil and Water Conservation, 11(3): 210 - 217.

Pramanik, S. and S.K. Patra (2014).Influence of Fertigation on Fruit Yield, Water use and Distribution Efficiency and Economics of Guava (Psidiumguajava L). *J. Soil and Water Conservation,* 13 (2): 164-169.

Pramanik, S. and S.K. Patra (2016). Growth, Yield, Quality and Irrigation Water use Efficiency of Banana Under Drip Irrigation and Fertigation in The Gangetic Plain of West Bengal. World Journal of Agricultural Sciences, 12(3): 220 - 228.

Pramanik, S., S.K. Tripathi R. Ray and H. Banerjee (2014).Economic Evaluation of Drip-Fertigation System in Banana cv. Martaman (AAB, Silk) Cultivation in New Alluvium Zone of West Bengal. *Agricultural Economics Research Review,* 27: 103-109

Rajput, R.K. (1983). Research on Water Management Progress Report. Project on Water Management, pp. 331.

Ramniwas, R.A. Kaushik and D.K. Sarolia (2012). Response of Irrigation and Fertigation Scheduling on Flowering, Physiological Parameters and Fruit Yield of Guava (*Psidiumguajava*L.) under High Density Planting *Annals of Agriculture Research New Series,* 33(3): 1- 6.

Ramniwas, R.A. Kaushik, S. Pareek, D.K. Sarolia and V.Singh (2013).Effect of Drip Fertigation Scheduling on Fertilizer use Efficiency, Leaf Nutrient Status, Yield and Quality of Shweta

Guava (*PsidiumguajavaL.*) under Meadow Orcharding.*National Academy Science Letter*, 36(5): 483- 485.

Ramniwas, R.A., D.K. Kaushik, S. S. Pareek and V. Singh (2012).Effect of Irrigation and Fertigation Scheduling on Growth and Yield of Guava (*PsidiumguajavaL.*) under Meadow Orcharding. African J Agricultural Research, 47 (7): 6350 – 6356.

Rzekanowski, C.Z. and S.T. Rolbiecki (2000). The Influence of Drip Irrigation on Yield of Some Cultivars of Apple Trees in Central Poland under Different Rainfall Conditions During The Vegetation Season. *ActaHorticulturae*, 537: 929-928.

Salvin, S., K. Baruah and S. K. Bordoli (2000). Drip Irrigation Studies in Banana Cv. Barjahaji. *Crop Research* (Hissar).,20(3): 489-493.

Sarolia, D.K., A.K. Shukla, P. Singh and N.P. Upadhyay (2005).Response of Micro-irrigation on Plant Growth of Sardar Guava under Semi- Arid Conditions of Rajasthan. In: Proc. of Inter. Conference on Plastic and Precision Farming. 17-21 November, 2005 at IARI, New Delhi. P: 134 - 138.

Serrano, L., X. Carbonell, R. Save, D. Marfa and J. Penuelas (1992).Effect of Irrigation Regimes on the Yield and Water use of Strawberry. *Irrigation Science*, 13(1): 45-48.

Sharma, I.P., S. Kumar and P. Kumar (2005). Effect of Drip Irrigation and Mulches on Yield, Quality and Water-use Efficiency in Strawberry under Mid Hill Conditions. *ActaHorticulturae*, 696: 259-264.

Sharma, K. and Kispotta (2014).Assessment of The Impact of Irrigation and Fertigation on Growth and Yield of Guava (*Psidiumguajava* L.) under Meadow Orcharding. *Int. J. Irrigation and Water Manage*, 7: 122-124.

Sharma, S. (2009).Studies on Drip vs. Flood Irrigation and Nitrogen Dynamics in Guava (*Psidiumguajava* L.) in New Alluvial Zone of West Bengal. Bidhan Chandra Krishi Viswavidyalaya, Department of Soil and Water Conservation, Faculty of Agriculture. Mohanpur, Nadia. P: 27-28.

Shashidhara, K.K., A. Bheemappa, L.V. Hirevekanagoudar and K.C. Shashidhar (2007). Benefits and Constraints in Adoption of Drip Irrigation Among the Plantation Crop Growers. Karnataka Journal of Agricultural Science, 20 (1): 82- 84.

Shelke, D. K., V. G. Vaishaava, S. R. Oza and G. S. Jadhav (1998). Management of Irrigation in Banana through Drip Irrigation System.*J. Maharashtra Agric. Univ.*, 23(3): 317-318.

Shirgure, P.S, A.K. Srivastava and S. Singh (2001). Effect of Pan Evaporation Based Irrigation Scheduling on Yield and Quality of Drip Irrigated Nagpur Mandarin (*Citrus Reticulate*). Indian J Agric. Sci., 71(4): 264–266.

Shirgure, P.S. 2013.Yield and Fruit Quality of Nagpur Mandarin (Citrus Reticulata Blanco. as Influenced by Evaporation Based Drip Irrigation Schedules. *Scientific J. Crop Sci.*, 2(2): 28-35.

Shirgure, P.S., A.K. Srivastava and A.D. Huchche (2014). Water Requirements in Growth Stages and Effects of Deficit Irrigation on Fruit Productivity of Drip Irrigated Nagpur Mandarin (*Citrus Reticulata*). Indian J Agric. Sci., 84 (3): 317-322.

Shirgure, P.S., Srivastava, A.K., Singh and A. Shyam (2003). Irrigation Scheduling and Fertigation in Acid Lime (Citrus Aurantifolia. *Indian J. Agri. Sci.*, 73: 363-367.

Shukla, A.K., D.K. Sarolia, R.A. Kaushik and V. Singh (2017).Effect of Micro Irrigation on Growth, Yield and Quality of Sardar Guava under Semi Arid Conditions of Rajasthan. Journal of Agriculture and Ecology, 3: 33-37.

Singh, B.K., K.N. Tiwari, S.K. Chourasia and S. Mandal (2007).Crop Water Requirement of Guava (Psidiumguajava L.) CvKaji under Drip Irrigation and Plastic Mulch. *ActaHortic.*, 735: 56 -57.

Singh, V.K., M.K. Soni and Anurag Singh (2015).Effect of Drip Irrigation and Polyethylene Mulching on Fruit Yield and Quality of Guava cv. Allahabad Safeda under Meadow Orcharding. Indian Journal of Horticulture, 72 (4): 479 – 484.

Sivanappan, R.K. (1993). Increased Production and Income in Banana Crop through Drip Irrigation-a Case Study. Technical Journal, All India Symp. on Spriakla and Drip Irrigation IEI, 21 (1): 105-106.

Srinivas, K. (1996 a).Growth, Yield and Water use of Papaya under Drip Irrigation. *Indian J. Hort.*, 53(1): 19-22.

Srinivas, K. (1996 b). Plant Water Relations, Yield and Water use of Papaya at Different Evaporation-replenishment Rates under Drip Irrigation. *Tropical Agriculture,* 73(4):264-269.

Srinivas, K. (1998). Standardization of Micro Irrigation in Fruit Crops – An Overview. In Proc. Micro Irrigation and Sprinkler Irrigation Systems. 28-30 April, 1998, CBIP, New Delhi, pp. II 30-33.

Srinivas, K. and D.M. Hedge (1990). Drip Irrigation Studies in Banana. In: *Procs. XI International Congress*. pp. 151-157.

Srivastava, P.K., M.M. Parikh, N.G. Sawani and S. Raman (1999).Response of Banana to Drip Irrigation, Mulches and Irrigation Scheduling in South Gujarat. *Agril. Engg. Today*, 23: 29-38.

Sujatha, S., J. Rao and N.N. Reddy (2006).Effect of Drip Irrigation and Nutrient Management of Mango (Mangiferaindica. in Alfisols of semi- arid tropics.*The Indian J. Agri. Sci.*, 76: 10 - 13.

Suresh, R. and D. P. Saha (2004).Effect of Mulching and Drip Irrigation on Papaya in Calcareous Soil of North Bihar. *Progressive horticulture*, 36 (1):76-81.

Tank, R.V. and N.L. Patel (2013). Influence of Fertigation on Yield and Nutrient Status in Soil and Leaf of Papaya (Carica Papaya L.var. Madhu Bindhu under South Gujarat Condition. *Asian J. Hort.*, 8 (1): 170-173.

Tekinel, D., R. Kanber, S. Onder, N. Baytorun, R. Bastug, J.R. Rydzewsjd and C.F. Ward (1989). The Effect of Trickle and Conventional Irrigation Method on Some Crops, Yield and Water use Efficiency under Cukurova Conditions. *Irrigation Theory and Practice,* P:641-651.

Thadchayini, T. and S. Thiruchelvam (2005). An Economic Evaluation of a Drip Irrigation Project for Banana Cultivation in Jaffna District. Water Professional Day Symposium. Water Resources Research in Sir Lanka.

Tiwari, K.N., M. Kumar, D.T. Santosh, V.K. Singh and M.K. Maji (2014). Influence of Drip Irrigation and Plastic Mulch on Yield of Sapota (Achraszapota) and Soil Nutrients. Irrigation & Drainage Systems Engineering., 3 (1): 116 - 124.

WTC (1985-2003). Annual Reports of Water Technology Centre, Tamil Nadu Agricultural University, Coimbatore.

Young, S.C.H., T.W. Sammins and I. Wu (1985). Banana Yield as Affected by Deficit Irrigation and Patterns of Lateral Layouts. Transactions of ASAE., 28:507-510.

Yuan, B.Z., J. Sun and S. Nishiyama (2004).Effect of Drip Irrigation on Strawberry and Yield Inside a Plastic Greenhouse. *Biosystems Engineering,* 87(2): 237- 245.

Horticulture and Ecology - ***Studies & Management*** **Pages 116-129**
Edited by: **Dr. Alka Chauhan and Dr. Pawan Kumar 'Bharti'**
ISBN: 978-93-88854-09-2
Edition: **2019**
Published by: **Discovery Publishing House Pvt. Ltd., New Delhi (India)**

6

Post Harvest Technology of Citrus Fruit

[1]Awadhesh Kumar, [2]Bhagwan Deen and [3]Pragya Ojha

ABSTRACT

All the technologies are applied from harvesting of fruits to its final consumption is called as post harvest technology. Development of processing industry takes care of surplus produce as well as of those fruits that are of lower quality. With the development of processing industry citrus fruits can be utilized for the production of wide range of commercial products. The large variability in physico-chemical characteristics of citrus fruits provides an opportunity to select desirable types for commercial exploitation. In India citrus fruit is available in large quantity that can be processed in to different processed products very easily. The fresh citrus fruits are not consumed in large quantity as fresh fruit due to high acidic in taste. The post-harvest technology including value addition would provide opportunity for commercial exploitation of the citrus fruits and leads to the marketing and processing in to quality products.

Keywords: Post harvest technology, Processing, Physiological disorders, Squash, Cardial, Marmalade.

Introduction

In developing country like India post harvest losses of citrus fruits are in the range of 25-30% as against 5-10% in developed citrus growing countries like Brazil, USA, Australia, Spain and Israel. This is mainly due to the unscientific practices of picking, handling, packaging, transport and storage. In order to improve its post harvest technology system, an understanding of the nature of citrus fruit, various factors influencing the post harvest shelf-life and quality and the state of post harvest technology will be a pre-requisite. Citrus is generally characterized as less perishable fruit in comparison to loquat, litchi,

1 Technical Assistant, Department of Agriculture, Government of Uttar Pradesh, Faizabad District (UP), India
2 Professor, Department of Horticulture, N.D. University of Agriculture and Technology Faizabad, U.P. India
3 Subject Matter Specialist, Krishi Vigyan Kendra Banda, Banda University of Agriculture and Technology Banda, U.P., India

fresh fig (Kader and Arpaia, 2002). According to Murata (2001) respiration of citrus fruits, this is an important determinant of the fruit shelf-life, influenced by temperature, humidity movement of air composition of gases bruises and microbial infection. Post harvest losses of citrus fruits can be minimized by adopting the proper harvesting and handling practices and storage conditions.

In tropical and subtropical countries developed fruits are affected by the temperature. Maturity of the rind and maturity of the flesh of the fruit are not synchronized. The fruit is edible even when the rind still remains green. Mature fruit vary in size, even those on the same tree. With sweet orange such as Valencia, harvesting should begin with the smaller fruit which mature first. Some time a chemical treatment is applied of the fruit before storage, to reduce the incidence of post harvest diseases. Application of plant growth regulator and fungicide at pre-harvest stage reduces the colour development and microbial spoilage. The treatment with 2, 4-D improved the maintaining colour for longer duration during storage period. Treatment of ethephon resulted the decay loss due to *Aspergillus niger*, *Penicillium italicum* in citrus fruits. Thus the long quantity of highly nutritive fruits is lost due to poor handling practices and inadequate storage and processing facilities. Since the cost involved in preventing the losses is always cheaper than the cost of production, therefore post harvest technology receives greater attention. In this chapter several post harvest technologies have been summarized to minimize the post harvest losses of citrus fruits.

Changes During Maturation/Ripening of Citrus

(A) Physical Changes

1. Size of fruits: Usually the greatest increase in diameter precedes the attainment of prime eating condition. The volume and weight of the citrus fruits increase simultaneously.

- Sweet oranges- Diameter and weight increases up to November.
- Mandarin orange- Increases up to November to December.
- Grape fruit- Increases up to December.
- Sweet lime- Diameter and weight increase up to September.
- Lemons- In spring season set fruit develops more rapidly than fall set fruit.

2. Weight: The fruit weight increases with the maturation of citrus fruits or when fruit is in prime eating quality due to an increase in pulp weight and in amount of soluble solids and sugars in the juice. In over mature fruits weight decreased due to dryness of juice vesicles.

3. Rind thickness: Rind thickness increases gradually from immature stage to large and over ripe stage. In mandarin, grape fruit and sweet lime rind thickness decreased gradually with the maturity of fruits.

4. Rind colour: Slightly rind colours changing in different colours are below:

(*i*) **Sweet lime:** Deep green changes to yellow colour or slight orange yellow colour.

(*ii*) **Lemon:** Green to different shades of yellow colour.

(*iii*) **Mandarin:** Skin colour changes from green to orange and harvesting from December to January.

(*iv*) **Grape fruits:** Appear of pink colour due to lycopene in red fleshed variety such as Ruby.

5. Colour and texture of flesh: No abrupt change occurs in mandarin orange it changes from yellow to orange.

6. Juice content: Juice content increases up to maturity of prime eating condition. It decreases in over ripe fruits. According to International Standards Organization (ISO) juice content at maturity stage should be as under in following fruits.

(*i*) Sweet oranges as Washington Navel orange and Thomson Navel 30 per cent and other varieties are 35 per cent.

(*ii*) Mandarin minimum juice content 33 per cent.

(*iii*) Grapefruit must be 35 per cent.

(*iv*) Lemon should be not less than 25 per cent.

7. Rag and peel content: In citrus fruit usually rag and peel content decreased at ripening period.

B. Chemical Changes

1. **pH and acidity:** The pH value (the measure of active acidity) gradually increases as fruit ripened in mandarins (2.8 to 4.0) and sweet orange (3 to 4.2). Similarly pH value increases in sweet lime, lemon and grape fruit. Total titratable acidity content decreases during ripening of fruits.
2. **Ascorbic acid:** Highest amount of ascorbic acid per unit of the juice was found in immature fruits. The fruits ripened it gradually decreased and lowest values were found late in the season or over ripe fruits.
3. **Sugars**: non-reducing sugar content increases slowly up to maturity in sweet orange, mandarin orange and grape fruit. Level remains constant up to prime eating quality thereafter decreases in over ripe fruits.
4. **Total soluble solids:** Increases up to maturity in sweet orange, mandarin orange and grape fruit thereafter level decreases in over ripe fruits.
5. **TSS/ acid ratio:** TSS/acid ratio increases in sweet and mandarin oranges as the fruits mature because of an increase in TSS content and decrease in acidity level.
6. **Total Ash:** Higher in immature fruits, decreases during maturation period and a slight increase can be noticed in very ripe fruits of grape fruit.

7. **Carotene:** Increases in lime, lemon (1mg/100g), sweet orange and mandarin orange.
8. **Chlorophyll:** Chlorophyll content both a and b decreases and reached to zero at maturity stage.
9. **Pectin:** Pectin content increases in citrus up to maturity and decreases in post (as a Ca pectate) maturity period.

Maturity Standards

Maturity: Stage of fruit development during which fruit attains full growth and development is called maturity.

Ripening: It refers terminal period of maturation of fruits during which fruits attain maximum aesthetic and edible quality.

Citrus fruits should be harvested at right stage of maturity since it decides the quality, storage life and transportation of fruits.

In India citrus fruit is generally harvested on the basis of colour. Fruits are considered fully mature for harvesting when they change colour from green to yellow. However, the colour break cannot be always taken as the reliable criteria to judge the maturity for oranges. Colour breaks depends upon the climatic conditions and it is observed that in the high rain fall regions fruits may sometime remain green externally but internally pulp has sweetened and colour changed. In such circumstances few fruit should be plucked from the tree and should be examined for their characteristics flavor and taste of the variety then it should be picked. In other counties citrus fruits are harvested on the basis of size, colour, juice content, TSS, titratable acidity and TSS/acid ratio.

Limitations: Maturity standards varies from:

1. Region to region
2. Species to species
3. Varieties to varieties
4. Position of the fruit (out and inner of canopy)
5. Climatic conditions
6. Area of production

Causes of Post Harvest Spoilage in Citrus Fruits

Post harvest spoilage of citrus fruits is problem of considerable significance in countries characterized by tropical conditions. Post harvest losses are characterized by high wastage i.e. 20-40 per cent. These losses occur at different stages in the chains of picking, packing transport, poorly equipped market, insufficient storage and poor stage of processing.

The most important causes of spoilage are classified in following categories:

1. **Mechanical injury:** Fruits may be bruised or injured during various stage of post harvest handling particularly at the time of harvesting. Spoilage can also occur during packaging and transportation if, precaution is not taken. Injured fruits do not fetch good price and they become the source of entry to micro-organism. Green mold (*Penicillium digitatum*) and Blue mold (*Penicillium italici*)enter through injury and causes serious spoilage.
2. **Physiological disorder after harvesting of citrus fruit:** Physiological disorders significantly influence the quality of citrus fruits in the markets. Post harvest factors affect the occurrence of physiological disorders of the fruits (Grierson, 1981). Post harvest factors humidity, temperature, mechanical stress, gaseous composition and ageing affect occurrence of physiological disorders. The physiological disorders are briefly summarized as following.
   (*a*) **Oleocellosis:** This disorder mostly found in all varities of citrus fruit but specially attacks in lemon, limes and orange. Oleocellosis appears when the temperature is high (Calero *et al.*, 1981).Bruising causes the liberation of oil cells in the rind. This brings superficial brown spitting over the peel known as Oleocellosis and lowers the market value of the fruits particularly limes and lemons. Care should be taken that fruit should not be injured during harvesting and handling.
   (*b*) **Red Blotch:** Black regular spots appear on the surface of fruits particularly in lemon fruit during storage period. Harvest fruits at green mature stage.
   (*c*) **Watery breakdown:** Watery break down is a kind of low temperature disorder occurs when fruits stored at below 4.5°C temperature. Affected fruits produced off flavor of fermentation when stored fruits transferred from the cold storage to ambient temperature. The flesh and rind of citrus fruits affected with watery breakdown are soft and spongy is the symptoms of the disorder.
   (*d*) **Black buttons:** When fruits are stored in polythene bag particularly without ventilation colour of buttons becomes black due to high humidity. Application of 2, 4-D at 100 ppm as post harvest treatments checks these problems.
   (*e*) **Chilling injuries:** It occurs mostly in lemon, lime, grape fruit and pummelo (Eaks, 1980 and Murata, 1990). It starts to 10°C in Lemon and 4.4°C in Kagzi lime. Symptoms of chilling injury in citrus fruits are pitting, superficial brown staining of the rind, discoloured patches, browning of the albedo and watery breakdown. Chilling injury can be affected by delayed storage, packaging and treatment

with CO_2, ethylene, vegetable oils and sugar esters as well as by low temperature. This disorder can be alleviated by temperature conditioning (McDonald *et al.*, 1993), sucrose fatty acid esters (Murata, 1990) and by film packaging (McDonald, 1986)

(*f*) **Puffiness:** Puffiness disorder is common in mandarins and rare in lemon and oranges. Puffiness shows itself as a separation of the peel from the pulp during storage (Grierson, 1981 and Murata, 1981). As the result of advanced maturity, vigour of the tree and high humidity in the storage room, the rind become thickened and separates from the pulp. Incidence of this disorder can be managed by the air movement in the storage room (Murata, 1981).

(*g*) **Granulation:** The granulation occurs at high level of humidity, high as well as low temperatures, age and vigour of tree, nutritional status, late harvesting in the season or from young trees. A symptom of the disorder is that extractable juice is severely decreased due to gel formation within the vesicles. Spray of 2, 4-D at 12 ppm and/or application of copper and zinc reduces the granulation problem.

3. Post harvest diseases: Citrus fruits are susceptible to invasion by fungi bruises and skin breaks. In particular, *Penicillium spp.,* which causes serious damage of blue-mould and green-mould rotin all varieties of citrus fruits, is a typical fungus of wound infection. It is important to reduce the distribution of micro-organisms on the fruit surface by use of fungicidal spray before harvest. The following diseases of citrus fruits are due to fungal infection are summarized as below:

1. Green Mould: This disease is caused by *Penicillium digitatum* it is important post harvest disease of citrus fruit in storage. Its pathogen attack on tree or in packaging house, transit, storage and market. *Penicillium digitatum* pathogen are wound parasites but will spread by contact of the affected fruit.

(*i*) **Source of entering:** Stem end of the fruit is source of entry, and it is major source of post harvest decay in fruit and is responsible for the wide spread of post harvest diseases in citrus fruit known as citrus rot.

(*ii*) **Symptoms**: Peel of fruits become soft, watery, breaks easily with pressing and fungus growth is olive-green in colour, surrounded by a broad zone of white mycelium.

Control: Spray with 0.1-0.2% benlate or benomyl and 6 to 9% waxol before harvest of the fruit.

2. Blue mould: It is plant pathogen but it is post harvest disease commonly associated with citrus fruits. Blue mould pathogens are grows at temperatures too low in storage house. Blue mould is more common in long term storage at low temperature. Blue mould is caused by *Penicillium italicum* and mode of infection is similar to green mould. In this case fungus growth in blue colour mycellium and surrounded by white mycelium, almost up to the edge.

Management: Inoculation of healthy fruit can be diminished and controlled by careful picking, handling and packaging of the citrus so that the rinds are not damaged. Without of injury infected on the fruit, the conidia are unable to again access, and thus unable to germinate in to infectious pathogen. Spray of 10 ppm of GA_3 before harvest checks the infection of this fungus during storage.

3. Aspergillus rot: This rot is caused by *Aspergillus niger* and 10-15% limes are spoiled through this fungus. Its spread is very fast in high humidity. Prevent injury during harvest. Remove injured fruits if any before packing and storage are the effective control measures of as pergillus rot.

4. Black rot: The *Alternaria citri* is the causal organism of black rot. Specially certain lemon, lime, orange, mandarin and grape fruit species are susceptible hosts for this pathogen. The fruit infected by black rot produces blackish-green mycelium on the surface in Satsuma mandarins. There are no external symptoms of this disease.

Management: Fruit harvesting at optimum maturity is advisable by clipping the fruit and not snapping it. Snapping refers to the act of pulling the fruit and damaging the stalk end of the fruit. Treat the fruits with wax emulsion containing 2, 4-D at 100 ppm.

5. Stem end rot: It is common post harvest diseases of citrus that is caused by *Botryodiplodia theobromate*. Malta fruits are more affected by stem end rot. This disease occurs mostly in warm, humid regions. Symptoms appear as water-soaked spots near the stem end of the fruit, which then turn tan to blackish-brown. Treat the fruits with 6 to 9 % borax or preharvest spray of benlate (500ppm) effectively controls the rot.

(C) Post Harvest Treatments

1. Waxing: Waxing of fruits is done for prevention of wilting, shriveling, mold infection checking and prolong storage life.

2. Plant Growth Regulators-

(*i*) **Ethephon:** Used for decomposing the green pigment in fruits. Decomposing of green pigments is known as degreening. Degreening practices are mostly done in limes and lemons. Degreening can be obtained by applying ethephon at 500-1500 ppm.

(*ii*) **2, 4-D (2, 4 Dichlorophenoxy acetic acid):** The treatment of 2, 4-D is given to extend the storage life of lemon fruits.

(*iii*) **GA_3:** This plant growth regulator is applied for degreening of citrus fruits.

3. Chemicals-

Sorbic acid: Application of sorbic acid checks the spoilage in Nagpur orange during storage.

Wax: Coating of fruits with wax emulsion increases storage life and marketability of Coorg mandarin and Sath-gudi orange.

Borax: Application of borax (0.8%) reduces Penicillium rot.

Grading

The fruit are inspected during grading and unripe, immature, undersized, damaged or decayed fruits are discarded. For local market, the citrus fruits are graded as per the size in to small, medium and large grades. The differences between categories will depend on the type of fruit. For exports of Nagpur mandarins, the various grades recommended are the follows:

Grade size (mm)	No. of fruits/10 kg packing
50-55	115
55-60	98
60-65	84
65-70	76
70-75	64

Packaging: Packaging adds value to citrus fruit as it protects the fruit at all stages of transportation, storage and marketing. Efficient packaging can increase shelf-life of fruits at both room and low temperature. Packaging does not improve citrus fruit quality but it retains quality.

Packaging Containers

A wide range of packaging containers used for the marketing of citrus fruits.

Packaging containers	Citrus fruits
Gunny bags and fiber carton	Sweet orange, lemon, lime
Wooden boxes	Mandarin
Plastic Boxes/ crates	Kinnow, mandarin

Storage: Fruit after harvest respires and have life. It is difficult to stop the life process but it can be minimized. The principle aims of storage are to control the rate of respiration, transpiration, ripening and also undesirable biochemical changes and diseases infection. One of the effective methods of storage of fresh produce after harvest is low temperature and high humidity storage.

The optimum storage temperature and relative humidity for citrus fruit in low temperature storage areas under.

Fruit	Temperature (°C)	Humidity (%)	Storage life (weeks)
Sweet orange	6-7	85-90	16
Mandarins	6-7	85-90	8

Processing of Citrus Fruits

Edible Products

1. Juices: (*i*) Bottling or canning: Both Mandarin and Sweet orange can be used.

Fruits
↓
Washing
↓
Peeling (hand peeling)
↓
Separation of segments and their cleaning
↓
Juice extraction (Screw type juice ex tractor or motorizedextractor)
↓
Straining
↓
Heating (175-1800F)
↓
Bottling or canning
↓
Crown corking or cane sealing
↓
Pasteurization(20-25 minutes) as simmeringwaterStorage
↓
Storage

Sweet oranges, such as Malta, Mosambi give a good canned juice free from any bitterness. The juice from mandarin oranges however, often develops on heating a characteristic bitter taste in the cane or bottle. This bitterness is not acceptable. Limonin is the chemical substances which impart bitterness to the juice or heat processing.

The bitterness in the juice can be reduced considerably by extracting the juice from the segments dipped in 2% boiling alkali (NaOH) for 30 to 60 seconds to remove the outer covering of the segments and the fibrous materials which cause bitterness in the juice when the juice is extracted from the segments in a screw type juice extractor. Addition of 5 to 6% sugar also helps in reducing the bitter taste of the canned juice.

To improve the quality and retain its vitamin-C content the juices is generally deairated and flesh pasteurized. Preservation of orange juice in its purity with all its natural flavor is still a technical problem.

(*ii*) Orange juice concentrate: In some countries concentration of pure fruit juice is highly popular. Citrus juice concentrates are in great demand in U.K., Europe and USA for feeding children (as source of Vitamin-C) for carbonation and for use in ice creams etc.

Juices are concentrated either by freezing and centrifuging or by evaporation under reduced pressure at low temperature so that their original flavors are not completely lossed. Frozen orange juice concentrate of 4:1 strength is a highly popular product in the USA. It is reconstituted into orange juice and is served.

In the freezing process known as cores process the juice is frozen into a mushy mixture of Ice crystals and juice or into a solid cake of ice which is broken up later. On centrifuging the broken mass in a basket-type centrifuge, ice crystals are retained in the basket where as the concentrated juice passes through centrifuged and partially concentrated juice is again frozen and recentrifuged to remove more of water and raise the Brix to 50 degrees. This concentrate either be held in cold storage or pasteurized to prevent spoilage.

***(iii)* Carbonated juice:** Juices can be carbonated directly. Carbonated beverage keep well for about a week without the addition of any preservative.

***(iv)* Fermented Juice** (Orange wine): Orange juice sweetened with cane sugar, can be fermented to make a fairly good wine. The method of preparation is practically similar to that employed in the case of grape wine.

***(v)* Squash:** Squash is a type of fruit beverage prepared by fruit pulp, sugar and acidity. Squashes are diluted 3 times with water before serving. Orange, lime and lemons, specifications for beverage making are:

Sl.No.	Product Name	Juice %	TSS ^{0}Brix	Acidity	Preservative
1	Squash	25	45	1.00	350 ppm SO_2
2	Crush	25	55	1.20	350 ppm SO_2
3	Syrup	25	65	1.20	350 ppm SO_2, if syrup TSS 70% not SO_2 is required
4	Lime juice, Cordial	25	35	1.50	350 ppm SO_2
5	Lemon Barley water	25	45	1.50	350 ppm SO_2
6	RTS (Mandarin orange)	10	13-15	0.30	70 ppm SO_2
7	Lemon juice	5	13-15	0.30	70 ppm SO_2

***(vi)* Cordial:** It is a type of fruit beverage which contains fruit juice, sugar, preservatives and colours. It is clear sparkling sweetened clarified juice with gelatin and prepared same as squash but the suspended pulp particles are totally removed by filtration.

***(vii)* Citrus marmalade:** The term marmalade is generally associated with the product made from citrus fruits such as Orange and Lemon, in which shredded peels is used as a suspended material.

In the home, marmalade can be prepared by following combination:

(*i*) Khatta or lime 0.5 kg

(*ii*) Sweet orange (Malta)-1 kg

After pectin extraction

(*i*) Sugar 750g

(*ii*) Shredded peel 62 g

(*iii*) Pectin extracts 1L

Citrus marmalades are classified in to jelly marmalades and jam marmalades:

Jelly marmalade: Following combination can give good jelly marmalades.

(*a*) Sweet orange (Malta) and Khatta or sour orange (*Citrus aurantium* L.) in 2:1 by weight shreds used from Malta.

(*b*) Mandarin orange and Khatta in 2:1 by weight shreds used from Malta.

(*c*) Sweet orange (Malta) and galgal (*Citrus limonia* L.) in 2:1 by weight shreds from Malta.

The following flow chart can be used for the preparation of jelly marmalade-

Ripened fruit
↓
Washing
↓
Peel outer yellow (flavedo) portion thinly
↓
Cut out yellow portion into fine shreds
↓
Peeled fruits are cut into slices 0.3 to 0.45 cm think or Crush into pulp and grater, to facilitate pectin extraction.
↓
Boiling for extraction of pectin (boiling in 2-3 times its weight of water 45-6 0 minutes) Strain the juice or clear it
↓
Test for its pectin content (alcohol test)
↓
Add sugar as per pectin test Cooking continuously up to 103°C temperature
↓
Add prepared shreds (peel is cut into shreds and shredded peel is boiled for 10-15 minutes in
↓
several changes of water remove bitterness) and softening
↓
Boiling till jellying point (62g/kg of extract)
↓
Test for end point sheeting/drop/temperature test i.e. 105°C
↓
Cooling (82-880C)
↓
Flavouring
↓
Filling
↓
Scaling
↓
Storage

Jam marmalade: The method of preparation of the jam type marmalade is practically the same as that for making jelly marmalade. In this pectin extract of fruit is not clarified. The whole pulp mass is used.

Pickle: The preservation of food in common salt or vinegar is called pickling. Spices and oil may also be added to the palatability of the meals. Salt, vinegar and lactic acid are the important ingredients and act as preservatives. Citrus pickles are prepared from Lime and lemon.

Lime pickle: There are two types of lime pickle

1. Hot lime pickle, and 2. Sweet lime pickle

Hot Lime Pickle

S.No.	Ingredients	Amount
1	Lime	1 kg
2	Salt	60 g
3	Red chillies powder	120 g
4	Mustard seed	30 g
5	Turmeric powder	5 g
6	Vinegar	300 mL
7	Gingeeli oil	1 kg
8	Green chillies	250 g
9	Cumin (Jeera)	5 g
10	Cumey leaves	10-15 g

The following flow chart shows the process of hot lime pickle preparation:

Fruits
↓
Cut in quarters
↓
Dry in sun for 2 days after sprinkling salt over them
↓
Grund all ingredients except green chillies in vinegar
↓
Heat oil
↓
Green chillies and cumey leaves a littled lengthwise and added followed by other ingredients
↓
Finally lime piece are added and boiled for just 5-10 minutes
↓
Filled in clean glass jars
↓
Cap it
↓
Storage

Sweet Lime Pickle

Sl.No.	Ingredients	Amount
1	Limes	1 kg
2	Jiggery	1 kg
3	Salt	30 g
4	Red chillies powder	30 g

Flow chart for sweet lime pickle making:

Fruits

↓

Cut in to small pieces and mixed with salt and chilli powder

↓

Put in alternate layer of jaggery

↓

Heat the contents and boil for 5minutes

↓

Fill into clean dry glass jars

10. Citrus peel candy: Candied peels are prepared for bakery and confectionary products. Only thick skined fruits like citron, grape fruit and pumelo are suitable for candy making. The method described in following flow chart can be used for candy making:

Peel (Remove rages white pithy portion)

↓

Cured in 5-10 % salt solution for 10-15 days

↓

Store in 12% salt solution with 1000 ppm of potassium metabisulphite

↓

Washed cured peel by repeated washing and soaking in warm water (for free of salt)

↓

Peel caps are pricked with forks

↓

Dipped in 30°Brix

↓

Raise 60° Brix

↓

Add citric acid 1.25g/kg of peel

↓

Syrup strength is raised up 75°Brix

↓

Peels are left insyrup for 2-3 weeks

↓

Dried on trays at room temperature till they are no longer sticky

(B) By Products

Essential oil from peel: Used for flavouring and perfumery trade

Fixed oil: Manufacture of soap and plastic materials and medicinal value

Pectin: Pectin is one of the most important by-products used in manufacturing of jam, jellies and marmalade

Citric acid: It is used as acidulents in fruits and vegetable processing industry.

Citrus molasses: 45% total sugar as in rest sugars.

Flavanoids: 30 flavanoids have been found in citrus fruit.

(*i*) **Hesperidin:** Blossom, small unripe fruits and peel of mature sweet orange. It is also found in lemon, mandarins and citron. It is therapeutic agent in pharmaceutical industry.

(*ii*) **Naringin:** Grapes fruit and pumelo it is extreme bitterness. Naringin is used in preparation of beverage drinks.

(*iii*) **Tanegeration**: Tanegerines.

(*iv*) **Limonin:** Lemon.

REFERENCES

Calero FA, Guillen C, Escriche. Physiological Disorders in the Storage of Lemon Fruits. Proceedings of the International Society of Citriculture. 1981; 2: 768-772.

Eaks IL. Effect of Chilling Respiration and Volatiles California Lemon Fruit. Journal of American Society Horticulture Science. 1980; 105: 865-869.

Grierson W. Physiological Disorders of Citrus Fruits. Proceedings of the International Society of Citriculture. 1981; 2: 764-767.

Kader AA. and Arpaia ML. Postharvest Handling Systems of Subtropical Crops, In A. A. Kader, ed. Postharvest Technology of Horticultural Crops, 3 ed. University of California, Agriculture and Natural Resources Publication. 2002; 3311.

McDonald RE, McCollum TG, Nordby HE. Temperature Conditioning and Surface Treatment of Grapefruit Affect Expression of Chilling and Gas Diffusion. Journal of the American Society for Hort Science. 1993; 118: 490-496.

McDonald RE. Effects of Vegetable Oils, CO_2 and Film Wrapping on Chilling Injury and Decay of Lemons. Hort Science. 1986; 24: 475-477.

Murata T. Relation of Chilling Stress to Membrane Permeability. Chilling Injury of Horticultural Crops. In: Wand CY (ed.) CRC Press Inc, Boca Raton, Florida. 1990; 201-209.

Murata T. Citrus, In SK Mitra, ed. Postharvest Physiology and Storage of Tropical and Subtropical Fruits. CAB International. 2001; 21-46.

Horticulture and Ecology - *Studies & Management* **Pages 130-139**
Edited by: **Dr. Alka Chauhan and Dr. Pawan Kumar 'Bharti'**
ISBN: 978-93-88854-09-2
Edition: **2019**
Published by: **Discovery Publishing House Pvt. Ltd., New Delhi (India)**

7

Ecological Status of Pteridophytes at Nagaon District of Assam

[1]Dr. Ashok K. Rathoure

ABSTRACT

Nagaon is the most populous district of Assam and one of the largest in area. It is known as the rice bowl of Assam. Nagaon district spreads in 3993 sq. km having 28,26,006 populations, Kaziranga National Park and Lowkhowa Wildlife Sanctuary. *Pteridophytes*, the seedless vascular plants, had a very flourishing past in dominating the vegetation on the earth about 280-230 million years ago. Although they are now largely replaced by the seed bearing vascular plants in the extant flora today. In view of variable climatic and altitudinal variations the Indian sub-continent represents Himalayas, Gangetic plains and Thar Desert as biodiversity centres. All the *pteridophytes* have economic importance. The *pteridophytes* grow in different habitats like moist or dry rocks and boulders, on tree trunks, as hydrophytes in lakes, ponds, *etc.*, on forest floors and edges, along perennial streams and deep ravines, grasslands, tea and coffee estates, inside dark area, *etc*. The industrial sector growing day by day mainly cements plants in Nagaon District. Tree fens need special attention for conservation.

Keywords: Nagaon, Pteridophyte, Biodiversity, Nutrition, Indicator.

Introduction

Biodiversity refers to the variety of life forms at all levels of organization, from gene through species to higher taxonomic forms and also includes the variety of ecosystems and habitats as well the processes occurring therein. Biodiversity is fundamental to the fulfillment of human needs - a biodiversity rich region offers wide options and opportunities for sustaining human welfare including adoption to changes. India is one of the 17 Mega biodiverse countries in the world and accounts for 7-8% of the recorded species. The State of Assam is a constituent unit of the Eastern Himalayan Biodiversity Region; one of the two biodiversity "Hot Spots" in the country. The climatic condition and wide variety in physical features witnessed in Assam have resulted in a diversity of ecological habitats such as forests, grasslands, wetlands, which harbour and sustain wide ranging floral and faunal species placing.

[1] Eco Group of Companies, Surat (GJ) India

The climatic conditions cause prevalence of not and highly humid weather in this part of country and coupled with heterogenic physiography make possible luxuriant growth of a number of plant communities imparting Assam a distinct identity phyto-geographically, many a species are endemic to this region and it is also the center of origin for commercially important plants including Banana, Citrus, Mango, Zizyphus, and Tea. The array of floristic richness has prompted many a scholars to describe Assam as the "Biological Gateway" of North East. The eminent Plant Taxonomist and Plant Geographer Armen L. Takhtajan observed, "Cradle of flowering plants lies in between Assam and Fiji".In the "Revised Survey of Forest Types in India", Champion and Seth categorized as many as fifty one different forest types/sub types for this region. But, the species diversity is so spectacular that it becomes often difficult to clearly identify separate riche to existing plant formations. However, broadly speaking the forest in Assam can be described into following types/sub types.

(*i*) Tropical Wet Evergreen Forests.

(*ii*) Tropical Semi Evergreen Forests.

(*iii*) Tropical Moist Deciduous Forests.

(*iv*) Sub-tropical Broadleaf Hill Forests.

(*v*) Sub-tropical Pine Forests.

(*vi*) Littoral and Swamp Forests.

(*vii*) Grassland and Savannahs.

Tropical Wet Evergreen Forests are found in the districts of Golaghat, Jorhat, Sibsagar, Tinsukia, Dibrugarh and in a narrow stretch in Lakhimpur and Dhemaji districts along foot hills. These forests also occur in the southern part of the State at lower elevations in Borail Range, and in Loharbund, Sonai, Longai and Dholia Reserve Forests in Cachar and Karimganj Districts.Nagaon district extends from 250-45′ to 260 -45′ N Latitude 920 -33′ to 920 -6″ E Longitude with total area 4435.3 Sq.Km and is bounded by Sonitpur district and the Brahmaputra river in the north, West KarbiAnglong and North Cachar Hills in the south, East KarbiAnglong and Golaghat district in the east. The major rivers are The Brahmaputra, Kalong, Sonai, Nanoi, Jamuna, Kopili and Barpani. There are several beels, marshy lands and swamps are there, these are in reality old abandone channels of Kalong and Kopili rivers of Nagaon district. These are Marikalong, Potakalong/Haribhanga, Jongalbalahu, Samoguribeel, Urigadang and Nawbhanga.These beels are major unused resources of the district. There are nearly more than two hundred numerous marshy land exist here which should be used for development of the area.

The soil is mainly clayey loam mixed with silt. The soil is acidic and pH varies from 4.36-6.86. The average annual rainfall remains around 2000 mm and about 70% occurs during June-September. The relative humidity varies between 65-95% and is lowest during the month of March. The present paper deals with the floristic diversity of the study site. The present study reveals the presence of 373 species of Angiosperms. The dicotyledonous plants belong to 74 families, 178 genera and 267 species, and the monocotyledonous to 18 families, 80 genera and 106 species. In addition to this 16 species of ferns were identified these belong to 12 families and 15 genera. Poaceae is the largest family in the sanctuary followed by Euphorbiaceae and Papilionaceae as the 2ndand 3rd largest families respectively.

Biodiversity is the characteristics of nature and is the basis for ecological stability. Biodiversity refers to the variety and variability among living organization, the ecological complexes in which they occur, and the ways in which they interact with each other and their environment. At present, biodiversity is a result of a series of turnovers in the rate of evolution and extinction since the geological past. One of the greatest challenges facing society today is the need to address the unsustainable use of natural resources. In an ideal world, all biodiversity conservation needs should be addressed without jeopardizing human aspirations for social and economic development. Thus, conservation is becoming the crisis discipline. Deciding what, where and for whom to conserve is an essential first step in managing the crisis. India has a rich and varied heritage of biodiversity, encompassing a wide spectrum of habitats from tropical rain forests to alpine vegetation to coastal wetlands. India figured with two hotspots - the Western Ghats and the Eastern Himalayas; out of 25 biodiversity hotspots identified by Myers (2000). In addition, India has 26 recognized endemic centers that are home to nearly one third of all the flowering plants identified and described till now.

Pteridophytes are vascular plants and have leaves (known as fronds), roots and sometimes true stems and tree ferns have full trunks. Examples include ferns, horsetails and club-mosses. Fronds in the largest species of ferns can reach some six meters in length. Many ferns from tropical rain forests are epiphytes, which mean they only grow on other plant species; their water comes from the damp air or from rainfall running down branches and tree trunks. There are also some purely aquatic ferns such as water fern or water velvet (*Salvinia molesta*) and mosquito ferns (*Azolla*species). *Pteridophytes* do not have seeds or flowers either instead they also reproduce via spores. The pteridophytes which dominated the earth during carboniferous are survived today by about 12,000 species comprising 305 genera. Amongst of which most numerous are the homosporous ferns comprised of approximately 11,500 species, whereas rest 500 as fern-allies known globally. In India the Pteridophytes have been found to grow in almost all climatic zones under different habitats and represented by approximately 1200 species falling under 191 genera. In addition to species composition the Pteridophytes are very diverse in their habitat as well as occupancy (Page, 1997).

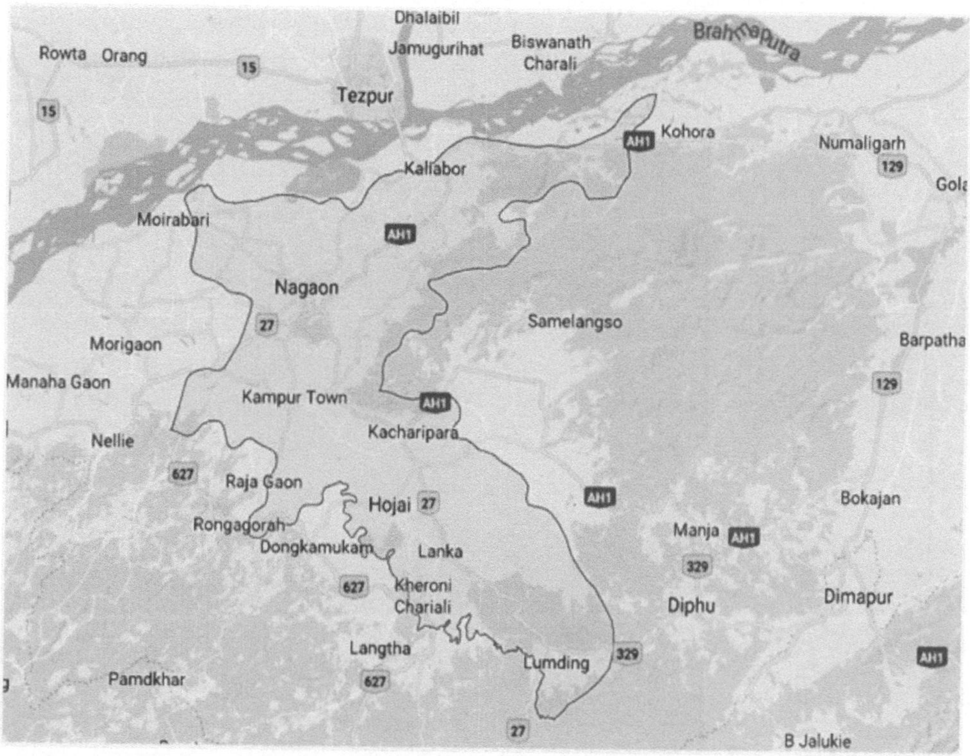

Fig. 7.1: Map showing Nagaon District in Assam

Period of the Study

The baseline study, for the evaluation of the floral and faunal biodiversity of the terrestrial environment of the study area in Nagaon District has been conducted during 2013-2014. This study was a part of Environmental Impact Assessment for Cement Units at Nagaon (Assam).

Methodology

The primary objective of survey was to describe the floral and faunal communities within the study area. The sampling plots for floral inventory were selected randomly in the suitable habitats within the study area. Emphasis has been placed on presence of endemic species, threatened species if any present in the study area. Desktop literature review was conducted to identify the representative spectrum of threatened species and floral communities listed by BSI (Kumar and Srivastava 2012; Kumar, 2013; 2014); Kumar and Aggarwal 2013a;b; Kumar *et al.*, 2013).

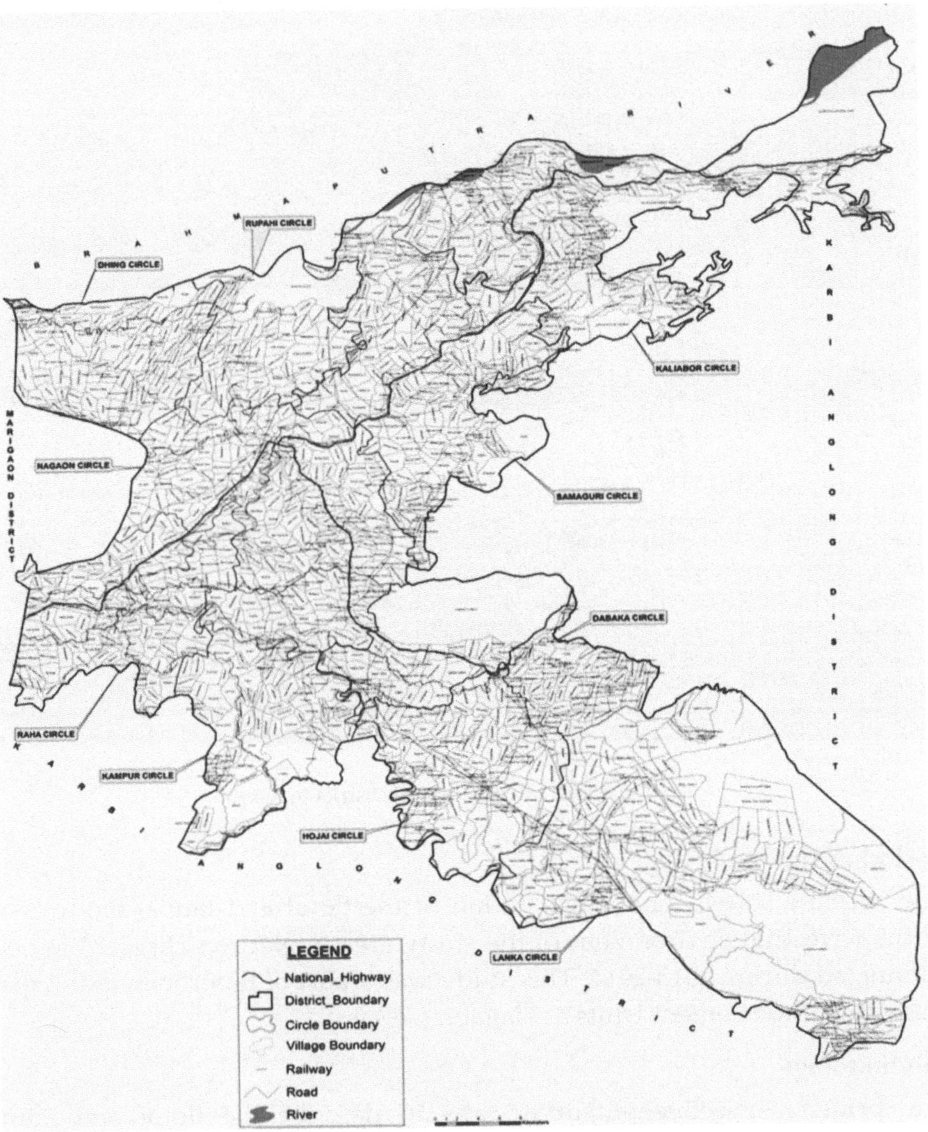

Fig. 7.2: Typical Map of Nagaon district showing the circles

Results and Discussion

The study area, Nagaon district, is agricultural land. The few villages in the study area are engaged in Paddy and Tea cultivation. Villages are scattered in between the large patches of agriculture lands especially for paddy due to heavy rainfall for six month. The tea garden was dominated over the study area. The tree cover in the study area is scanty restricted only in the habituated areas of the village and few along the boundary of the agricultural fields and road sides. It was observed that most of the villages in the study area was with large village "beel" (water bodies) used in rain water harvesting. One village was distributed in parts of two or three (tripartite) due to development of Tea Estate. The study area is also characterized by many water logged regions occupied by hydrophytes. Majority of the area covered in the present investigation was suitable of paddy crop and other part is developed for tea gardens. Almost entire south-east are occupied by forest, while north-west occupied by the large patch of scrub land with sparse population of *Areca catechu, Cocusnucifera, Bombaxceiba* and *Ficusreligiosa.* The fern species were found near the water bodies.

Flora

Shrubs are the dominant perennials of this area, represented mainly:

(*i*) *Prosopisjuliflora,*
(*ii*) *Lowsoniaintermis,*
(*iii*) *Dichorostachyscinera,*
(*iv*) *Mimosa hamata,*
(*v*) *Calotropisprocera,*
(*vi*) *Calotropisgigantea,*
(*vii*) *Maytenusemarginata,*
(*viii*) *Lantana camara,*
(*ix*) *Zizyphusnummularia,*
(*x*) *Cassia auriculata,*
(*xi*) *Ipomoea fistulosa,*
(*xii*) *Euphorbia nivulia*
(*xiii*) *Capparis decidua.*

The low lying area along the fringes of agriculture lands were dominated by thick ground cover of herbaceous species:

(*i*) *Hygrophilaauriculata,*
(*ii*) *Echinopsechinatus,*
(*iii*) *Tridexprocumbens,*
(*iv*) *Xanthium strumarium,*
(*v*) *Cressacretica,*
(*vi*) *Cyperussps*
(*vii*) *Abutilon indicum,*
(*viii*) *Cortalariameicaginea,*
(*ix*) *Indigoferaoblongifolia,*

(*x*) *Tephrosiapurpurea,*

(*xi*) *Tephrosiatinctoria*

(*xii*) *Phragmites karaka,*

(*xiii*) *Triumfettapentandra*

(*xiv*) *Typhaangustata.*

Aquatic Plant Diversity

The aquatic plants species belongs to diverse habits and have distinctive characteristics. More than 9 aquatic species have been identified and they can be described into following broad categories.

- Free floating hydrophytes: *Eichhorniacressipes, Lemnamino.*
- Suspended submersed hydrophytes: *Ceratophyllumdemersum, Utriculariagibba.*
- Anchored submerged hydrophytes: *Hydrillaverticillata, Potamogeton-crispus, P. pectinatus.*
- Anchored hydrophytes with floating shoots: *Ludwigia aquarium, Ipomeaaquatica.*
- Emergent amphibious hydrophytes: *Sagittarialatifolia.*

Fig. 7.3: Images showing mixed flora: top left to right Water hyacinth & Lantana; Down left to right silver fern & Bamboo

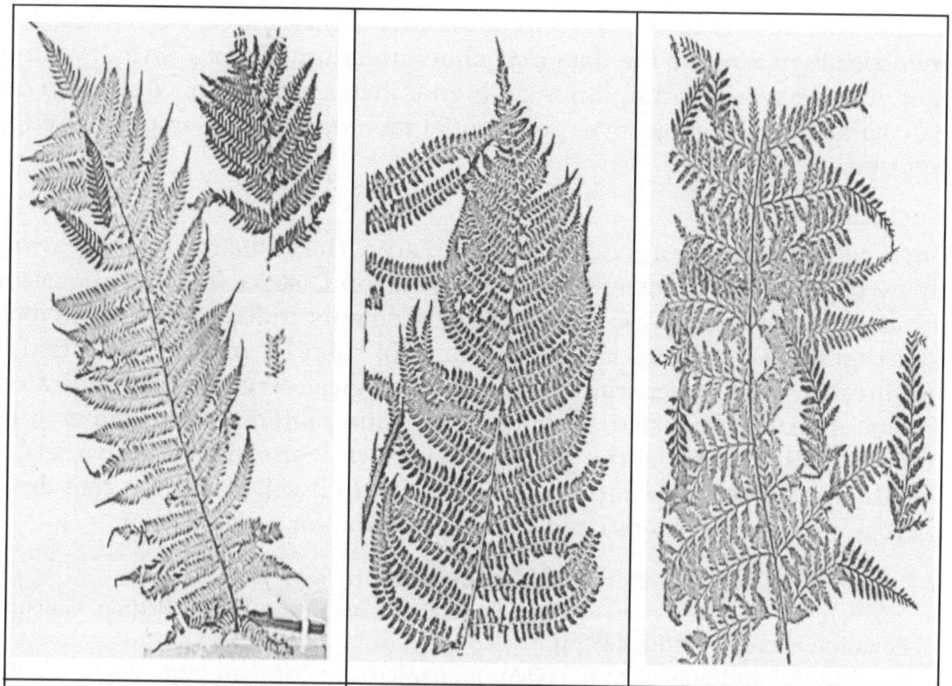

Cyatheadealbata	Polystichumdiscretum	Aspleniumbulbiferum

Fig. 7.4: Specimen of Ferns Spotted

The IUCN Red List is the world's most comprehensive inventory of the global conservation status of plant and animal species. It uses a set of criteria to evaluate the extinction risk of thousands of species and subspecies. These criteria are relevant to all species and all regions of the world. With its strong scientific base, the IUCN Red List is recognized as the most authoritative guide to the status of biological diversity. Out of 17000 species of higher plants known to occur in India, nearly 614 higher plant species were evaluated by IUCN. Among them 247 species are under threatened category (IUCN, 2008). Among the enumerated flora in the study area, none of them were assigned any threat category by Red data book of Indian Plants (Jain and Sastry, 1984; Nayar and Sastry, 1987; 1988; 1990; Oldfield *et al.*, 1998; Kholia and Bhakuni, 2009) and Red list of threatened Vascular plants (IUCN, 2010). De Candolle (1855), Swiss botanist, first used the concept of Endemic, which is defined as an area of a taxonomic unit, especially a species which has a restricted distribution or habitat, isolated from its surrounding region through geographical, ecological or temporal barriers. Out of 17000 species of known flowering plants of India nearly 5000 species are said to be endemic. Nearly 58 genera and 1932 taxa are found to be endemic to peninsular India (Nayar, 1980; Ahmedullah and Nayar, 1986; 1987; Jain 1992; Nayar, 1996; Vijaya Shankar *et al.*, 2005; Nautiyal *et al.*,

2009a,b; Shendage *et al.*, 2010). Tree community (Species-area) curves based on phytosociology fitted to the data may show unnatural shapes, with levelling-off or even decrease in sampling sizes higher than average. This distortion can be explained by the subjective, preferential method of field sampling used in phytosociology.

Conclusion

The Nagaon district has a good diversity of Ferns. The industrial sector growing day by day especially cements plants in Nagaon District. The dust emission and air pollutants (PM, Sox, Nox) from Cements industries have adverse impact on ferns. The ferns are the indicator of vascular plant composition in rain forests. Ferns in general provide an ecological service as bio-indicators for habitat health because of their sensitivity and preference for temperature, humidity, soil type, moisture, pH, light levels, *etc*. Ferns thrive in a variety of habitats that flowering plants would often fail to dwell in such as tree limbs and rock crevices. Tree fens need special attention for conservation.

REFERENCES

Ahmedullah, M. and M.P. Nayar (1987). Endemic Plants of the Indian Region. Culcutta: Botanical Survey of India. 147 pp.

Ahmedullah, M. and Nayar, M.P. (1986). Endemic Plants of the Indian Region. VoI.1. Peninsular lndia. Bot. Surv. of India, Calcutta.

Anderson, T. (1867). An Enumeration of the Indian Species of Acanthaceae. Journal of Linnaean Society 9: 425–454.

IUCN (1994). IUCN Red List Categories. Prepared by the IUCN Species Survival Commission. IUCN, Gland, Switzerland.

IUCN (2001). IUCN Red List Categories and Criteria : Version 3.1. IUCN Species Survival Commission. IUCN, Gland, Switzerland and Cambridge, UK.

IUCN (2003). Guidelines for Application of IUCN Red List Criteria at Regional Levels: Version 3.0. IUCN Species Survival Commission. IUCN, Gland, Switzerland and Cambridge, UK.

IUCN (2008). Red List of Threatened Species. (www.iucnredlist.org).

IUCN (2010). Guidelines for Using the IUCN Red List Categories and Criteria, Version 8.1 (August 2010), Prepared by the Standards and Petitions Subcommittee of the IUCN Species Survival Commission: on www. http://intranet.iucn.org/webfiles/doc/SSC/RedList/ RedListGuidelines.pdf

Jain, S. K. (1991). Dictionary of Indian Folk Medicine and Ethnobotany. Deep Publications, New Delhi.

Jain, S.K. (1968). Medicinal Plants Nation Book Trust, New Delhi. Jain, S.K. 1983. Rare and Endangered Specles: Observation on Rare, Imperfectly Known Endemic Plants. In the Sacred Groves of Western Maharashtra. Calcutta; Bot. Sur of India 169-178.

Jain, S.K. (1992). The Problem of Endangered Species. Concepts, Problems and Solutions. *In:* Tropical Ecosystems: Ecolosv and Management (Eds. K.P. Singh and J.S. Singh.), Iiley Eastern Limited, New Delhi, 69-80.

Jain, S.K. and Rao, R.K. (1983). An Assessment of Threatened Plants of India. Bot. Surv. of India. Calcutta.

Jain, S.K. and Sastry, A.R.K. (1980). Threatened Plants of India - A State of the Alf Report Bot. Surv. of India. New Delhi.

Jain, S.K. and Sastry, A.R.K. (1984). Safeguarding Plant Diversity in Threatened Natural Habitats. In Conservation of Threatened Natural Habitats. (Ed. Anthony V. Hall). African Nat. Sci. Prog. Report. 92.

Kholia, B. S. and Bhakuni, K. (2009). Western Himalaya a New Range of Distribution for a Critically Endangered Fern, Dryopsis Manipurensis (Bedd.) Holttum et P. J. Edwards. Nelumbo, Bulletin of the Botanical Survey of India 51:245–248.

Kumar Ashok (2013). Butterfly (Lepidoptera: Insecta) Diversity from Different Sites of Jhagadia, Ankleshwar, District-Bharuch, Gujarat, *Oct. Jour. Env. Res.* 1(1):09-18.

Kumar Ashok (2014). Environmental Management Plan for Chemical Industries Especially Resin Manufacturing Unit, *Oct. Jour. Env. Res.* 2(3): 262-273.

Kumar Ashok and Aggarwal Savita Goyal (2013a). Ecology and Biodiversity Status of Sachin Gidc and Its Surroundings with Special Reference to Conservation Measures for Indian Peafowl (Pavo cristatus) schedule –I Bird Species, *Oct. Jour. Env. Res.* 2(1): 82-100.

Kumar Ashok and Aggarwal Savita Goyal (2013b). Study of Common Property Resources (CPR) With Special Reference To Water And Biological Resources At Projected Area Near Village Ninat, Bardoli, District-Surat, *Oct. Jour. Env. Res.* 1(4): 319-331.

Kumar Ashok and Srivastava Meena (2012). Diversity of Medicinal Plants in Uttarakhand and their Conservation Strategy with Special Reference to Orchids, *In*: Proceeding of National Conference on Environementla Health: Challaneges and Management, Jan. 20-21, 2012, Organized by Pt. Deendayal Upadhyay Govt. PG College Rajajipuram, Lucknow. pp. 139-142.

Kumar Ashok, Srivastava Meena and Goyal Savita (2013). The Biodiversity At Sandi Bird Sanctuary, Hardoi With Special Reference to Migratory Birds. *Oct. Jour. Env. Res.* 1(3): 173-181.

Myers, N. Mittermeier, R.A., Mittermeier, C.G., Fonseca, G.A.B. & Kent (2000). Biodiversity Hot Spots for Conservation Priorities. Nature, 403:853-858.

Nayar MP and ARK Sastry (1987). Red Data Book of Indian Plants. Vol. I. Botanical Survey of India, Calcutta.

Nayar MP and ARK Sastry (1988). Red Data Book of Indian Plants. Vol. II. Botanical Survey of India, Calcutta.

Nayar MP and ARK Sastry (1990). Red Data Book of Indian Plants. Vol. III. Botanical Survey of India, Calcutta.

Nayar, M.P. (1980). Endemism and Patterns of Distribution of Endemic Genera (Angiosperms) in India. J. Econ. Tax. Bot. I: 99-110.

Nayar, M.P. (1996). Hotspots of Endemic Plants of India, Nepal and Bhutan. Thiruvanathapuram: Tropical Botanical Garden and Research Institute. 204 pp.

Ohasi H (1975). Flora of Eastern Himalaya, Third Report. University Museum of University of Tokyo Bulletin 8:1-458.

Oldfield, S., Lusty, C. and MacKinven, A. (1998). The World List of Threatened Trees. World Conservation Press, Cambridge.

Page C.N. (1997). Pteridophytes as Field Indicators of Natural Biodiversity Restoration in the Scottish Flora. Botanical Journal of Scotland, 49(2):405-414.

Vijaya Sankar, R., Ravikumar, R. and N.M. Ganesh Babu (2005). On the Collection of a Peninsular Endemic, Barleria Stocksii (Acanthaceae), After a Century. Zoo's Print 20:1820.

Horticulture and Ecology - *Studies & Management* **Pages 140-146**
Edited by: **Dr. Alka Chauhan and Dr. Pawan Kumar 'Bharti'**
ISBN: 978-93-88854-09-2
Edition: **2019**
Published by: **Discovery Publishing House Pvt. Ltd., New Delhi (India)**

8

Ecology and Ethnobotany of Ceratopteris thalictroides (L.) Brongn.

[1]Bhasker Joshi, Sona Tewari*, Anupam Srivastava, Rajesh Kumar Mishra**

ABSTRACT

Ceratopteris thalictroides (L.) Brongn., is an important pteridophyte, have high medicinal value and used in various parts of the world. The whole plant is used as medicine. Less information is available about this plant. The present article provides various informations like distribution, description and ethnobotanical uses of this plant.

Keywords: *Ceratopteris thalictroides* (L.) Brongn., Ecology, Ethnomedicinal uses and Kumaun Himalaya.

Introduction

Indigenous knowledge of plant use is considered as an important component of the world's cultural heritage. It can make a significant contribution to sustainable development (Mewari and Joshi, 2013). Pteridophytes (ferns and fern allies) are called as reptile group of plant kingdom and are one of the earliest groups of vascular plants (Karthik *et al.*, 2011). More than 1200 species of ferns and fern allies have been reported from India (Dixit, 1984; Chandra, 2000). They are used in Homeopathic, Ayurvedic and Unani medicines and provided insecticides, antibiotics, food and ornamentation but due to habitat destruction by human being more than 10% species are now endangered (Benniamin, 2011). Therefore the aim of this article is to highlight the habitat, description and ethnobotanical uses of *Ceratopteris thalictroides* (L.) Brongn. reported from foothills of Kumaun Himalaya near Kashipur, Uttarakhand.

Ceratopteris thalictroides (L.) Brongn. in Bull. Sci. Soc. Philom. Paris 8: 186. 1821; Pande & Pande, Ill. Fern Flora Kumaon Himalaya 2: 116. 2002; Dixit & Kumar, Pteridophytes of Uttaranchal 65-66. 2002; Pande & Pande, Ill. Fern Flora

[1] Patanjali Herbal Research Department, Patanjali Research Foundation, Haridwar, Uttarakhand, 249405, India

* Department of Botany, Kumaun Kesari Pt. Badri Dutt Pandey Govt. P.G. College Bageshwar-263642 (Kumaun University, Nainital), Uttarakhand, India

** MD Scholar, Dravyaguna Department, Patanjali Bhartiya Ayurvigyan Evum Anusandhan Sansthan, Haridwar, Uttarakhand, 249405, India

Kumaon Himalaya 1: 147-148. 2003; Joshi *et al.*, Biodiversity Conservation and Envir. Management 178. 2012. *Acrostichum thalictroides* L., Sp. Pl. 2: 1070. 1753. *Acrostichum siliquosum* L., Sp. Pl. 2: 1070. 1753. *Pteris thalictroides* (L.) Sw. in J. Bot. (Schrader) 1800(2): 65. 1801. *Belvisia siliquosa* (L.) Mirb., Hist. Nat. Vég. 5: 473. 1802. *Pteris siliquosa* (L.) P. Beauv., Fl. Oware 1: 63. 1804. *Pteris cornuta* P. Beauv., Fl. Oware 1: 63, pl. 37. 1809. *Ceratopteris gaudichaudii* Brongn. in Bull. Sci. Soc. Philom. Paris 8: 187. 1821. *Teleozoma thalictroides* (L.) R. Br., Narr. Journey Polar Sea 767. 1823. *Ellobocarpus cornuta* (P. Beauv.) Kaulf., Enum. 148. 1824. *Furcaria cornuta* (P. Beauv.) Desv. in Mém. Soc. Linn. Paris 6: 292. 1827. *Furcaria thalictroides* (L.) Desv. in Mém. Soc. Linn. Paris 6: 292. 1827. *Onychium cornutum* (P. Beauv.) Hassak., Tijdschr. Nat. Geschied. 10: 115. 1843. *Ceratopteris deltoidea* Benedict in Bull. Torrey Bot. Club 36: 472. 1909. *Ceratopteris siliquosa* (L.) Copel. in Philipp. J. Sci. 56(2): 107. 1935.

Vernacular Name

It is commonly known as "Water Sprite, Water Fern, Oriental Water fern, Water Stag-horn fern and Water Hornfern". In the Philippines it is called *pakung-sungay*. Japanese Rômaji: mizu-warabi; Spanish (Peru): helecho de Sumatra; Swedish: smal vattenbräken (Source: U.S. National Plant Germplasm System).

Etymology

Genus name *Ceratopteris* derived from Greek word *keras, keratos* means 'horn' and *pteris* means 'fern'; referring to the foliage and to the appearance of this plant (Quattrocchi, 2000). Species name *thalictroides* means the leaves are similar to those of genus *Thalictrum* (Canadian Wildflowers, 2016).

Geographical Distribution

This fern is mostly found in Africa, Asia-Temperate, Asia-Tropical, Australasia, Northern America, Pacific and Southern America (Source: U.S. National Plant Germplasm System). It is reported in many localities in India from Chamba and Kangra (Himachal Pradesh), Dehra Dun (Garhwal), Nainital, Almora and Pithoragarh (Kumaun), Meghalaya, Nagaland, Kohima, Madhya Pradesh, Rajasthan, Karnataka, Tamil Nadu and Andaman Nicobar Islands (Singh *et al.*, 2015). In present study it was reported from the forest of Tarai and Bhawar area of Kumaun Himalaya adjacent to Kashipur. This site situated in the foothills of Shivalik mountain of the outer Himalaya and south-east to Corbett National Park between 29°14′43.6″ N to 29°19′50.5″ N and 79°03′22.6″ E to 79°04′23.2″ E at an elevation of 250 to 265 meter above the sea level, in the district Udham Singh Nagar and occupies the middle reaches of the river Kosi and Dabaka. (Source: Office of Tarai West Forest Division, Kumaun, Ramnagar, Uttarakhand). This study was conducted in rainy season of year 2009.

Habitat, Distribution and Ecology

Ceratopteris thalictroides (L.) Brongn. is an aquatic fern, free-floating or rooted, growing in estuarine and other marshes through the tropics and subtropics. In India it is very common in Bengal and Tarai region of Himalaya. Swampy areas, swamp forests, swamps, marshes, natural and man-made ponds, mostly in stagnant water bodies or in still pockets along slow flowing rivers, full sun to moderate shade, from sea level to 1300 m, but mostly less than 500 m altitude. In some areas it exhibits a degree of seasonality, reaching maturity and shedding spores during the dry season (Gangulee and Kar, 2010). Plants have lost nearly all sterile fronds by this stage. The species has been reported to functionally be an annual, repopulating from spore the next season, but it is clearly of indefinite lifespan in cultivation. It is a common species of sluggish streams and a widespread weed in rice-fields (Masuyama, 2007) and in recent revision of the species aggregate in Asia the Himalayan tetraploid, also present in other parts of India etc., is recognised as a distinct entity with a distinct morphology, especially in its stipe to blade length, which may be appropriately treated at the specific rank (Chandra *et al.*, 2008). Plant has a very short life cycle. The whole cycle from spore to spore can be completed in less than 30 days. Apart from spores, the plant reproduces by bulbils growing on the leaves (Prota).

Plate 1. A Sub-tropical forest of Ramnagar Range of outer Himalaya

Botanical Description

Plants polymorphic, unbranched aquatic or semi-aquatic usually rooted in mud, green in colour. Rhizome erect, short. Root thick long, fibrous, fleshy. Viviparous buds grow into new plants from floating or submerged leaf margins. Leaves (fronds) dimorphous. Fertile fronds large, lanceolate to ovate to deltate or cordate and dissected like a stag-horn. Stipes 3 to 15 mm diameter in mature plants, spongy and air filled. Sterile fronds shorter than the fertile, lanceolate to lance-ovate to ovate to deltate or cordate, pale green, thin, flaccid and spreading with 4 to 60 cm long, including a stipe. Half this length, fertile fronds are pale green to brown when over mature and erect, with 15 to 100 cm long. Sporangia usually crowded between segment midvein and revolute margin, covered with reflexed margin of lobe, brown. (Source: Wikipedia, Flora of China, Flora of North America, India Biodiversity Portal, The DNA of Singapore).

Chemical Composition

It contains L-arginine monohydrochloride, L-Hydroxyproline, L-Glutamic acid, DL-Valine and L-Tyrosine amino acids (Mandal and Mondal, 2012).

Uses

Fronds of *Ceratopteris thalictroides* (L.) Brongn. are cooked and eaten as a vegetable in Madagascar and raw as a salad in Micronesia. However, the plant is believed to contain carcinogenic chemicals. It is widely used in aquarium and highly prized for its versatility. In the Sepik region of New Guinea fronds are used as a personal decoration. Fresh juice of leaves is applied on fresh wounds effectively to stop bleeding immediately. Fronds are used as poultice in skin diseases (Rout *et al.*, 2009). The whole plant parts are grounded into paste and mixed with turmeric, mixture is applied over the affected places to treat skin diseases and wounds (Karthik *et al.*, 2011; Mithraja *et al.*, 2012). The fronds are used as poultice in skin diseases (Benniamin, 2011; Jain and Rao, 1983). They are reported to be toxic and styptic to stop bleeding (Singh, 1999). Young fronds are eaten as vegetable (Sen and Ghosh, 2011). Paste of whole plant applied for effective blood clotting in fresh cut and wound (Barukial and Sarmah, 2011).

Conclusion

The study shows that Tarai and Bhawar region of Kashipur, U.S. Nagar is rich is floristic diversity. Numerous medicinal and rare plants are found in this area (Joshi, 2011a, b). It is one of the rare plant reported from this area. This area highly suffers from anthropogenic pressure (Joshi and Kumar, 2011). Therefore an immediate conservation strategy is required for conservation of medicinal and rare plants of this area for the benefit of human beings in future.

Plate 2. Seedling Stage

Plate 3. Vegetative Stage of Plant showing Dimorphous leaves

Plate 4. Young Plant

Plate 5. Plant in Natural Habitat

Plate 6. Mature Plant

Plate 7. Plant with Mature Fronds

REFERENCES

Barukial, J. and Sarmah, J.N. (2011). Ethnomedicinal Plants Used by the People of Golaghat District, Assam, India. *Int. J. Med. Arom. Plants*, 1(3):203-211.

Benniamin, A. (2011). Medicinal Ferns of North Eastern India with Special Reference to Arunachal Pradesh. *Indian Journal of Traditional Knowledge*, 10(3):516-522.

Canadian Wildflowers Fleurs sauvages du Canada. (2016). *Caulophyllum thalictroides*. Retrieved May 06, 2016 from http://www.fleurssauvages.ca/berberidaceae/caulophyllum_thalictroides.html

Chandra, S. (2000). *The Ferns of India* (Enumeration, Synonyms & Distribution). International Book Distributors, Dehra Dun, India. pp. 459.

Chandra, S., Fraser-Jenkins, C.R., Kumari, A. and Srivastava, A. (2008). A summary of the status of threatened Pteridophytes of India. *Taiwania*, 53(2): 170-209.

Dixit, R.D. (1984). *A Census of the Indian Pteridophytes*. Flora of India, Ser. 4, Botanical Survey of India, Howrah (Calcutta). India, pp. 1-177.

Flora of China. (n.d.). *Ceratopteris thalictroides* (L.) Brongn. Retrieved May 06, 2016 from http://www.efloras.org/florataxon.aspx?flora_id=2&taxon_id=200003558.

Flora of North America. (n.d.). *Ceratopteris thalictroides* (L.) Brongn. Retrieved May 06, 2016 from http://www.efloras.org/florataxon.aspx?flora_id=1&taxon_id=200003558.

Gangulee, H.C. and Kar, A.K. (2010). *College Botany*, Vol. II. New Central Book Agency (P) Ltd. pp. 1028-1029.

India Biodiversity Portal. (n.d.). *Ceratopteris thalictroides* (L.) Brongn. Retrieved May 06, 2016, from http://indiabiodiversity.org/species/show/226820.

Jain, S.K. and Rao, R.R. (1983). *An Assessment of Threatened Plants of India*, In: Proceeding of the Seminar Held at Dehradun, BSI, Botanical Garden, Howrah.

Joshi, B. and Kumar, P. (2011). Resource Utilization and Anthropogenic Pressure in a part of Submontane forest of Outer Himalaya, Uttarakhand. *Environment Conservation Journal*, 12(1&2): 43-47.

Joshi, B. (2011 a). Medicinal Plants of Submontane Forest in a Part of Tarai and Bhawar of Kumaun Himalaya. *Nature and Science*, 9(5):95-99.

Joshi, B. (2011 b). Ecology and Medicinal Uses of *Helminthostachys zeylanica* (L.) Hook. "An Endangered Flora of India" Reported at Foothills of Kumaun Himalaya (Kashipur), Uttarakhand. *Researcher*, 3(4):51-54.

Karthik, V., Raju, K., Ayyanar, M., Gowrishankar, K. and Sekar, T. (2011). Ethnomedicinal Uses of Pteridophytes in Kolli Hills, Eastern Ghats of Tamil Nadu, India. *J. Nat. Prod. Plant Resour.*, 1(2): 50-55.

Mandal, A. and Mondal, A.K. (2012). Qualitative Analysis of Free Amino Acids of Some Pteridophytes with Special Reference to their Ethnomedicinal Uses in West Bengal, India. *International Journal of Science and Nature*, 3(4):819-823.

Masuyama, S. (2007). Morphological Characteristics of the *Ceratopteris thalictroides* Complex, a Polymorphic Aquatic Fern. In: Amoroso, V. B. (ed.), 4th Symposium on Asian Pteridology and Garden Show, Abstracts. Central Mindanao University, Musuan, Bukidnon, Philippines, pp. 64.

Mewari, N. and Joshi, B. (2013). *Ethnobotany: An Approach to Nature*. In "Ethnobotany and Medicinal Plants" Edited by Pawan Kumar 'Bharti and Avnish Chauhan (eds.). Ancient Publishing House, Delhi, pp. 6-27.

Mithraja, M.J., Antonisamy, J.M., Mahesh, M., Paul, Z.M. and Jeeva, S. (2012). Chemical Diversity Analysis on Some Selected Medicinally Important Pteridophytes of Western Ghats, India. *Asian Pacific Journal of Tropical Biomedicine*, S34-S39.

PROTA4U. (2016). *Ceratopteris thalictroides* (L.) Brongn. Retrieved May 06, 2016, from http://www.prota4u.org/protav8.asp?fr=1&p=Ceratopteris+thalictroides+.

Quattrocchi, U. (2000). *CRC World Dictionary of Plant Names*, Vol. I (A-C). Florida: CRC Press, Boca Raton.

Rout, S.D., Panda, T. & Mishra, N. (2009). Ethnomedicinal Studies on Some Pteridophytes of Similipal Biosphere Reserve, Orissa, India. *International Journal of Medicine and Medical Sciences*, 1(5):192-197.

Sen, A. & Ghosh, P.D. (2011). A Note on the Ethnobotanical Studies of Some Pteridophytes in Assam. *Indian Journal of Traditional Knowledge*, 10(2):292-295.

Singh, H.B. (1999). Potential Medicinal Pteridophytes of Indian and their Chemical Constituents. *J. Econ Tax. Bot.*, 23(1): 63-78.

Singh, S.K., Gautam, R.P., Srivastava, S.K. & Rajkumar, S.D. (2015). A Diploid Cytotype of *Ceratopteris thalictroides* (l.) Brongn. (Parkeriaceae-Pteridophyta) from Uttar Pradesh, India. *Int. J. Curr. Microbiol. App. Sci.*, 4(10): 711-715.

The DNA of Singapore. (2016). *Ceratopteris thalictroides* (L.) Brongn. Retrieved May 06, 2016, from http://lkcnhm.nus.edu.sg/dna/organisms/details/597.

The Plant List. (2013). *Ceratopteris thalictroides* (L.) Brongn. Retrieved May 06, 2016, from http://www.theplantlist.org/tpl1.1/record/tro-26600076.

U.S. National Plant Germplasm System. (n.d.). *Ceratopteris thalictroides* (L.) Brongn. Retrieved May 06, 2016, from https://npgsweb.ars- grin.gov/gringlobal/taxonomydetail.aspx?400378#common.

Wikipedia. (2013). *Ceratopteris thalictroides*. Retrieved May 06, 2016 from https://en.wikipedia.org/wiki/Ceratopteris_thalictroides.

Horticulture and Ecology - ***Studies & Management*** **Pages 147-186**
Edited by: **Dr. Alka Chauhan and Dr. Pawan Kumar 'Bharti'**
ISBN: 978-93-88854-09-2
Edition: **2019**
Published by: **Discovery Publishing House Pvt. Ltd., New Delhi (India)**

9

Ecological Status for Ratapani and Singhori Wild Life Sanctuary, Raigad (MP) India

[1]Dr. Ashok K. Rathoure

ABSTRACT

The baseline study was conducted for the evaluation of the floral and faunal biodiversity of the terrestrial as well as aquatic environment of the study area, it comprises of total 5 reserved forest and 3 protected forest including Ratapani and Singhori Wildlife Sanctuary falls Dist-Raigad, Madhya Pradesh, India. It is strongly recommended to prepare the conservation plan for schedule-1 Fauna (listed 9 animals and 1 bird) and it is ensure to implement the conservation plan during construction and operation phase of railway track. Moreover, there is an urgent need of public awareness for the importance of wildlife, as illegal hunting, killing or capturing of wild animals was recorded from locals living in the forest and nearby villagers.

Keywords: Tiger, Leopard, Reserve Forest, Railway track, Wildlife Sanctuary.

Introduction

Plants and animals are more susceptible to environmental stress. A change in the composition of biological communities is reflected by a change in the distribution pattern, frequency, density and abundance of natural species of flora and fauna existing in the ecosystem. These changes over a span of time can be quantified and related to the existing environmental factors. Natural flora and fauna are important features of the environment. They are organized into natural communities and are sensitive to outside influences. Integrating ecological thinking into the planning process is urgent need in the context of deterioration of natural environment, which is unwanted but direct consequence of development. Study area comprises of reserved and protected forest including wildlife sanctuary. There are five reserved forest and 3 protected forest including Ratapani and Singhori Wildlife Sanctuary.

[1] Ecology & Biodiversity Expert, Eco Chem Sales & Services Ecosystem Resource Management Pvt. Ltd. Surat Gujarat, India

Methodology

The primary objective of survey was to describe the floral and faunal communities within the study area. The sampling plots for floral inventory were selected randomly in the suitable habitats (Anderson, 1867; Jain and Rao, 1983; Dixit, 1984; Wilson and Reeder, 2005; Kumar, 2013; Kumar *et al.*, 2013). The methodology adopted for faunal survey involve random survey, opportunistic observations, diurnal bird observation, active search for reptiles, faunal habitat assessment, active search for scats and foot prints, animal call, and review of previous studies. The aim was to set baselines in order to monitor and identify trends after the commissioning of the cargo handling activity. Emphasis has been placed on presence of endemic species, threatened species if any present in the study area. The qualitative study has been carried out only. The listed of villages covered for survey is presented in Table 8.1 and the detailed method and parameters covered for the said study has been highlighted in Table 9.2.

Desktop literature review was conducted to identify the representative spectrum of threatened species, population and ecological communities listed by IUCN, WCMC, ZSI, BSI and Indian Wild life Protection Act, 1972 (Bentham and Hooker, 1862-1883; Hunter, 1879; Dixit, 1984; Ghosh *et al.*, 2004; Lushington, 1915; Wilson and Reeder, 1993; BirdLife International, 2000; BirdLife International, 2004a, b; Wilson and Reeder, 2005; BirdLife International, 2010; Kumar and Srivastava, 2012; Kumar, 2013; Kumar *et al.*, 2013; Kumar and Aggarwal, 2013a,b). The status of individual species was assessed using the revised IUCN/SSC category system (WCMC, 1988; IUCN, 1994; WCMC, 2000; IUCN, 2001, 2003, 2008, 2010).

Table 9.1: Sensitivity of the Study Area

S.No.	Area/Track/Zone	Name of Forest/ HotSpots	Remarks
1.	Rail track	Project Site/Length 26.70 km	Proposed third line is parallel to Existing (2 lines - up & down) railway track passing through Wildlife Sanctuary.
2.	Obedullahganj	Chakla RF	Reserved and protected forest fall in the study area, majorly teak;open mixed, dense forest.
3.	Obedullahganj	Diwattiaya PF	
4.	Obedullahganj	Gohar Ganj RF	
5.	Obedullahganj	Obedullahganj PF	
6.	Obedullahganj	Obedullahganj RF	
7.	Budani	Budani PF	
8.	Budani	Budani RF	
9.	Budani	Ramnagar RF	

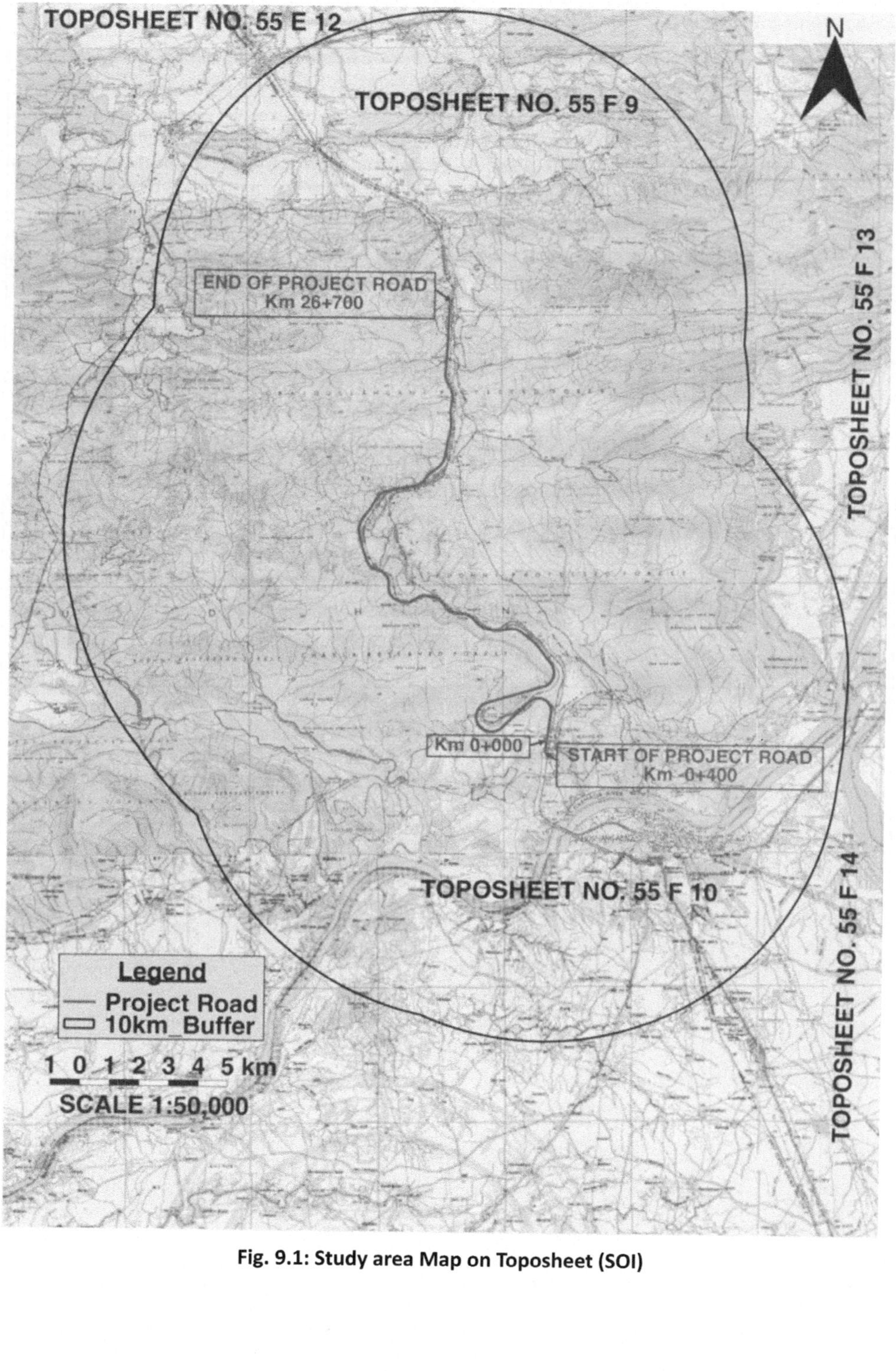

Fig. 9.1: Study area Map on Toposheet (SOI)

Table 9.2: Mode of Data Collection and Parameters Considered During the Survey

Sl. No.	Aspect/s	Data	Mode of Data Collection	Parameters Monitored	Remarks
1.	**Terrestrial Ecology**	Primary data collection	By Field Survey Hutto et al., 1986; Welsh, 1987; Thommpson *et al.*, 1989; Welsh *et. al.*, 1991; Allen *et al.*, 1996; Misra, 2013.	**For Floral diversity, Vegetation measurements:** Tree, Shrub, Herbs, Grasses, Climbers, Cultivated plants in the study area, Floristic composition of the study area, Medicinal plants of the study area, Status of the forest, their category in the study area, Rare and endangered flora in the study area. Endemic plants in the study area. **For Fauna in the study area:** -Reptiles, -Amphibians, -Birds, -Fresh water fishes-Mammals,-Butterflies. Rare and Endangered fauna in the study area, Endemic fauna in the study area, Wild life and their conservation importance in the study area.	Random survey, opportunistic observations, diurnal bird observation, active search for reptiles, faunal habitat assessment, active search for microhabitat, scats, foot prints, animal call, pug marks, debarking sign, Nesting, Claws, Dung, etc. and information from local villagers.
2.		Secondary data collection Secondary data collection	• Barkhera Range and Budani Range Forest Division· • Data of Fisheries department. • Literature like research papers, books published by research/ academic Institutions.·	Interpretation of secondary data for Ecological Sensitive Areas such as national forests, wild life sanctuaries, lakes, ravines, hills, hillocks and reserve forest, vegetation, type, importance etc.	Bentham and Hooker, 1862-1883; Hunter, 1879; Dixit, 1984; Ghosh *et al.*, 2004; Lushington, 1915; Wilson and Reeder, 1993; BirdLife International, 2000; BirdLife International, 2004a, b; Wilson and Reeder, 2005; Bird Life International, 2010; Kumar and Srivastava, 2012; Kumar, 2013; Kumar *et al.*, 2013; Kumar and Aggarwal, 2013a,b). The status of individual species was assessed using the revised IUCN/ SSC category system (WCMC, 1988; IUCN, 1994; WCMC, 2000; IUCN, 2001, 2003, 2008, 2010.

3.	**Evaluation of Ecological sensitivity**	Secondary	Review and Discussion	Wild life importance, Floral Endemicity, Faunal Endemicity, State of Terrestrial vegetation, State of wet land vegetation, Mangrove vegetation, Conservation importance, Legal status (National park, Wild life sanctuary, Reserve forest, Wetlands, Agricultural lands) Lakes / reservoirs/dam, Natural lakes and Swamps, Breeding ground of Migratory and Residential birds.	-

Results and Discussion

Terrestrial Floral and Faunal Components of the Study Area

Agro-ecological regions by the National Bureau of Soil Survey & Land Use Planning (NBSS & LUP) have been delineated. Delineation of agro-climatic zones based on soil, water, rainfall, temperature etc. is the first essential step for sustainable production. The National Bureau of Soil Survey & Land Use Planning (NBSS & LUP) came up with twenty agro-ecological zones based on the growing period as integrated criteria of effective rainfall, soil groups, delineated boundaries adjusted to district boundaries with a minimal number of regions. Subsequently, these twenty agro-ecological zones were sub-divided into 60 sub-zones. As per the map provided in figure 4, the study area fall under Central Highlands (Malwa, Bundelkhand and Eastern Satpura) which represents tropical dry deciduous forest cat 5 & 3 with hot sub humid climate with black and red soil (length of cropping period is 150-180 days) favorable for mustard, wheat, pulses. Vegetation in the Malwa Plateau is tropical dry forest, with scattered teak (*Tectona grandis*) forests. The other main trees are Butea, Bombax, Anogeissus, Acacia, Buchanania and Boswellia. The shrubs or small trees include species of *Grewia, Ziziphus mauritiana, Casearia, Prosopis, Capparis, Woodfordia, Phyllanthus,* and *Carissa*. The Malwa plateau is considered to be an extension of the Deccan Traps and was formed at the end of Cretaceous period. Black, Brown and Bhtatori or stony soil is abundant in the Malwa Plateau. The black soil requires less irrigation because of its high capacity for moisture retention. The other two soil types are lighter and have a higher proportion of sand. Ratapani and Singhori Wildlife Sanctuary contains 129 tree species, 73 herbs and shrubs species, 33 climbers and parasites, 35 grasses and bamboo species, 35 mammals, 205 birds, 14 fish, 33 reptiles and 10 species of amphibians have been recorded in Ratapani and Singhori Wildlife Sanctuary. The major crop in the study area is Rabi and Kharif; this cropping pattern depends on water from Narmada River. The forest land is involved in the railway track. There is no any major crop in the forest area, only Maize was observed at some places where tribal living.

Fig. 9.2: Location of Wildlife Sanctuary in Map of Madhya Pradesh

Fig. 9.3: View of Rail Track passing through wild life sanctuary

Fig. 9.4: Wildlife Presence in the Forest (WLS)

Fig. 9.5: Pug marks of Tiger Movement

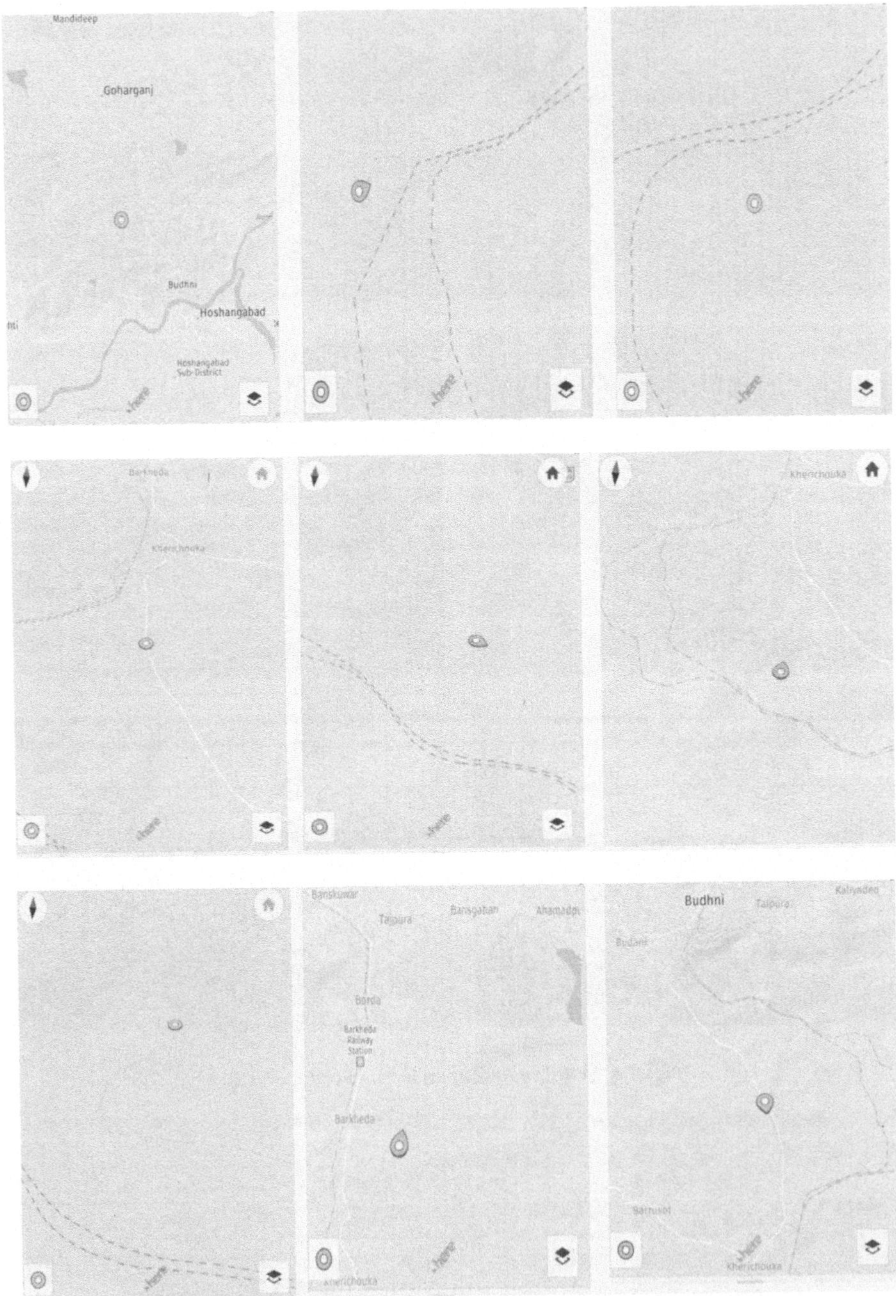

Fig. 9.6: GPS location of Wildlife Presence within forest (WLS)

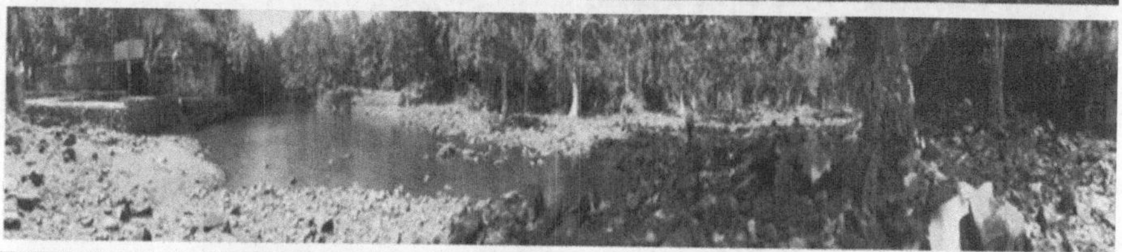

Fig. 9.7: Aquatic Habitat of the Study Area

Fig. 9.8: Tree Distribution and pattern in the Forest

गडरिया
GADARIYA
BRIDGE NO. 791/4

Fig. 9.9: Glimpses of Local information and Confirmation from Locals/Villagers

Floral Diversity of the Study Area

The objective of this floral inventory of the study area is to provide necessary information on floristic structure in the study area for formulating effective management and conservation measures. The climatic, edaphic and biotic variations with their complex interrelationship and composition of species, which are adapted to these variations, have resulted in different vegetation cover, characteristic of each region (Ohasi, 1975). The tree species, herbs, shrubs, climbers and major crops, were documented during this base line study (Jain, 1968; 1991).

Trees and Shrubs: A tree is a perennial plant with an elongated stem or trunk, supporting branches and leaves in most species. Trees tend to be long-lived, some reaching several thousand years old. While a shrub or bush is a small to medium-sized woody plant. They are distinguished from trees by their multiple stems and shorter height and are usually less than 6 m (20 ft) tall. The dominant trees in the study area are *Tectona grandis* (Sagaun/teak), *Butea* *monosperma (Palas), Acacia nilotica (*Babool*), Mangiferaindica* (Aam), *Pongamia glabra* (Karanj), *Zizyphus mauratiana(Ber)*. Total 101 species of trees belong to 37 families are enumerated from the study area.

Table 9.3: Trees in the Study Area (Natural Vegetation)

Sl. No.	Family	Vernacular name	Botanical Name
1.	Anacardiaceae	Chironji	*Buchanania lanjan*
2.		Aam	*Mangifera indica*
3.	Jhingan	*Lannea coromendelica*	
4.	Anonaceae	Ashok	*Polyalthia longifolia*
5.		Kari	*Saccopetalum tomentosum*
6.		Sitafal	*Anona squamosa*
7.	Apocynaceae	Dudhi/Karayja	*Wrightia tinctoria*
8.	Bignoniaceae	Padar	*Sterospermum suaveolens*
9.	Bixaceae	Kakai	*Flacourtia ramontchi*
10.		Galgal	*Cochlospermum religiosum*
11.	Boraginaceae	Datraga	*Ehretia laevis,*
12.		Lasoda	*Cardia myxa*
13.	Burseraceae	Keked	*Garuga pinnata*
14.		Salai	*Boswellia serrata*
15.	Capparidaceae	Barna	*Crataeva unilocularis*
16.	Celastraceae	Jamrasi	*Elaeodendron glaucum*
17.	Combreteceae	Arjun	*Terminalia arjuna*
18.		Dhavada	*Anogeissus latifolia*
19.		Bahera	*Terminalia belerica*
20.		Kardhai	*Anogeissus pendula*
21.		Saaj	*Terminalia tomentosa,*
22.	Cornaceae	Akol	*Ailangium lamarchii*
23.	Ebenaceae	Tendu	*Diospyros melanoxylon*
24.		Bhaktendu	*Diospyros cordifolia*
25.	Euphorbiaceae	Aanvla	*Emblica officinalis*
26.		Kasai	*Bridelia retusa*
27.	Euphorbiaceae	Thuar	*Euphorbia neriifolia*
28.		Ratanjot	*Jatropha curcus*
29.	Euphorbiaceae	Roli	*Mallotus philippinensis*
30.		Sahand	*Euphorbia nivulia*
31.	Lauraceae	Maida lakdi	*Litsea glutinosa*
32.	Lecythidaceae	Kumbhi/Kalindi	*Careya arborea*

33.	Leguminosae	Amaltas	*Cassia fistula*
34.		Anjan	*Hardwickja binata*
35.		Asta	*Bauhinia racemose*
36.		Imli	*Tamarindus indica*
37.		Karanj	*Pongamia glabra*
38.		Kachnar	*Bauhinia variegata*
39.		Kalasiris	*Albizzia lebbek*
40.		Keyolar	*Bauhinia spp.*
41.		Kheir	*Acacia catechu*
42.		Khejra	*Prosopis juliflora*
43.		Gulmohar	*Delonix regia*
44.		Chhekur	*Prosopis spicigera*
45.		Chhichva	*Albizzia odoratissima*
46.		Tinsa	*Ougeinia dalbergiodes*
47.		Dhovin	*Dalbergia paniculata*
48.		Palas	*Butea monosperma*
49.		Pagra	*Erythrina suberosa*
50.		Babool	*Acacia nilotica*
51.		Bijasaal	*Pterocarpus marsupium*
52.		Renja	*Acacia leucophloea*
53.		Safed siris	*Albizzia procera*
54.		Safed khair	*Acacia ferruginae*
55.		Sehra	*Bauhinia retus*
56.		Bhisom	*Delbergia latifolia*
57.		Sissu	*Delbergia sissoo*
58.	Lythraceae	Seja	*Lagerstroemia parviflora*
59.	Malvaceae	Pula	*Kydia calycina*
60.		Kullu	*Sterculia lanceolata*
61.	Meliaceae	Neem	*Azadirachta indica*
62.		Bakain	*Melia azedarach*
63.		Rohan	*Soymida febrifuga*
64.	Moraceae	Gular	*Ficus glomerate*
65.		Pakar	*Ficus infectoria*
66.		Paraspeepal	*Ficus retusa*
67.		Peepal	*Ficus religiosa*
68.		Bargad/vad	*Ficus bengalensis*

69.		Bhahtoot	*Morus laevigates*
70.	Moringaceae	Sahjana	*Moringa pterygosperma*
71.	Myrtaceae	Jamun	*Syzygium cuminii*
72.		Gum tree	*Eucalyptus sp.*
73.	Oleaceae	Mokha	*Schrebera swietenioidas*
74.	Palmae	Khajoor	*Phoenix humilis*
75.	Rhamnaceae	Ghont	*Zyphus xylopyra*
76.		Ber	*Zizyphus mauratiana*
77.	Rubiaceae	Aal	*Morinda tintoria*
78.		Kem	*Mitragyana parvifolia*
79.		Dikamali	*Gardenia licisa*
80.		Tilwan	*Wendlandia exserts*
81.		Papra	*Gardenia latifolia*
82.		Feitara	*Gardenia turgida*
83.		Bhawarsal	*Hymenodictyon excelsum*
84.		Haldu	*Adina cordifolia*
85.		Lokhandi	*Ixora parviflors*
86.	Rutaceae	Keth	*Feronia Limonia*
87.		Bel	*Aegle marmelos*
88.		Bilsena	*Limonia Crenculata*
89.		Meethneem	*Murrasya koenigii*
90.	Salmaliaceae	Semal	*Salmalia malabarcum*
91.	Salvadoraceae	Peelu	*Salvadora oleodides*
92.	Sapindaceae	Kusum	*Schleiehera trijuga*
93.		Reetha	*Sapindus laurifolius*
94.	Sapotaceae	Mahuva	*Madhuca indica*
95.		Molsari	*Mimusops elangi*
96.	Simaroubaceae	Maharukh	*Ailanthus excelsa*
97.	Tiliaceae	Dhaman	*Grewia tiliaefolia*
98.	Ulmaceae	Chirol	*Holoptelea integrifolia*
99.	Verbenaceae	Gamari	*Gmelina arborea*
100.		Morpaye	*Vitex peduncularis*
101.		Sagaun/Teak	*Tectona grandis*

Herbs: Total 37 herbaceous species belongs to 29 family (agricultural crops not included) were recorded from the study area enlisted in table below.

Table 9.4: List of Herbaceous Species Observed in the Study Area

S. No.	Family	Vernacular name	Scientific name
1.	Acanthaceae	Maruadona	*Strobilanthes callosus*
2.	Amaranthaceae	Chirchita	*Achyranthes aspera*
3.	Anacardiaceae	Adusa	*Adhatoda vasica*
4.	Apocynaceae	Karonda	*Carissa spinarum*
5.		Kurchi	*Holarrhena antidysenterica*
6.	Asciepiadaceae	Oak	*Calotropdis gigantea*
7.	Berberidaceae	Sarkata	*Argemone mexicana*
8.	Cactaceae	Nagfani	*Optuttia dillenii*
9.	Capparidanceae	Heens	*Capparis horrida*
10.		Kareel	*Capparis aphylla*
11.	Celastraceae	Bekal	*Gymnosporta montana*
12.	Compositae	Gokhuru	*Xanthium aspera*
13.	Euphorbiaceae	Jhondharli	*Antidesina ghacsehilla*
14.		Chakhetan	*Fluggca microcarpa*
15.	Fabaceae	Tarwar	*Cassia auriculata*
16.		Chumui	*Mimosa rubicaulis*
17.		Chipti	*Desmodium pulchellum*
18.	Lamiaceae	Puwar	*Vitex negundo*
19.	Leguminosae	Nirgud	*Indigolera pulchella*
20.		Tovara	*Cassia tora*
21.	Liabiatae	Kala Bansa	*Colebrookea oppositifolia*
22.		Kora	*Pogostemon plectranthoides*
23.	Lythraceae	Dhawai	*Woodfordia floribunda*
24.	Malyaceae	Banakpas	*Thespesia lampus*
25.	Myrsinaceae	Babrang	*Embelia robusta*
26.	Myrtaceae	Jamun	*Eugenia heyncana*
27.	Rhamnaceae	Jharberi	*Zityphtis rotundifolia*
28.	Rutaceace	Ratanjot	*Clausena pantaphylla*
29.	Salicaceae	Bansa	*Salix tetrasperama*
30.	Sapindaceae	Khareta	*lodonoca visocosa*
31.	Sterculiaceae	Marorfali	*Helicteres isora*
32.	Tamaricacene	Jhau	*Tamarix dioica*
33.	Tiliaceae	Gursakari	*Grewia hirsuta*
34.	Bandi	*Grewia scabrophylla*	
35.	Verbenaceae	Harsingar	*Nyctanthes arbortristis*
36.	Vitaceae	Hathi kand	*Leea macrophylla*
37.	Zygophyllaceae	Hingota	*Balanites roxburghiii*

Creepers: Total 19 Creepers species belongs to 7 families (agricultural crops not included) were recorded from the study area enlisted in table below.

Table 9.5: List of Creepers Observed in the Study Area

S.No.	Family	Vernac4ular name	Scientific name
1.	Asclepiadaceae	Gudmar	*Gymnema sylvestris*
2.		Chikti	*Marsdenia tenacissima*
3.	Combntaceae	Hathi Sandan	*Combretum ovalifolia*
4.		Peevarvel	*Combreturn decandrum*
5.	Dioscoreaceae	Baichandi	*Dioscorea daemons*
6.	Leguminosae	Kavach	*Mucuna pruriens*
7.		Karanj	*Caesalpinia sepiaria*
8.		Gaanj	*Melletia auriculata*
9.		Rathi	*Abrus precatorius*
10.		Gurar	*Acacia cassia*
11.		Palas Bel	*Butea superba*
12.		Mahul	*Bauhinia vahlii*
13.		Ravni	*Acacia pennata*
14.		Nasbel	*Spatholobus roxbarghii*
15.	Liliaceae	Agnishikha	*Gloriosa superba*
16.		Satavari	*Asparagus racemosa*
17.	Menispermaceae	Giloy	*Tinospora cordifolia*
18.	Rhamnaccae	Makoy	*Zizyphus oenoplia*
19.		Kevti	*Ventilago calyculata*

Grasses and parasitic plant: Total 22 Grass species belongs to Gramineae family (agricultural crops not included) and 4 parasitic plants belongs to 3 families were recorded from the study area enlisted in table below.

Table 9.6: List of Grasses and Parasitic Plant Observed in the Study Area

S.No.	Family	Vernacular name	Scientific name
1.	Gramineae	Kus	*Eragrostis nees*
2.		Kusal	*Heteropogon contortus*
3.		Kunda	*Ischaemum pilosum*
4.		Kaus	*Saccharum spointaneum*
5.		Kush	*Desmostachya bipinnata*
6.		Khas	*Vetiveria zizaniodes*
7.		Gararu	*Coix gigentea*
8.		Gadela	*Coix lacrymajobi*

9.		Guner	*Themada quadrivalvis*
10.		Chikula	*Chrysopogon montanus*
11.		Chhir	*Imperata cylindrica*
12.		Dub	*Cynodon dactylon*
13.		Poniya	*Schima sulcatum*
14.		Phuli	*Apluda varis*
15.		Phusel	*Iseilema laxum*
16.		Phooli	*Apluda mutica*
17.		Baas	*Dendracalamus strictus*
18.		Katang baas	*Bambusa bamboos*
19.		Basu	*Sorghum halepense*
20.		Bhurbushi	*Eragrostis tenella*
21.		Marvel	*Dichanthium annulatum*
22.		Gather	*Bothriochloa pertusa*
23.		Sen	*Cenchrus ciliaris*
Parasitic plant			
24.	Coonvolvulaceae	Amarbel	*Cuscuta reflexa*
25.	Orchidaceae	Archid	*Vanda tessellata*
26.	Loranthaceae	Banda	*Vascum nepalense*
27.		Bada	*Dendrophthoe falcata*

Cultivated Plants in the Study Area

The prevalent cropping systems of this area are the cumulative results of past and present decisions by individuals; these decisions are usually based on experience, tradition, expected profit, personal preferences and resources, and so on. The crop occupying the highest percentage of the sown area of this region is taken as the major crop and all other possible alternative crops which are sown in this region either as substitutes of the base crop in the same season or as the crops which fit in the rotation in the subsequent season, are considered as minor crop. It is observed that, the different parts of the study area were practicing different crop pattern based on the season and availability of irrigation facility. The general crop patterns practiced in the study area were Maize, Wheat etc.

Major Horticultural Crops: Plantation of Chikku (*Manilkara zapota*), Kela (*Musa sp.*) Papaya (*Carica papaya*), Amla (*Phyllanthus emblica*) and Mango trees (*Mangifera indica*) were observed at some localities. Mango trees (*Mangifera indica*) were observed adjacent to the residential area and also along the road side at almost all villages.

Major Vegetable Corps: The major vegetables grown in the study area were:

- Bhindi (*Abelmoschus escelentus*),
- Brinjal (*Ringana Solanum melongena*),
- Cabbage (*Brassica oeraceae*),
- Tomato (*Lycopersicon lycopersicum*),
- Karela (*Momordica charantia*),

Pulses: The pulses cultivated in this region were Gram (*Cicer arietinum*); Mug (*Vigna acontifolia*), Arhar (*Cajanus cajan*).

Rare and Endangered Flora in the Study Area: The IUCN Red List is the world's most comprehensive inventory of the global conservation status of plant and animal species. It uses a set of criteria to evaluate the extinction risk of thousands of species and subspecies. These criteria are relevant to all species and all regions of the world. With its strong scientific base, the IUCN Red List is recognized as the most authoritative guide to the status of biological diversity. Out of 17000 species of higher plants known to occur in India, nearly 614 higher plant species were evaluated by IUCN. Among them 247 species are under threatened category (IUCN, 2008).

As per list of 2012; plants seemed to be the most threatened life form with 60 species being listed as Critically Endangered and 141 as Endangered in India.

Among the enumerated flora in the study area, none of them were assigned any threat category by Red data book of Indian Plants (Jain and Sastry, 1984; Nayar and Sastry, 1987; 1988; 1990; Old field *et al.*, 1998; Kholia and Bhakuni, 2009) and Red list of threatened Vascular plants (IUCN, 2010).

Endemic Plants of the Study Area: De Candolle (1855), Swiss botanist, first used the concept of Endemic, which is defined as an area of a taxonomic unit, especially a species which has a restricted distribution or habitat, isolated from its surrounding region through geographical, ecological or temporal barriers. Out of 17000 species of known flowering plants of India nearly 5000 species are said to be endemic. Nearly 58 genera and 1932 taxa are found to be endemic to peninsular India (Nayar, 1980; Ahmedullah and Nayar, 1986; 1987; Jain 1992; Nayar, 1996; Vijaya Shankar *et al.*, 2005; Nautiyal *et al.*, 2009a,b; Shendage *et al.*, 2010).

The flora of India is one of the richest in the world due to the country's wide range of climate, topology, and environment. There are over 15,000 species of flowering plants in India which account for 6% of all plant species in the world. Many plant species are being destroyed, however, due to their prevalent removal. Roughly 1/4 of all plant species in the world are at risk of being endangered or going extinct. The combination of global warming and habitat destruction is the sole reason for the disappearance of many plants. Though there are thousands of interesting and unusual plants, here are some common plants which have become rare and endangered species in the past 30 years due to habitat destruction.

Among recorded plant species none can be assigned the status of endemic plant of this region. Tree community (Species-area) curves based on phytosociology fitted to the data may show unnatural shapes, with leveling-off or even decrease in sampling sizes higher than average. This distortion can be explained by the subjective, preferential method of field sampling used in phytosociology. When making releves in species-poor vegetation, one probably tends to use larger plots in order to include more species. The reason for this may be that a higher number of species gives a higher probability of including presumed diagnostic species, so that the releve can be more easily classified in the Braun-Blanquet classification system. This may has at least two consequences: in phytosociological data bases species-poor vegetation types are underrepresented or releves are artificially biased towards higher species richness; the suitability of phytosociological data for species richness estimation is severely limited.

Status of the Forest, Their Category in Study Area

According to the Champion and Seth, the forest tropical high deciduous of this region fall into the following categories:

- 5A / CIII - Southern tropical dry Deciduous Mixed Forest,
- 5A / DSI - Southern tropical dry Deciduous Scrub (Degradation Stage),
- 5 / DS4 - Southern tropical dry Deciduous Forest (Degradation Stage).

Following are the forest (WLS/RF/PF) has been recorded for the study area.

(*i*) Ratapani and Singhori Wild Life Sanctuary
(*ii*) Chakla RF
(*iii*) Diwattiaya PF
(*iv*) Gohar Ganj RF
(*v*) Obedullahganj PF
(*vi*) Obedullahganj RF
(*vii*) Budani PF
(*viii*) Budani RF
(*ix*) Ramnagar RF

Ratapani/Singhori Wildlife Sanctuary

Ratapani and Singhori Wildlife Sanctuary spreads over an area of 1201.29 Square Kilometers is located in Raisen district in the State of Madhya Pradesh. Ratapani and Singhori Wildlife Sanctuary is extremely rich in flora and fauna and harbours a number of endemic species. Ratapani and Singhori Wildlife Sanctuary are rich in biodiversity. These wildlife areas are classified into semi-arid wildlife zone - IV B Gujarat Rajputana under Roger and Pawar classification. The sanctuary is inhabited by all the usual animals of the region, such as Tiger (*Panthera tigris*) leopard (*Panthera pardus*), Wolf (*Canis lupus*), Jackal (*Canis aureus*), Indian fox (*Vulpes bengalensis*), Striped hyena (*Hyaena hyaena*) Sloth bear (*Melursus ursinus*) among carnivores and spotted deer (*Axis axis*), Sambhar (*Cervus unicolor*), Nilgai (*Boselaphus tragocamelus*), Chinkara (*Gazella gazelle bennetti*), Wild pig (*Sus scrofa*), Chowsingha (*Tetracerus quadriconis*) and Blackbuck (*Antelope cervicapra*), amongst herbivores. Apart from these, crocodiles/gharials can also be seen in Ratapani and Singhori Wildlife Sanctuary. Ratapani and Singhori Wildlife Sanctuary contains 129 tree species, 73 herbs and shrubs species, 33 climbers and parasites, 35 grasses and bamboo species, 35 mammals, 205 birds, 14 fish, 33 reptiles and 10 species of amphibians have been recorded in Ratapani and Singhori Wildlife Sanctuary.

Coordinates for Ratapani and Singhori Wildlife Sanctuary

Corners	Latitude (N)	Longitude (E)
A	23° 2′ 21.742″	77° 20′ 9.817″
B	22° 48′ 58.759″	77° 25′ 39.132″
C	23° 8′ 30.593″	78° 16′ 31.158″
D	23° 17′ 47.545″	78° 12′ 19.342″

Coordinates for Eco Sensitive Zone of Ratapani and Singhori Wildlife Sanctuary

Corners	Latitude (N)	Longitude (E)
A	23° 2′ 12.670″	77° 19′ 2.020″
B	22° 48′ 24.792″	77° 25′ 38.686″
C	23° 8′ 28.575″	78° 17′ 7.044″
D	23° 18′ 53.787″	78° 12′ 43.135″

It is necessary to conserve and protect the area to the extent and boundaries of which is specified in paragraph 1 of this notification, around the protected area of Ratapani and Singhori Wildlife Sanctuary as Eco-sensitive zone from ecological, environmental and biodiversity point of view and to prohibit industries or class of industries and their operations and processes in the said Eco-sensitive Zone.

Extent and boundaries of Eco-sensitive Zone: The extent of Eco-sensitive Zone is one kilometer in the revenue area and two kilometer in the surrounding forest area from the boundary of Ratapani and Singhori Wildlife Sanctuary. The area of Eco sensitive Zone is 546.52 square kilometers which has 72 villages.

List of Villages on EcoSensitive Zone of Ratapani and Singhori Wildlife Sanctuary

Sl.No.	Division	Village
1.	**Bhopal**	Rabiyawad
2.		Vurthi
3.		Prabadhan
4.		Stahphan
5.		Punha
6.		Banpur
7.	**Obedullahganj**	Alampur
8.		Amchha Kalan
9.		Amchha Khurd
10.		Ankalpur
11.		Baheria
12.		Bamhori
13.		Bamuila
14.		Bansgahan
15.		Bari
16.		Bhiyanpur
17.		Bineka
18.		Biptanagar
19.		Bithori
20.		Borpani
21.		Chora Kamraura
22.		Damdongri
23.		Dehgaon
24.		Dhabla
25.		Dimria
26.		Ghana Kalan
27.		Ghatpipaliya
28.		Ghoti
29.		Goripura
30.		Jalkhera
31.		Jatanpur
32.		Jet
33.		Karakbani
34.		Karitalai
35.		Kesalwara

36.		Khari
37.		Kumhariya
38.		Kumri
39.		Mahwakheri
40.		Mokalwara
41.		Nishankhera
42.		Nishankhera
43.		Niwari
44.		Panagar
45.		Ratanpur
46.		Tajpura
47.		Thanwari Ghatkheri
48.		Udayagiri
49.		Umariya
50.	**Raisen**	Bandral
51.		Jaipura
52.		Jamgarh
53.		Madhamau
54.		Padariya
55.		Samnapur
56.	**Sehore**	Amargarh
57.		Amdoh
58.		Babariakhal
59.		Bardha
60.		Barijhiri ka Pathar
61.		Budhni
62.		Imaliya
63.		Johliapur
64.		Karkadehri
65.		Kheri
66.		Maljhar
67.		Midghat
68.		Nadiakheda
69.		Neemwalakheda
70.		Patni
71.		Sirwara
72.		Yaarnagar

Activities Prohibited or to be Regulated within the Eco-sensitive Zone

All activities in the Eco sensitive Zone shall be governed by the provisions of the Environment (Protection) Act, 1986 (29 of 1986) and the rules made there under including the Coastal Regulation Zone (CRZ), 2011 and the Environmental Impact Assessment (EIA) Notification, 2006 and other applicable laws including the Forest (Conservation) Act, 1980 (69 of 1980), the Indian Forest Act, 1927 (16 of 1927), the Wildlife (Protection) Act 1972 (53 of 1972), and amendments made thereto and be regulated in the manner specified.

Prohibited Activates in Eco Sensitive Zone

Commercial Mining: All new and existing (minor and major minerals), stone quarrying and crushing units are prohibited with immediate effect except for meeting the domestic needs of bona fide local residents including digging of earth for construction or repair of houses and for manufacture of country tiles or bricks for housing and for other activities. The mining operations shall be carried out in accordance with the order of the Hon'ble Supreme Court dated 04.08.2006 in the matter of T.N. Godavarman Thirumulpad vs. UOI in W.P.(C) No.202 of 1995 and dated 21.04.2014 in the matter of Goa Foundation Vs. UOI in W.P.(C) No.435 of 2012.

Setting of industries causing pollution (Water, Air, Soil, Noise, etc.): No new industries and expansion of existing polluting industries in the Eco-sensitive zone shall be permitted. Only non-polluting industries shall be allowed within ESZ as per classification of Industries in the Guidelines issued by Central Pollution Control Board in February 2016, unless so specified in this notification. In addition, non-polluting cottage industries shall be promoted.

Establishment of major hydroelectric project: Prohibited (except as otherwise provided) as per applicable laws.

Use or production or processing of any hazardous substances: Prohibited (except as otherwise provided) as per applicable laws.

Discharge of untreated effluents in natural water bodies or land area: Prohibited (except as otherwise provided) as per applicable laws.

Setting of new saw mills: No new or expansion of existing saw mills shall be permitted within the Eco-sensitive Zone.

Setting up of brick kilns: Prohibited (except as otherwise provided) as per applicable laws.

Use of polythene bags: Prohibited (except as otherwise provided) as per applicable laws.

Commercial use of firewood: Prohibited (except as otherwise provided) as per applicable laws.

New wood based industry: Prohibited (except as otherwise provided) as per applicable laws.

Fishing: Prohibited (except as otherwise provided) as per applicable laws.

Faunal Biodiversity of Study Area

For the documentation of the faunal biodiversity of the study area with respect to birds, reptiles, amphibians, and butterfly species, a baseline survey had been conducted.

Birds: The sighting of bird species was very lass during the study period. The most commonly spotted bird species of this area were Eurasian Collared-Dove, Cattle Egret, Red-wattled Lapwing, Intermediate Egret, Rock Pigeon, Chestnut-headed Bee-eater, Bank Myna and Common Myna. Water birds are common near to Ratapani Lake. The Indian Peafowl was observed which is listed as schedule–I as per IWPA, 1972 and others listed as schedule IV as per IWPA, 1972.

Total 1,224 bird species reliably recorded from India, together with their status categories. In total there are 1219 extant native species including migrants and vagrants (but excluding 3 species now known to be extinct in the country and 2 introduced species). There are 923 breeding species (911 residents, plus 12 suspected residents). IUCN evaluated 1254 bird species from India and categorized 77 species as threatened (13 species as critically endangered, 10 species as Endangered and 54 species as Vulnerable). No one sighted birds were evaluated as near threatened by IUCN, 2010 and BirdLife International, 2010. A taxon is Near Threatened, when it has been evaluated against the criteria but does not qualify for Critically Endangered, Endangered or Vulnerable categories, but is close to qualifying or is likely to qualify for a threatened category in the near future. List of schedule -1 as per Wild life Protection Act 1972, species is given in the Table 9.7. Systematic account of the birds in the study area with the status of occurrence is given in the Table 9.8.

Table 9.7: Schedule –I Bird(s) of Study Area

Species	As IWPA 1972	IUCN	CITES
Indian Peafowl *(Pavo cristatus)*	Schedule I; Part –III; 11	Least Concern ver 3.1	Not listed

Table 9.8: Systematic Lists of Birds in the Study Area with Status

Sl. No.	Family	Vernacular Name	Scientific Name	Status
1.	Accipitridae	Black-winged kite	*Elanus caeruleus*	R
2.		Black kite	*Milvus migrans*	R
3.		Shikra	*Accipiter badius*	V
4.		Changeable hawk-eagle	*Nisaetus cirrhatus*	O
5.		Tawny eagle	*Aquila rapax*	E
6.		Crested serpent eagle	*Spilornis cheela*	E
7.	Alaudidae	Ashy-crowned sparrow-lark	*Eremopterix griseus*	R

8.	Alcedinidae	Pied kingfisher	*Ceryle rudis*	R
9.		Common kingfisher	*Alcedo atthis*	R
10.		White-throated kingfisher	*Halcyon smyrnensis*	V
11.		Black-capped kingfisher	*Halcyon pileata*	R
12.	Anatidae	Eurasian teal	*Anas crecca*	O
13.		Northern shoveller	*Anas clypeata*	O
14.		Cotton teal	*Nettapus coromandelianus*	R
15.		Knob-billed duck	*Sarkidiornis melanotos*	R
16.	Apodidae	Alpine swift	*Tachymarptis melba*	R
17.		Little swift	Apus affinis	R
18.	Ardeidae	Grey Heron	*Ardea cinerea*	R
19.		Indian pond heron	*Ardeola grayii*	R
20.		Cattle egret	*Bubulcus ibis*	R
21.		Little egret	*Egretta garzetta*	R
22.		Large egret	*Egretta garzetta*	R
23.	Artamidae	Ashy woodswallow	*Artamus fuscus*	V
24.	Campephagidae	Small minivet	*Pericrocotus cinnamomeus*	W
25.		Scarlet minivet	*Pericrocotus speciosus*	V
26.		Black-faced cuckooshrike	*Coracina novaehollandiae*	V
27.	Caprimulgidae	Indian nightjar	*Caprimulgus asiaticus*	R
28.	Charadriidae	Red-wattled lapwing	*Vanellus indicus*	R
29.	Chloropseidae	Blue-winged leafbird	*Chloropsis cochinchinensis*	R
30.	Ciconiidae	White stork	*Ciconia ciconia*	W
31.	Cisticolidae	Ashy prinia	*Prinia socialis*	V
32.	Columbidae	Grey-fronted quail-dove	*Geotrygon caniceps*	R
33.		Yellow-footed green pigeon	*Treron phoenicoptera*	R
34.		Rock pigeon	*Columba livia*	R
35.		Eurasian collared dove	*Streptopelia decaocto*	R
36.		Spotted dove	*Spilopelia chinensis*	R
37.	Coraciidae	Indian roller	*Coracias benghalensis*	R
38.	Corvidae	Jungle crow	*Corvus macrorhynchos*	R
39.	Cuculidae	Common hawk-cuckoo	*Hierococcyx varius*	R
40.		Koel	*Eudynamys scolopaceus*	R

41.		Greater coucal	*Centropus sinensis*	R
42.	Dicaeidae	Fire-breasted flowerpecker	*Dicaeum ignipectus*	V
43.	Dicruridae	Fork-tailed drongo	*Dicrurus adsimilis*	R
44.		White-bellied drongo	*Dicrurus caerulescens*	R
45.		Greater racket-tailed drongo	*Dicrurus paradiseus*	R
46.	Estrildidae	Red avadavat	*Amandava amandava*	V
47.		Tricoloured munia	*Lonchura malacca*	O
48.	Gruidae	Common crane	*Grus grus*	R
49.		Sarus crane	*Grus antigone*	R
50.	Hirundinidae	Wire-tailed swallow	*Hirundo smithii*	S
51.	Laniidae	Long-tailed shrike	*Lanius schach*	R
52.	Leiothrichidae	Jungle babbler	*Turdoides striata*	R
53.	Megalaimidae	Crimson-fronted barbet	*Megalaima rubricapilla*	R
54.	Meropidae	Green bee-eater	*Merops orientalis*	R
55.		Blue-tailed bee-eater	*Merops philippinus*	R
56.	Motacillidae	Grey wagtail	*Motacilla cinerea*	R
57.		White wagtail	*Motacilla alba*	R
58.		White-browed wagtail	*Motacilla maderaspatensis*	R
59.		Western Yellow Wagtail	*Motacilla flava*	V
60.	Muscicapidae	Tickell's blue flycatcher	*Cyornis tickelliae*	R
61.		Black redstart	*Phoenicurus ochruros*	S
62.		African stonechat	*Saxicola torquatus*	W
63.		Pied bush chat	*Saxicola caprata*	R
64.		Blue-capped rock thrush	*Monticola cinclorhyncha*	R
65.		Oriental magpie-robin	*Copsychus saularis*	R
66.		Indian robin	*Saxicoloides fulicatus*	R
67.	Nectariniidae	Purple sunbird	*Cinnyris asiaticus*	R
68.	Oriolidae	Eurasian golden oriole	*Oriolus oriolus*	O
69.	Passeridae	House sparrow	*Passer domesticus*	R
70.	Phalacrocoracidae	Little Cormorant	*Phalacrocorax niger*	V
71.		Large Cormorant	*Phalacrocorax carbo*	V
72.	Phasianidae	Black Partridge	*Francolinus francolinus*	R
73.		Grey francolin	*Francolinus pondicerianus*	V
74.		Jungle bush quail	*Perdicula asiatica*	R

75.		Red spurfowl	*Galloperdix spadicea*	R
76.		Red junglefowl	*Gallus gallus*	O
77.		Indian peafowl	*Pavo cristatus*	R
78.	Picidae	Black-rumped flameback	*Dinopium benghalense*	R
79.		Yellow fronted pied woodpecker	*Leiopicus mahrattensis*	R
80.	Pittidae	Indian pitta	*Pitta brachyura*	R
81.	Ploceidae	Baya weaver	*Ploceus philippinus*	R
82.	Psittacidae	Alexandrine parakeet	*Psittacula eupatria*	R
83.		Rose-ringed parakeet	*Psittacula krameri*	R
84.		Blossom-headed parakeet	*Psittacula roseata*	R
85.	Pycnonotidae	Red-vented bulbul	*Pycnonotus cafer*	R
86.	Recurvirostridae	Black-winged stilt	*Himantopus himantopus*	R
87.	Rhipiduridae	White-browed fantail	*Rhipidura aureola*	W
88.	Rostratulidae	Greater painted-snipe	*Rostratula benghalensis*	R
89.	Scolopacidae	Common redshank	*Tringa totanus*	R
90.		Common snipe	*Gallinago gallinago*	W
91.	Sittidae	Indian nuthatch	*Sitta castanea*	S
92.	Strigidae	Eurasian eagle-owl	*Bubo bubo*	O
93.		Jungle owlet	*Glaucidium radiatum*	O
94.	Sturnidae	Chestnut-tailed starling	*Sturnia malabarica*	V
95.		Brahminy starling	*Sturnia pagodarum*	V
96.		Pied myna	*Gracupica contra*	R
97.		Jungle myna	*Acridotheres fuscus*	R
98.		Common myna	*Acridotheres tristis*	R
99.	Threskiornithidae	White Ibis	*Threskiornis sp.*	R
100.	Timaliidae	White-browed scimitar babbler	*Pomatorhinus schisticeps*	R
101.	Upupidae	Hoopoe	*Upupa epops*	R

Note: Key to Status

R	Resident
V	Vagrant
S	Summer only
W	Winter only
P	Spring or autumn passage
O	Occurs most years
VS	Vagrant summer

VP	Vagrant passage
PB	Passage and breeds
PW	Passage and winter
E	Escape

Butterflies from the study area: Butterflies from three families observed during the present study are documented in the table below.

Table 9.9: Butterflies in the Study Area

Scientific Name and Family	Common Name	Relative Abundance
Family Asclepiadaceae		
Danaus genutia Cramer	Striped Tiger	Common
Family Papilionidae		
Papilio polytes	Common Mormon	Common
Family Pieridae		
Eurema hecabe	Common Grass yellow	Very Common
Ixias Marianne	White orange tip	Common
Family: Nymphalidae		
Danaus chrysippus	Plain Tiger	Common
Phalantha phalantha	Common Leopard	Fairy Common
Hypolimanas misippus	Danaid egg fly	Common
Mycalesis perseus	Common bush brown	Uncommon
Cynthia cardui Linnaeus	Painted Lady	Uncommon
Junonia hierta Fabricius	Yellow pansy	Common
Junonia orithya Linnaeus	Blue pansy	Fairy Common

Herpetofauna: In amphibian group, the toads were sighted during the study period. The reptiles Common Garden Lizard, House Gecko, Fan-Throated Lizard, Common rat Snake, Indian Monitor, Crocodile, etc. were observed in the region is given in the table below.

Table 9.10: Reptiles and Amphibian in the Study Area

S.No.	Common Name	Scientific name	Schedule as IWPA, 1972
1.	Toad	*Bufo bufo*	Not listed
2.	Common Indian Krait*	*Bungarus caeruleus*	Schedule II
3.	Indian chameleon	*Chameleon calcaratus*	Schedule II
4.	Rock Python*	*Python molurus*	Schedule II
5.	Russel Viper*	*Vipera russellii*	Schedule II
6.	Crocodile	*Crocodle crocodylus*	Schedule I; Part II 1D
7.	Common Garden Lizard	*Calotes versicolor*	Not listed

8.	Fan-Throated Lizard	*Sitana ponticeriana*	Not listed
9.	House Gecko	*Hemidactylus flaviviridis*	Not listed
10.	Brahminy Skink*	*Mabuya carinata*	Not listed
11.	Common Rat Snake	*Ptyas mucosus*	Schedule II
12.	Indian Cobra*	*Naja naja*	Schedule II
13.	Indian Monitor	*Varanus bengalensis*	Schedule II

*Not sighted but included as per the secondary information from the villagers.

Mammals: The wild mammals observed other than the domesticated ones are given in the table below.

Table 9.11: Mammals in Study Area

Sl. No.	Family	Scientific Name	Common Name	Status as per IWPA 1972
1.	Antilopinae	*Antilope cervicapra*	Black buck	Schedule – I; Part –I; 2
2.		*Boselaphus tragocamelus*	Blue bull	Schedule-III
3.		*Tetracerus quadricornis*	Four horned Antilope	Schedule – I; Part –I; 8A
4.		*Cervus unicolor*	Sambhar	Schedule - III
5.	Bovidae	*Gazella gazellabennetti*	Chinkara	Schedule – I; Part –I; 5B
6.	Canidae	*Canis aureus*	Jackal	Schedule - II
7.		*Vulpes bengalensis*	Indian fox	Schedule - II
8.		*Cuon alpinus*	Wild Dog/Dhole	Schedule - II
9.		*Axis axis*	Spotted deer	Schedule - III
10.	Circopthecidae	*Macaca mulatta*	Rhesus macaque	Schedule - II
11.	Cotobidae	*Presbytis entellus*	Common Languor	Schedule - II
12.	Einaceidae	*Hemiechinus auritus*	Hedgehog	Schedule - IV
13.	Felidae	*Panthera tigris*	Tiger	Schedule - I; Part-I; 39
14.		*Panthera pardus*	Panther/Leopard	Schedule - I; Part-I; 16B
15.		*Felis chaus*	Common Jungle cat	Schedule - II
16.	Herpestidae	*Herpestes edwardsii*	Common Mongoose	Schedule - II
17.	Hyaenidae	*Hyaena hyaena*	Striped hyena	Schedule - III

18.	Hystricidae	*Hystrix indica*	Common Indian Porcupine	Schedule IV
19.	Leporidae	*Lepus nigricollis*	Common Indian Hare	Schedule IV
20.	Manidae	*Manis crassicaudata*	Scaly ant eater	Schedule-I; Part-I; 28
21.	Muridae	*Bandicota bengalensis*	Field Rat	Not listed
22.		*Golund ellioti*	The Indian bush rat	Not listed
23.	Mustelidae	*Mellivora capensis*	Indian Ratel/ Honey Badger	Schedule-I; Part-I; 29
24.	Pteropodidae	*Cynopterus sphinx*	Shot nosed fruit bat	Schedule V
25.		*Pteropus giganteus*	Indian Flying fox	Schedule IV
26.	Sciuridae	*Funambulus Pennanti*	Common 5 Striped Squirrel	Schedule IV
27.	Suidae	*Sus scrofa*	Wild Boar	Schedule - II
28.	Ursidae	*Melursus ursinus*	Sloth Bear	Schedule-I; Part-I; 31C

Domestic Animals

The domestic animals *viz.* dog, cow, buffalo, goat, sheep and chicken observed in the study area.

Insects like Wasps, Honeybees and Signature spider was also recorded.

Fisheries

Narmada River is Major River in the study area, one lake *i.e.* Ratapani Water Lake and Natural Drain (Gadariya Nala) are the water bodies in the study area. The fishes observed in study area are listed in table below.

Table 9.12: List of Fishes Reported from the Study Area

S. No.	Common Name	Scientific Name
1.	Katla (Komal, Bhakhar)	*Catla catla*
2.	Rohu	*Labco rohita*
3.	Mrigal (Narain)	*Cirrhisus mregala*
4.	Samval (Saul)	*Chana marulius*
5.	Samval (Kabra)	*Chana striatus*
6.	Samval	*Chana punctalus*
7.	Karra	*Chana gachua*
8.	Padin	*Wallago attu*
9.	Gangarwar (Pabda)	*Ompak bimaculatus*
10.	Singhad	*Mystus singhala*

11.	Aur	*Nystus aor*
12.	Bleekeri	*Mystus bleekeri*
13.	Cavacius	*Mystus cavacius*
14.	Gengra	*Rita rita*
15.	Andus	*Bagarus bagarius*

*not seen directly.

Rare and Endangered Fauna of Study Area: The IUCN Red List is the world's most comprehensive inventory of the global conservation status of plant and animal species. It uses a set of criteria to evaluate the extinction risk of thousands of species and subspecies. These criteria are relevant to all species and all regions of the world. With its strong scientific base, the IUCN Red List is recognized as the most authoritative guide to the status of biological diversity. IUCN, (2008) has evaluated 1976 animal species from India, among them 313 have in recognized as threatened species. Among them one species is considered as extinct, while 44 species are in critically endangered (CR) category, 88 is in endangered category (EN), while 181 is considered as vulnerable (VU). Wild Life (Protection) Act, 1972, amended on 17th January 2003, is an Act to provide for the protection of wild animals, birds and plants and for matters connected therewith or ancillary or incidental thereto with a view to ensuring the ecological and environmental security of the country. Total 10 species of the sighted fauna were given protection under Schedule –I by the Indian Wild Life (Protection) Act, 1972 listed in Table 9.13.

Table 9.13: List of Schedule –I Fauna Observed During the Survey

Sl.No.	Scientific Name	Common Name	Schedule As Per (WPA, 1972)	IUCN Category	CITES Listing
1.	Panthera tigris	Tiger	Schedule-I; Part-I; 39	Endangered A2abcd; C1 ver 3.1	Appendix I
2.	Manis crassicaudata	Scaly ant eater	Schedule-I; Part-I; 28	Endangered A3d+4d ver 3.1	Appendix I
3.	Panthera pardus	Panther/ Leopard	Schedule-I; Part-I; 16B	Vulnerable A2cd ver 3.1	Appendix I
4.	Melursus ursinus	Sloth Bear	Schedule-I; Part-I; 31C	Vulnerable A3c ver 3.1	Appendix I
5.	Tetracerus quadricornis	Four horned Antilope	Schedule-I; Part-I; 8A	Vulnerable C2a(i) ver 3.1	Appendix III
6.	Gazella gazellabennetti	Chinkara	Schedule-I; Part-I; 5B	Least Concern ver 3.1	Appendix III

7.	Antilope cervicapra	Black buck	Schedule-I; Part-I; 2	Least Concern ver 3.1	Appendix III
8.	Mellivora capensis	Indian Ratel	Schedule-I; Part-I; 29	Least Concern ver 3.1	Appendix III
9.	Pavo cristatus	Indian Peafowl	Schedule-I; Part-III;11	Least Concern ver 3.1	Not listed
10.	Crocodle crocodylus	Crocodile	Schedule I; Part II 1D	Not Assessed yet	Not listed

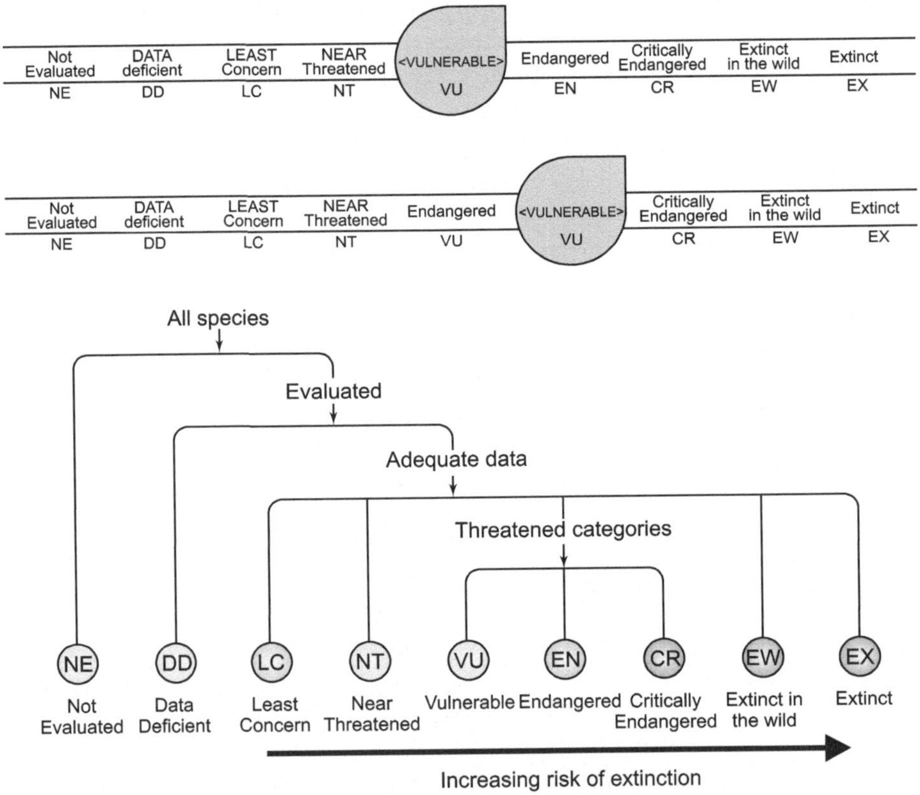

Fig. 9.10. Representation of Risk of Extinction as per IUCN

Recommendations and Conclusion

The study area is ecologically sensitive having protected and reserved forest and notified wildlife sanctuary. The railway track is passing through Ratapani & Singhori Wildlife Sanctuary which has rich biodiversity and endangered species. These wildlife area are classified into semi-arid wildlife zone-IVB Gujarat Rajputana under Roger and Pawar classification. The sanctuary is inhabited by all the usual animals of the region, such as Tiger (*Panthera tigris*) leopard (*Panthera pardus*), Wolf (*Canis lupus*), Jackal (*Canis aureus*), Indian fox

(*Vulpes bengalensis*), Striped hyena (*Hyaena hyaena*) Sloth bear (*Melursus ursinus*) among carnivores and spotted deer (*Axis axis*), Sambhar (*Cervus unicolor*), Nilgai (*Boselaphus tragocamelus*), Chinkara (*Gazella gazelle bennetti*), Wild pig (*Sus scrofa*), Chowsingha (*Tetracerus quadriconis*) and Blackbuck (*Antelope cervicapra*), amongst herbivores. Apart from these, crocodiles/gharials can also be seen in Ratapani and Singhori Wildlife Sanctuary. Ratapani and Singhori Wildlife Sanctuary contains 129 tree species, 73 herbs and shrubs species, 33 climbers and parasites, 35 grasses and bamboo species, 35 mammals, 205 birds, 14 fish, 33 reptiles and 10 species of amphibians have been recorded in Ratapani and Singhori Wildlife Sanctuary.

Panthera tigris(Tiger) and *Manis crassicaudata* (Scaly ant eater) are endangered species listed by IUCN and protected under Schedule-1 as per Wildlife Protection Act 1972. *Panthera pardus* (Leopard), *Melursus ursinus* (Sloth Bear) and *Tetracerus quadricornis* (Four horned Antilope) are vulnerable species listed by IUCN and protected under Schedule-1. Other species protected under schedule-1 are *Gazella gazellabennetti* (Chinkara), *Antilope cervicapra* (Black buck), *Mellivora capensis* (Indian Ratel), *Crocodle crocodylus* (Crocodile) and one bird *Pavo cristatus* (Indian Peafowl). The illegal tree cutting by villagers and contractors was observed during study. The 8 tiger death was reported by RFO last year (2016-17) on Railway track. The major reason was in search of food i.e. Monkey. The people travelling in train are disposing food items and people working in pantry are also used to dispose the waste food in the forest. The food item attract to monkeys and they are killed by running train on railway track, the blood and meat of money attract to tigers/panthers and also they were killed by running train on railway track mostly in night.

It is strongly recommended to prepare the conservation plan for schedule-1 Fauna (listed 9 animals and 1 bird) and it is ensure to implement the conservation plan during construction and operation phase of railway track. Moreover, there is an urgent need of public awareness for the importance of wildlife, as illegal hunting, killing or capturing of wild animals was recorded from locals living in the forest and nearby villagers. People coming from outside are giving the greed of money and other necessary provision to villagers for hunting. It's an environmental crime against the natural resources.

REFERENCES

Ahmedullah M. and Nayar M.P. (1987). Endemic Plants of The Indian Region. Culcutta: Botanical Survey of India. 147 pp.

Ahmedullah M. and Nayar M.P. (1986). Endemic Plants of The Indian Region. VoI.1. Peninsular India. Bot. Surv. of India, Calcutta.

Anderson, T. (1867). An Enumeration of The Indian Species of Acanthaceae. Journal of Linnaean Society 9: 425–454.

APHA (1971). Standard Methods for The Examination of Water and Waste Water. American Public Health, Association, New York.

B. Welsh, H.H., Jr. 1987. Monitoring Herpetofauna in Woodlands of North Western California and South West Oregon: a Comparative Strategy. pp. 203-213.

Batten, SD, Clarke R, Flinkman J (2003). CPR Sampling: The Technical Background, Material and Methods, Consistency and Comparability. Progress in Oceanography, 58, 193-215.

Bentham, G. and Hooker, J.D. (1862-1883). Genera Plantarum. L Reeve and Co., London.

Bird Life International (2000). Threatened Birds of The World. Lynx Edicions and BirdLife International, Barcelona and Cambridge, UK.

BirdLife International (2004a). Threatened Birds of The World 2004. CD-ROM. Bird Life International, Cambridge, UK.

BirdLife International (2004b). State of The World's Birds 2004-Indicators for our Changing World. Bird Life International, Cambridge, UK.

BirdLife International (2010). The BirdLife Checklist of The Birds of The World, with Conservation Status and Taxonomic Sources. Version 3. Available from http://www.birdlife.info/docs/SpcChecklist/Checklist_v3_June10.zip

C. Welsh, H.H. Jr. and Lind, A. (1991). The Structure of the Herpetofaunal Assemblage in the Douglas-fir/hardwood Forests of Northwestern California and South Western Oregon. pp. 395-411.

Colebrook, J. M. (1960). Continuous Plankton Records: Methods of Analysis, 1950-59. Bulletins of Marine Ecology, 5:51-64.

D. Hutto, R.L., S.M. Pletsechel and P. Hendrick. 1986. A Fixed Radius Point Count Method for Non-breeding Season use. The Auk. 103: 593-602.

Dixit, R. D. (1984). A Census of The Indian Pteridophytes. Flora of India Series 4. Botanical Survey of India, Howrah (Calcutta).

E. Allen, L., Engeman, R. and Krupa, H. 1996 Evaluation of three Relative Abundance Indices for Assessing Dingo Population. Wildlife Research. 23: 197-206.

Edmondson WT (1974). A Simplified Method for Counting Phytoplankton. In: A Manual on Methods for Measuring Primary Production in Aquatic Environments (Ed. Vollenmeider RE) Balckwell Sci. Pub., Oxford, pp. 14-16.

F. Thommpson, I.D., Davidson, I.J., O' Donnell, S. and Brazeau, F. (1989). Use of Track Transects to Measure the Relative Occurrence of some Arboreal Mammals in Uncut Forest and Regeneration Stands. *Canadian Journal of Zoology*. 67:1816-1823.

Gamble, J.S. (1924). The Flora of Presidency of Madras 2. Culcutta: Botanical Survey of India. 743 pp.

Ghosh, S. R., Ghosh, B., Biswas, A. and Ghosh, R. K. (2004). The Pteridophytic Flora of Eastern India 1:1–591. *In:* Flora of India Series 4, Botanical Survey of India, Kolkata.

Hunter, W.W. (1879). Statsstical Account of Assani. Vol II Trubner and Co.

IUCN (1994). IUCN Red List Categories. Prepared by The IUCN Species Survival Commission. IUCN, Gland, Switzerland.

IUCN (2001). IUCN Red List Categories and Criteria: Version 3.1. IUCN Species Survival Commission. IUCN, Gland, Switzerland and Cambridge, UK.

IUCN (2003). Guidelines for Application of IUCN Red List Criteria at Regional Levels: Version 3.0. IUCN Species Survival Commission. IUCN, Gland, Switzerland and Cambridge, UK.

IUCN (2008). Red List of Threatened Species. (www.iucnredlist.org).

IUCN (2010). Guidelines for Using the IUCN Red List Categories and Criteria, Version 8.1 (August 2010), Prepared by the Standards and Petitions Subcommittee of the IUCN

Species Survival Commission: on www. http://intranet.iucn.org/webfiles/doc/SSC/RedList/ Red List Guidelines.pdf

Jain, S. K. (1991). Dictionary of Indian Folk Medicine and Ethnobotany. Deep Publications, New Delhi.

Jain, S.K. (1968). Medicinal Plants Nation Book Trust, New Delhi. Jain, S.K. 1983. Rare and Endangered Species: Observation on Rare, Imperfectly Known Endemic Plants. In the Sacred Groves of Western Maharashtra. Calcutta; *Bot. Sur of India* 169-178.

Jain, S.K. (1992). The Problem of Endangered Species. Concepts, Problems and Solutions. *In:* Tropical Ecosystems: Ecolosv and Management (Eds. K.P.Singh and J.S.Singh.), Iiley Eastern Iimited, New Delhi. 69-80.

Jain, S.K. and Rao, R.K. (1983). An Assessment of Threatened Plants of India. Bot. Surv. of India. Calcutta.

Jain, S.K. and Sastry, A.R.K. (1980). Threatened Plants of India - A State of The Alf Report Bot. Surv. of India. New Delhi.

Jain, S.K. and Sastry, A.R.K. (1984). Safeguarding Plant Diversity in Threatened Natural Habitats. In Conservation of Threatened Natural Habitats. (Ed. Anthony V. Hall). African nat. Sci. Prog. Report. 92.

Kholia, B. S. and Bhakuni, K. (2009). Western Himalaya a New Range of Distribution for a Critically Endangered Fern, Dryopsis Manipurensis (Bedd.) Holttum et P. J. Edwards. Nelumbo, Bulletin of The Botanical Survey of India 51:245–248.

Kumar Ashok (2013). Butterfly (Lepidoptera: Insecta) Diversity From Different Sites of Jhagadia, Ankleshwar, District-Bharuch, Gujarat, *Oct. Jour. Env. Res.* 1(1):09-18

Kumar Ashok (2014). Environmental Management Plan for Chemical Industries Especially Resin Manufacturing Unit, *Oct. Jour. Env. Res..* 2(3): 262-273

Kumar Ashok and Aggarwal Savita Goyal (2013a). Ecology and Biodiversity Status of Sachin Gidc and its Surroundings with Special Reference to Conservation Measures for Indian Peafowl (Pavo Cristatus) Schedule –I Bird Species, *Oct. Jour. Env. Res.* 2(1): 82-100

Kumar Ashok and Aggarwal Savita Goyal (2013b). Study of Common Property Resources (CPR) With Special Reference To Water And Biological Resources At Projected Area Near Village Ninat, Bardoli, District-Surat, *Oct. Jour. Env. Res.* 1(4): 319-331

Kumar Ashok and Srivastava Meena (2012). Diversity of Medicinal Plants in Uttarakhand and their Conservation Strategy with Special Reference to Orchids, *In*: Proceeding of National Conference on Environementla Health: Challaneges and Management, Jan. 20-21, 2012, Organized by Pt. Deendayal Upadhyay Govt. PG College Rajajipuram, Lucknow. pp 139-142

Kumar Ashok, Srivastava Meena and Goyal Savita (2013). The Biodiversity At Sandi Bird Sanctuary, Hardoi With Special Reference to Migratory Birds. *Oct. Jour. Env. Res.* 1(3): 173-181

Lackey J B. (1938). The Manipulation and Counting of River Plankton and Changes in some Organisms Due to Formalin Preservation. US Public Health Reports 53:2081-93.

Lushington, A.W. (1915). Vernacular List of Trees, Shrubs and Woody clrnbers of the Madras Presidency. Govt. Press, Madras

Misra, R. (2013, Reprinted in India). Ecology Workbook. Scientific Publishers. (Page 31 to 45).

Nautiyal DC, SK Sharma and MK Pandit (2009). Notes on the Taxonomic History, Rediscovery and Conservation Status of two Endangered Species of Ceropegia (Asclepiadaceae) from Sikkim Himalaya. Journal of Botanical Research Institute Texas 3(2): 815-822

Nautiyal DC, SK Sharmaand MK Pandit (2009). Notes on the Taxonomic History of two Rare Species of Begonia (Begoniaceae) from Sikkim Himalaya and their Conservation. Journal of Botanical Research Institute Texas 3(2): 823-830

Nayar MP and ARK Sastry (1987). Red Data Book of Indian Plants. Vol. I. Botanical Survey of India, Calcutta

Nayar MP and ARK Sastry (1988). Red Data Book of Indian Plants. Vol. II. Botanical Survey of India, Calcutta

Nayar MP and ARK Sastry (1990). Red Data Book of Indian Plants. Vol. III. Botanical Survey of India, Calcutta

Nayar, M.P. (1980). Endemism and Patterns of Distribution of Endemic Genera (Angiosperms) in India. J. Econ. Tax. Bot. I: 99-110.

Nayar, M.P. (1996). Hotspots of Endemic Plants of India, Nepal and Bhutan. Thiruvanathapuram: Tropical Botanical Garden and Research Institute. 204 pp.

Ohasi H (1975). Flora of Eastern Himalaya, Third Report. University Museum of University of Tokyo Bulletin 8:1-458.

Oldfield, S., Lusty, C. and MacKinven, A. (1998). The World List of Threatened Trees. World Conservation Press, Cambridge.

Shendage, S.M. and S.R. Yadav (2010). Revision of the Genus Barleria (Acanthaceae) in India. Rheedea 20(2):81–230.

Vijaya Sankar, R., Ravikumar, R. and N.M. Ganesh Babu (2005). On the Collection of a Peninsular Endemic, Barleria stocksii (Acanthaceae), After a Century. Zoo's Print 20:1820.

Vollenweider R A (Ed). (1969). A Manual of Methods For Measuring Primary Production in Aquatic Environment. IBP Handbook No. 12, Blackwell Scientific Publications.

Welch F S. (1948). Limnological Methods. McGraw Hill Book Co Inc., New York

Wilson, D.E. and Reeder, D.M. (eds). (1993). Mammal Species of the World a Taxonomic and Geographic reference. Second edition. Smithsonian Institution Press, Washington and London.

Wilson, D.E. and Reeder, D.M. (eds). (2005). Mammal Species of The World. A Taxonomic and Geographic Reference. Third Edition. Johns Hopkins University Press, Baltimore.

World Conservation Monitoring Centre (1988). The Conservation of Biological Diversity. WCMC., I.U.C.N., Cambridge, UK

World Conservation Monitoring Centre (2000). Global Biodiversity: Earth's Living Resources in the 21st Century. *By*: Groombridge B. and Jenkins, M.D. World Conservation Press, Cambridge.

Index

W

Z